Human Geography in the Making

Series Editor:

ALEXANDER B. MURPHY

Department of Geography,
University of Oregon, USA

SERIES PREFACE

To understand the rapidly changing world in which we live, the study of geography is essential. Yet the nature and importance of a geographic perspective can easily be misconstrued if geography is seen simply as a set of changing patterns and arrangements. Like the world around it, the discipline of geography itself has undergone sweeping changes in recent decades as its practitioners have confronted and developed new concepts, theories, and perspectives. Placing the contributions of geographic research within the context of these changes is critical to an appreciation of geography's present and future.

The *Human Geography in the Making* series was developed with these considerations in mind. Inspired initially by the influential 'Progress Reports' in the journal *Progress in Human Geography*, the series offers book-length overviews of geographic subdisciplines that are widely taught in colleges and universities at the upper division and graduate levels. The goal of each of the books is to acquaint readers with the major issues and conceptual problems that have dominated a particular subdiscipline over the past two to three decades, to discuss and assess current themes that are shaping the evolution of the subdiscipline, and to highlight the most promising areas for future research.

There is a widely recognized gap between topically focused textbooks and narrowly defined scholarly studies. The books in this series move into this gap. Through analyses of the intellectual currents that have shaped key subdisciplines of geography, these books provide telling insights into the conceptual and empirical issues currently influencing research and teaching. Geographic understanding requires an appreciation of how and why ideas have evolved, and where they may be going. The distinguished contributors to this series have much to say about these matters, offering ideas and interpretations of importance to students and professional geographers alike.

Alexander B. Murphy
Series Editor
Professor of Geography
University of Oregon

TITLES IN THE SERIES

Making Population Geography
(Adrian Bailey, University of Leeds, UK)

Making Political Geography
(John Agnew, UCLA, USA)

Making Development Geography
(Victoria Lawson, University of Washington, USA)

Making
Political
Ecology

RODERICK P. NEUMANN

Department of International Relations and Geography

Florida International University, USA

HODDER
EDUCATION
AN HACHETTE UK COMPANY

First published in Great Britain in 2005 by Hodder Education, an Hachette UK Company,
338 Euston Road, London NW1 3BH

www.hoddereducation.co.uk

British Library Cataloguing in Publication Data
A catalogue record for this book is available from the British Library

Library of Congress Cataloging-in-Publication Data
A catalog record for this book is available from the Library of Congress

ISBN 978-0-340-80939-6

Typeset in 10/14.5 Gill Sans by Dorchester Typesetting Group Ltd

What do you think about this book? Or any other Hodder Education title?
Please send your comments to the feedback section on www.hoddereducation.co.uk.

CONTENTS

ACKNOWLEDGEMENTS

In the course of writing this book I was fortunate to have the help of three outstanding graduate assistants from the Department of International Relations at Florida International University: Jorge Villegas, Cheeku Bhasin, and Jorge Gomez. Each was assigned in different semesters and thus worked on different aspects of the writing project. Collectively, they provided invaluable support in library research, assembling the bibliography, and editing the manuscript. Above all, they were a great pleasure to work with.

Several people offered encouragement, support, and advice along the way. Tom Bassett read parts of the manuscript and provided an enthusiastic response when I needed it most. Three anonymous reviewers provided extensive criticism of the initial prospectus that was immensely helpful in conceptualizing and writing the book. I think that the end product is vastly improved as a result of their input. I hope they will agree. Gail Hollander's contribution to this project is immeasurable. She was overly generous, as always, in sharing her ideas, providing critical but supportive responses to mine, carefully reading and rereading the manuscript, and offering her encyclopaedic knowledge of a wide range of literature. I am and will remain in her debt.

I would especially like to thank the series editor, Alec Murphy, for inviting me to join an outstanding group of human geographers in this project. I hope that I have hit the mark with this book and that it supports his vision for the series. I would also like to thank Abigail Woodman, Liz Gooster, Colin Goodlad and Deborah Edwards, the editors at Hodder Arnold, for their patience, responsiveness, and encouragement over the long months.

Rick Schroeder gave permission for Figure 4.5. Figure 2.2 is produced by permission of Blackwell Publishing, from Stonich, S. (1989) The dynamics of social processes and environmental destruction – a Central American case study, *Population and Development Review*, 15(2): 269–96. Figure 2.3 is produced by permission of John Wiley and Sons, from Blaikie, P. (1989) Explanation and policy in land degradation and rehabilitation for developing countries, *Land Degradation and Rehabilitation*, 1: 23–37. Figure 3.1 is produced by permission of John Wiley and

Sons, from Holling, C. (ed.) (1978) *Adaptive Environmental Assessment and Management*, New York: John Wiley and Sons. Figures 4.1 and 4.2 are produced by permission, from Bassett, T. and Koli Bi, Z. (2000) Environmental discourses and Ivorian savanna, *Annals of the Association of American Geographers,* 90(1): 67–95. Figures 4.3 and 4.4 are produced by permission of Blackwell Publishing, from Robbins, P. (1998) Authority and environment: institutional landscapes in Rajasthan, India, *Annals of the Association of American Geographers* 88(3): 410–35. Figure 5.1 is produced by permission of Cambridge University Press, from Turton, D. (1987) The Mursi and National Park development in the lower Omo Valley, in Anderson, D. and Grove, R. (eds) *Conservation in Africa: People, Policies and Practice*, Cambridge: Cambridge University Press, pp. 169–86. Figure 5.3 is produced by permission of Oxford University Press, India, from Poffenberger, M. (1998) The resurgence of community forest management in the Jungle Mahals of West Bengal, in Arnold, D. and Guha, R. (eds) *Nature, Culture, Imperialism: Essays on the Environmental History*, Delhi: Oxford University Press, pp. 336–69.

INTRODUCTION

1

The environment and how we acquire, disseminate, and legitimate knowledge about it are highly politicized, reflective of relations of power, and contested. Any doubts that this is so can be dispelled quickly by a survey of recent headlines. The debate on the science of climate change conducted in the US news media in 2003–2004 – replete with accusations of government censorship and attacks on the personal integrity of scientists – provides a compelling illustration. A good place to enter the debate is in June 2003 when an official of the United States Environmental Protection Agency (EPA) anonymously leaked to the New York Times a copy of the agency's draft report on the state of the environment that had been heavily edited by White House officials. 'Among the deletions were conclusions about the likely human contribution to [global] warming ... [and] a reference to a 1999 study showing that global temperatures had risen sharply in the previous decade' (Revkin and Seeyle, 2003: A1). The deletions were so numerous and so muddled the report's discussion on climate change that ultimately the EPA deleted the entire section, leaving a puzzling gap in its assessment of environmental trends. Responding to what they perceived as an overt effort to shape and direct scientific information for political ends, the Union of Concerned Scientists issued a report in 2004 claiming that the 'manipulation, suppression and misrepresentation of science by the Bush administration is unprecedented' (quoted in Revkin, 2004a: A9). A Harvard University-based psychologist concluded in a National Public Radio interview that US President George W. Bush's science advisor 'basically has become a prostitute' (quoted in Glanz, 2004: D1).

Interestingly, while one arm of the US government was suggesting that scientific findings about the existence and causes of global warming were at best inconclusive, another was contemplating the consequences of a rapid, near-term shift in climate conditions. As reported in detail in the pages of Fortune magazine, the US Department of Defense issued an unclassified report towards the end of 2003 that

explored the effects of a rapid change in global temperatures by 2020 on food pro-
duction, geopolitical conflict, human migration and natural resources availability.
Sponsored by 82-year-old defense planner Andrew Marshall, 'known as the
Defense Department's "Yoda"' (Stipp, 2004: 104), the report's findings led even
Fortune to suggest that government regulation of industry and reduced oil con-
sumption might be a wise move.

Stranger still is the most recent political flap over climate change science. Once
again the story begins with an anonymous leak to the *New York Times*, this one from
a senior scientist at NASA's Goddard Space Flight Center. In a peculiar confluence
of partisan political interests, environmental policy, science fiction and big budget
movie promotion, the newspaper reported that NASA scientists had been banned
from commenting on *The Day After Tomorrow*, a futuristic Hollywood disaster film
on the havoc wreaked by human-induced climate change. The NASA headquarters
directive states, 'No one from NASA is to do interviews or otherwise comment
on anything having to do with' the film (quoted in Revkin, 2004b: 14). The film,
which includes a fictional US Vice-President resembling then current Vice-
President Dick Cheney ridiculing climate change science as disaster unfolds,
presents a sort of instant-Ice-Age scenario induced by fossil fuel emissions.
NASA headquarters subsequently relaxed their stand somewhat, allowing
selected scientists to answer questions from the news media.

These news items highlight what this book, in broadest terms, is about. It is
about a field of human geography that explores the relationship between politics
and ecology. These articles indicate a number of ways in which this relationship is
manifested, such as the exercise of political power to control who has access to
environmental scientific knowledge and under what circumstances. They suggest
that the environment is increasingly being framed as a security issue to be
addressed through military institutions, in addition to or rather than political and
scientific institutions. They also suggest that our knowledge of the environment is
culturally mediated and that this mediation is infused in political struggles over the
environment in complex ways. Visual imagery, stories, myths, ideology and so
forth operate to position us – as individuals, as congeries of institutions, and as a
species – in relation to the non-human world. The book, of course, plumbs the
depths of the relationship of politics and ecology far below the surface of newspaper headlines and popular films. Among other ideas, it explores the ways that
political and economic interests are reflected in the very questions that science
asks about the direction and causes of environmental change. It asks how struggles
over human rights, social justice and poverty are linked to the politics of environ-

mental conservation and degradation. These and other paths of inquiry pursued within raise fundamental and challenging questions regarding the nature of human–environment relations, questions that collectively constitute the focus of political ecology.

The constitution of political ecology

Journal articles, edited volumes and books carrying the phrase 'political ecology' in their titles have been appearing in recent years at an accelerating pace across several academic disciplines. Even a cursory search of academic databases and library catalogues reveals an impressive number of political ecology studies on a fascinating, if puzzling, array of topics. To illustrate with just a few examples, we find a large collection of works with the phrase 'political ecology of' followed by: biodiversity (Brown, 1998); picking (Hansis, 1998); Agave (Burwell, 1995); the British Conservative Party (Turner, 1995); representation in English Canada (Eagles, 1998); the modern peasant (Anderson, 1994); flood hazard (Pelling, 1999); transboundary development (Dedina, 1995); bananas (Grossman, 1998); biogeography (Kirkpatrick, 2000); coastal planning (Lee, 1993); and tourism (Stonich, 1998). Can we locate a common theme, or read any sense of coherence in these titles? Would a political ecology of 'Agave' (an economically important plant) resemble in any way a political ecology of 'the British Conservative Party'? In their use of the term, political ecology, can all of these authors possibly be referring to the same thing?

The answer to these questions, at least for several of the examples provided above, is, no. There are significant differences in the way the term is used, some so significant that there is little overlap in meaning. For the sake of clarifying what this book is and is not about, it is important to briefly discuss the various uses of the term, some of which have little relation to the project at hand, while others share certain interests. We can begin by first eliminating those uses that have the least relevance here. One meaning for political ecology builds on the emphasis of place in political geography (Agnew, 1987), exploring how local ecology might influence the structure and conduct of politics. Specifically, the objective of this approach is 'to identify if there really is a local ecology of political life in Canada' (Carty and Eagles, 1998: 591). Another, slightly related, meaning is to apply the principles of ecology to politics, either metaphorically or in the sense that ecology provides 'a foundation of and restriction on political possibilities, even determines appropriate forms of politics' (Hayward, 1994: 11). Neither of these uses, though interesting and important in their own right, is of interest to us for the purposes of this book.

3

A more common and prominent usage of the term is in reference to environmentalism as a political movement, particularly as it has manifested in continental Europe in the form of 'Green' parties. Atkinson has provided a thorough review of this idea, defining political ecology as 'both a set of theoretical propositions and ideas on the one hand and on the other a social movement referred to as the "ecology movement" or, latterly, the Green movement' (1991: 18–19). Atkinson located the origins of the greens in the 1960s' *Zeitgeist*. Health threats from nuclear fallout, concerns over industrial pollution, new awareness about the ecological damage from pesticide use, and alarm over the rapid rate of population growth combined with the social and political activism of the 1960s to produce the environmental movement. Political ecology, in this sense, is a liberal political movement anchored in a reaction against industrialization and modernity. It is this conceptualization of the term that was the target of Enzensberger's (1974) 'critique of political ecology'. Enzensberger proposed that the core thinking of the movement could be summarized by the hypothesis: 'the industrial societies of the earth are producing ecological contradictions, which must in the foreseeable future lead to their collapse' (ibid.: 4). According to Enzensberger, the proposals for action to avoid this future – based as they are on a technological and scientific understanding of society – are a fatal flaw in the political logic of the movement. That is, in the absence of a critical understanding of social and economic life, the mainstream Green movement could not address the fundamental causes of the environmental crisis.

While the conceptualization of political ecology as a green movement is different from the meaning used in this book, it does include overlapping theoretical and conceptual elements. The career of René Dumont and the key role he played in the history of the Greens in France demonstrate this point. In 1974, Dumont was the first in France to run for presidential office on an ecology platform. Whiteside (1997) argues that Dumont had a pivotal influence on French political ecology, which has stood out among European Green movements for its relatively strong currents of social justice, concern for poverty and attention to unequal North–South power relations. Dumont was an agronomist by trade who had done much of his research and advising in colonial and postcolonial territories where he came to question the suitability of French agricultural advice for local conditions. His political ecology was sensitive to relations of dependency between the South and North, the vulnerability of the world's poorest countries to environmental hazards, and the social and ecological damage resulting from the accumulation of wealth. He was as convinced as anyone in the environmental

4

movement of the ecological limits of the modern industrial economy, but thought that it 'failed to communicate how the effects of those limits would be felt unequally' (Whiteside, 1997: 7).

Dumont's socialist leanings, his ideas for a green political movement, and his professional experience as an agricultural advisor working in the Third World bring us in closer proximity to the meaning of political ecology as it is used here. In this book, political ecology refers to a scholarly field that emerged in the 1980s among a group of primarily geographers and anthropologists based in the United States, Great Britain, and Australia. In Chapter 2 we will treat the origins and central concerns of the field at length. Suffice it for now to say that the progenitors of political ecology were specialists in rural development, cultural ecology, and ecological anthropology, many of whom were, like Dumont, conducting research in postcolonial territories and drawing similar conclusions about the relationship between poverty and environmental degradation, questioning the suitability of Northern technologies, and critiquing the purported benefits of deepening market relations. Their initial focus was on probing how the politics of access to and control over land and resources were related to environmental change. The main premise was that ecological problems were at their core social and political problems, not technical or managerial, and therefore demanded a theoretical foundation to analyze the complex social, economic, and political relations in which environmental change is embedded.

Two geographers, Harold Brookfield and Piers Blaikie, put a name to this field and defined it as follows. 'The phrase "political ecology" combines the concerns of ecology and a broadly defined political economy. Together this encompasses the constantly shifting dialectic between society and land-based resources, and also within classes and groups within society itself' (Blaikie and Brookfield, 1987: 17). This definition, however succinct, still leaves much room for discussion over what exactly political ecology entails. Scholars have referred to political ecology as a 'research agenda' (Bryant, 1992), an 'approach' (Warren et al., 2001; Zimmerer and Bassett, 2003a), and a 'perspective' (Rocheleau et al., 1996a; Kalipeni and Feder, 1999). There is also a proliferation of new modifiers attached to the term, which appear to be multiplying at an increasing rate. These include proposals for a political ecology that is 'poststructuralist' (Escobar, 1996), 'feminist' (Rocheleau et al., 1996b), 'Third World' (Bryant and Bailey, 1997), 'antiessentialist' (Escobar, 1999), 'critical' (Sayre, 1999; Forsyth, 2003), 'First World' (McCarthy, 2002), 'geographical' (Zimmerer and Bassett, 2003b), and 'urban' (Swyngedouw and Heynen, 2003). There is even the suggestion that 'liberation ecology' (Peet and

Watts, 1996a) might be a more apt term, better reflecting a growing interest in the relationship of the environment to new social movements for entitlements, livelihoods, and social justice. Is this ongoing proliferation of new modifiers a sign of a maturing field developing internal specializations, an expansion in the breadth of its practitioners' interests, or a process of academic Balkanization? The answer suggested in this book is that it reflects a healthy mix of the expansion of and specialization within political ecology's boundaries.

While the various approaches to political ecology will be discussed at length in the chapters that follow, it would be useful at this point to elaborate somewhat on the scholarly practices that collectively constitute this field of research. What do political ecologists *do* when they practise their trade? As we shall see, there is no single methodology for political ecology research, though multiscaler analysis has been a hallmark of political ecology, making it distinguishable from other approaches to human–environment relations. Other common methodological patterns can be discerned by evaluating key writings in the field. Among the most important are political-economic analysis, historical analysis, ethnography, discourse analysis and ecological field studies. Few political ecology studies incorporate all of these methodologies, or do so in the same relative proportions. Furthermore, the geographic scales at which each methodology is engaged may vary greatly within and among studies. Ultimately, an engagement with a combination of several of these methodologies is an important and distinctive characteristic of research in the field. Moreover, virtually by definition, political ecology research includes historical and political-economic analyses. Although this assertion will be elaborated throughout subsequent chapters, a brief discussion is warranted here.

If we start from the basic definition of political ecology as ecology plus political economy, certain concepts and analytics become central to explaining human–environment relations. Specifically, a focus on the respective roles and interactions of the state and the market and the influences on environmental outcomes is critical. In addition, some level of historical analysis has been integral to the conduct of political ecology research. In particular, political ecologists have been concerned with historical processes of formal colonialism and their influence in shaping contemporary structural relations between the state, civil society and the market. Historical analyses have also been important for uncovering land and resource management practices embedded in non-capitalist or pre-colonial indigenous socio-political systems.

Apropos of this last point, ethnography has played a crucial role in approaches to political ecology that are concerned with highlighting the differing and sometimes conflicting perspectives on the environment and environmental problems held among various actors operating at local, regional and global scales. In particular, much attention has been given to exploring the symbolic meanings ascribed to lands and environments and how these imbricate with struggles over control and access to material resources. Ethnographic analysis in political ecology is not simply a matter of interpreting the 'native' view of the world, but also of interrogating the role of ideology and the importance of cultural context in shaping the perceptions of scientists, policy makers and bureaucrats. As Moore explained, 'Ethnography provides a critical medium for exploring the dynamics of cultural politics which animate environmental conflicts' (1996: 126). From this perspective on political ecology, symbolic struggles over the meaning, definition and categorization of rights, responsibilities and benefits are at the core of material struggles over the environment (Carney, 1993). Much of this interest in cultural politics and symbolic meaning in political ecology can be traced to the emergence of poststructuralism. An exploration of poststructuralism will be conducted in later chapters, but it is important to briefly identify here the ways that it has shaped political ecology research.

Poststructuralism has introduced to political ecology an emphasis on new social movements based on socially constructed identities of race, gender and ethnicity and hence a conceptualization of politics that is much broader than a focus on elections and state offices. In particular, it has introduced the idea of discourse analysis in political ecology research and the importance of exploring and revealing the ways in which the environment and environmental problems are discursively constructed. While a great deal of debate about the precise role of discourse analysis in the field continues, over the past decade or so it has become widely recognized that material analyses in political ecology cannot be conducted in the absence of or separately from discursive analyses. In political ecology's engagement with discourse analysis, emphasis is placed on a critical perspective toward modernist notions of objectivity and rationality, on interrogating the relationship between power and scientific knowledge, and the recognition of the existence of multiple, culturally constructed ideas of the environment and environmental problems.

Finally, political ecology incorporates, albeit critically, theoretical perspectives and empirical findings from ecological science. Many political ecologists conduct field studies that typically include vegetation transects, plot sampling, soil tests, analysis of remotely sensed imagery, or the use of computerized geographic information systems (GIS). The use of remotely sensed imagery, including satellite images and aerial photographs, has played a particularly important role in studies that seek to identify the direction and cause of ecological change. Ecological methodologies thus have a strong temporal component, reinforcing political ecology's emphasis on historical analysis. Political ecology studies also incorporate pre-existing scientific ecological findings in two distinct ways: as a source of empirical evidence and as a subject of critical analysis. In cases of the latter usage, political ecology studies have analyzed the role of politics in the production of scientific knowledge, such as the way that 'natural' landscapes are historically and politically constituted in the application of GIS mapping techniques (McCusker and Weiner, 2003). In some approaches, political ecologists may use the same information source to critically evaluate the categories and assumptions used to produce representations of the environment as well as to confirm actual biophysical conditions. That is, sources are evaluated both for their role in the construction of discourse and for their usefulness in compiling biophysical data (Fairhead and Leach, 1996). Finally, as we shall see later in the book, new models and theories of non-equilibrium ecology are driving and being driven by new findings in political ecology and cognate fields.

Approaching political ecology

This book represents an effort to firmly establish political ecology as human geography's newest field. Like all human geography's fields, political ecology incorporates important contributions from related disciplines – mostly anthropology, environmental history, and ecology – while retaining a distinctly geographical perspective. Thus, there will be discussions throughout of critical contributions to the development of political ecology from scholarly work in other disciplines. Scholars have written many excellent (and occasionally divergent) accounts about the academic origins and development of political ecology (e.g., Bryant and Bailey, 1997; Watts, 2000a; Forsyth, 2003). There will be opportunities to incorporate and comment on several of these accounts later in the book. Without suggesting there is one correct narrative on the field's origins, the emphasis here will be on placing the emergence of political ecology in the context of a body of historically evolving human geographic thought.

Having identified environmental problems as simultaneously political and ecological, social and biophysical, we are faced with the challenge of defining a field that can incorporate the broad range of implied research questions. Given this breadth and the multiple disciplinary influences, it is not surprising that we should find numerous internal debates about proper methodologies, research agendas, and analytical foci of political ecology as the field matures (Paulson *et al.*, 2003). Some have argued that we need to 'put politics first' (Bryant, 1991: 164) or pointed to an 'absence of a serious treatment of *politics* in political ecology' (Peet and Watts, 1996a: 10, emphasis in the original). Alternatively, others have suggested that there is little ecology found in most political ecology studies and argued the need to incorporate specific ecological concepts into the study of human–environment relations (Peterson, 2000). Still another perspective claims that most political ecology uncritically accepts *a priori* concepts and explanations in ecology and argues for an approach that seeks 'to establish the political forces behind different accounts of "ecology" as a representation of biophysical reality' (Forsyth, 2003: 4). In a related argument, Blaikie has suggested that political ecology needs to 'take the scientific evidence seriously and at the same time to question its technical basis and its political use' (1995: 208).

While this book takes pains to incorporate the insights and contributions from scholars writing from a range of positions, it identifies political ecology as constructed primarily through the merger of cultural ecology with political economy. The central premise in this definition is that the human transformation of natural ecosystems cannot be understood without consideration of the political and economic structures and institutions within which the transformations are embedded. The relationship of nature and society is, in a word, dialectical. The book emphasizes attention to the multifaceted relationship of politics to ecology, without attempting to privilege one over the other. In this regard, it comes closest in agreement to Zimmerer and Bassett's insistence on the need to address the 'ecological and the political dimensions of environmental issues in a more balanced and integrated manner' (2003b: 1). Of particular importance, this integrated approach must be sensitive to the role of biophysical processes in shaping human–environment relations.

Underlying this position is the desire to somehow bridge the natural and social sciences in order to better understand human–environment relations. Harvey (1993) has pointed out, however, that past attempts to create a common language for science and politics have produced social Darwinism and Nazism and warned that deep shifts in the ontology and epistemology of both sides are required. In particular, an attempt to bridge the natural and social sciences in political ecology raises an ontological question regarding the existence of 'the environment' outside of human perception and knowledge. The philosophical stance taken in this book – and by increasing numbers of political ecologists – is known as 'critical realism'. Critical realism starts from the premise that the world exists independently of our knowledge of it and that its very independence means that human knowledge is not itself reality, but a representation of it (see Chapter 3).

The overarching position taken toward political ecology in this book is one of inclusiveness. The necessity and desirability of creating an ever-expanding typology of distinct political ecology approaches – 'geographical', 'urban', 'Third World' and so forth – are downplayed. While emphasizing political ecology as a field of human geography, the book borrows liberally from advances in a range of academic disciplines in the humanities, social sciences and biophysical sciences and does not attempt to claim the field as geography's alone. It suggests that the various attempts to define distinct approaches can be incorporated in a single political ecology defined broadly enough to contain the multiple theoretical and disciplinary influences that have constructed it over the past two decades. Nevertheless, every discipline has its biases and strengths, and geographers' interests in questions of scale, spatial relations and place will be emphasized throughout. In agreement with several prominent works in political ecology, it seeks to integrate urban as well as rural and First World as well as Third World studies into the field's core (e.g., Blaikie and Brookfield, 1987; Rocheleau *et al.*, 1996b; Zimmerer and Bassett, 2003a).

The danger of such an inclusive approach is to produce a political ecology that is unmanageably complex and theoretically incoherent. This danger can be minimized, however. The position taken in this book is that there are fundamental philosophical and theoretical starting points that provide the field with coherence, while at the same time leaving a great deal of space for exploration, difference and debate. First, the problem of complexity, when conducting multiscaler analyses of human–environment relations, is unavoidable. Rather than seek to reduce or repress complexity, however, the approach emphasized throughout the book is to focus on teasing out 'intersecting processes' operating at different spatial and temporal scales (Taylor, 1997: 122). With this approach, no two situations will share the same sets of processes with identical levels of importance and influence, yet there remains 'a role for some degree of social scientific generalization' (ibid.: 124). Second, the central theoretical challenge for political ecology is to integrate political and ecological dimensions, as well as material and discursive elements. As was previously suggested, critical realism provides the philosophical foundation for an approach to nature–society relations that acknowledges the ontological independence of the biophysical world while at the same time recognizing that our understanding of the natural world is partial, situational, and contingent. An analysis of intersecting processes from a critical realist perspective would thus recognize the materiality of nature while maintaining that our understanding of nature is discursively constructed.

The structure of the book

The book explores the emergence, internal debates, and future directions of political ecology by focusing on key works. Throughout the chapters, excerpts from some of these are highlighted to give readers a flavour of the contributions of individual scholars, their methods and their findings. The identification of key works proved to be a difficult task for such a dynamic, interdisciplinary field that is rapidly producing an expanding body of outstanding empirical and theoretical work. It involved not only an engagement with scholars who self-label their work 'political ecology', but also with many who do not, though their empirical studies or theoretical writings have provided important referents for the field. Largely for the sake of readability, the label of 'political ecologist' is liberally applied throughout the book to scholars who may not refer to themselves as such. In the interests of maintaining focus and a certain level of coherence, the book does not systematically address important works in related fields – such as environmental racism, environmental ethics, environmental security and environmental justice – as part of the core political ecology literature. A limited discussion of some of this literature is presented in Chapter 6, however, since efforts to seriously engage the concepts, analytics and findings of these fields are growing in political ecology.

Four core chapters, Chapters 2–5, anchor the book. Each is to a degree self-contained and understandable as a stand-alone work. Yet they are meant also to build one upon the other. Readers will be far better prepared to grasp political ecology's particular analyses of development and conservation that are presented in Chapters 4 and 5 if they have first read Chapters 2 and 3. In Chapters 2 and 3 efforts are made to identify not only the different theoretical and philosophical stances that have shaped political ecology, but also to clarify what each brings to our understanding of human–environment relations. Some of this material is conceptually challenging, particularly for readers with minimal exposure to either social theory or ecological science. The book is intended to present the material in those two chapters in an approachable manner and to articulate the meaning of key theoretical concepts. The intention is not only to keep the material accessible, but also to strive for clarity in purpose and meaning. The four core chapters are framed by this introductory chapter and, at the end, by a chapter that reflects on the future directions of the field. The structure and purpose of each chapter are briefly detailed below.

Chapter 2 explores political ecology's formative period, tracing its roots in older traditions of study in human geography and ecological anthropology. It locates one of the field's primary roots in cultural ecology, a speciality developed in the 1950s and 1960s primarily in anthropology, but overlapping and in dialogue with advances in human geography, including environmental hazards research. The first half of the chapter relates human geographers' critiques of the core concepts and assumptions of cultural ecology and environmental hazards research and explains how these critiques became a major building block in political ecology's founda-tion. The second half of the chapter demonstrates that the other major source of political ecology is found in the radical critiques of mainstream explanations of the environmental degradation in the global South. These critiques, originating in the 1970s, from scholars trained in geography, sociology and anthropology, claimed that the *ultimate* causes of environmental degradation could be explained using the principles and concepts of political economy, including questions about wealth dis-tribution, patterns of accumulation, the role of the state and power to control access to land and resources. Their central premise was that ecological problems are at their core social and political problems, not technical and managerial, and that what was required was a theoretical foundation to address the complex social, economic and political relations in which environmental degradation is embedded.

As studies employing a political ecology perspective proliferated from the late 1980s onward, developments in social and ecological theory shifted the intellec-tual terrain. Chapter 3 examines in depth some of the most important theoretical developments, highlighting along the way fundamental ontological and epistemo-logical problems confronting interdisciplinary political-ecological analyses. The first section concentrates on the way that political ecology has adopted, chal-lenged, or been revised by social theory, focusing particularly on differing concep-tualizations of nature and ecological change. It argues that social constructivist approaches have fundamentally altered political ecologists' understanding of nature, the kinds of questions asked about human–environment relations, and the methods deployed to answer them. The chapter then moves to address how envi-ronmental history, a recently emerged cognate field of political ecology, has dealt with the theoretical challenges of postmodernism and poststructuralism. The chapter argues that political ecology and environmental history share a focus on the materiality of nature and a scepticism of the concept of nature in balance that has brought them into a new kind of engagement with ecological science. The con-text for this new engagement is the profound transformation of ecology from a science governed by a paradigm of stable equilibrium to one governed by a paradigm of non-equilibrium complexity. The chapter's overall assertion is that political ecology emerged in the 2000s at the centre of an interdisciplinary effort to synthesize the insights of poststructuralism with the non-equilibrium model of ecology.

Having explored advances in social and ecological theory, Chapter 4 examines how these have shaped the kinds of questions and methodologies that political ecology brings to its analysis of the modern development project as it relates to the environment. The perspective taken on development in this chapter is that it is the manifestation of the continuous unfolding of capitalist modernity in particular places at particular times. This perspective is meant to expand the discussion beyond the limited notion of development as a post-World War II international aid programme for Third World national economies. The chapter stresses that political ecology has been an important source of critical analyses of the social and ecological effects of mainstream development. It deals at length with poststructuralist approaches to environment and development. Specifically, the chapter traces one of the most provocative debates within political ecology: the treatment of development as discourse. The penultimate section examines how patterns of economic development and environmental change relate to conditions of land tenure and property rights. Of particular interest to political ecology is how property rights are defined, negotiated and struggled over among different social groups – whether they are class, gender, or ethnic groupings – and how this helps to explain patterns and linkages among economic development and environmental conservation and degradation. The concluding section of the chapter argues that political ecology studies of development and environment have begun and must continue to move beyond the dualisms of urban–rural, industrial–agrarian, and First World–Third World.

Chapter 5, the last of the core chapters, examines the political ecology of biodiversity conservation, concentrating on analyses of territorially based conservation strategies. One goal of this chapter is to demonstrate that political ecology provides a powerful analytic to assess both the ecological efficacy of the territorial approach to biodiversity protection and the politics that produce and are produced by it. Territorially based biodiversity conservation strategies, the chapter argues, raise questions that are at the very core of political ecology. How is the relationship between society and nature defined and conceptualized, how is access to land and resources controlled, and how are environmental costs and benefits distributed? The first half of the chapter is organized around the three main groups of actors whose interactions drive the politics of global biodiversity conservation: the state, international organizations and institutions, and civil society. The chapter thus begins by introducing the interests of each of these in relation to the history and practice of nature conservation. The focus then shifts to the mainstream or 'fortress' model of territorially based biodiversity conservation and explores how political ecology and related fields have critically evaluated the ideologies, assumptions and practices of its advocates. The following section examines some of the new biodiversity conservation models of 'nature–society hybrids' that conservation planners have developed to address the political conflicts and ecologic limitations inherent in the fortress approach. Political ecology studies suggest four conceptual and philosophical challenges for global biodiversity conservation and these are discussed at length in the chapter's closing section.

In the final chapter, the current trends in research and shifts in the larger societal context for human–environment relations are assessed with the aim of suggesting future directions for political ecology. Future themes for political ecology are identified, based both on the prevailing research trajectories as well as on lacunae in knowledge. Six broad areas of investigation are identified, each of which raises particular theoretical and methodological concerns for future research. The six themes are urban, landscape and meaning, environmental security and violence, ethics, identity and environment, and biotechnology and biodiversity. The final chapter demonstrates that 'making' political ecology is an appropriate metaphor for a dynamic, growing field that is continuing to unfold in provocative new directions.

ROOTS AND BRANCHES

Political ecology is the most recent expression of geographers' long-standing interest in the ideological, material, and symbolic relationships of human society to the natural environment. This interest has taken many forms in the past one hundred years of the discipline's development, including environmental determinism, possibilism, human ecology and cultural ecology, some of which we will explore in this chapter. Geography, however, is not alone in its concern with human–environment relations. Political ecology has developed, in part, through contributions from and in dialogue with other disciplines, most notably ecological anthropology. One finds that it is often difficult (and perhaps rather pointless) to draw distinctions between the methods and concepts of anthropologists and geographers 'doing' political ecology. In tracing the roots of political ecology in the following pages, my emphasis will be on locating the field within human geography, without, however, neglecting the important contributions of other disciplines. My method, therefore, is to focus on key works, regardless of the authors' disciplines, that were important to the development and establishment of political ecology.

Geography's human–environment tradition

Fundamental questions about the relationship of human society to the natural environment were among the principal concerns of classical geographers. Greek, Roman and Arab Muslim scholars theorized the limits of the habitable Earth, mapped real and imaginary cultural geographies, and proposed causal linkages between environment and culture. In his sweeping treatise, *Traces on the Rhodian Shore,* geographer Clarence Glacken (1967) traced changing ideas of nature in Western culture from the ancients to the moderns. He found that Western philosophers and scholars have persistently asked three questions concerning the environment and their relationship to it. Is the Earth a purposefully designed creation? Have the climate and the physical features of the Earth influenced the moral and social character of individuals and cultures? In what ways have people altered the environment and the face of the Earth from a hypothetical pristine state? All three questions have continued to structure the development of modern geographic thought, but they have received varying degrees of emphasis. For example, throughout most of the period that Glacken investigated, the question of people's role in transforming the environment was not well developed. His investigation, however, ended near the close of the eighteenth century, just when 'the story becomes interesting' (Stoddart, 1986: 30). That is, the period under study ended just when an explosion of new technologies and scientific instruments increased both humanity's capacity to change the environment and to observe and monitor that change. Beginning with the publication in 1864 of George Perkins Marsh's *Man and Nature*, the modern period is distinguished by a growing concern with the impact of human activities on the environment.

The gradual shift in interest toward human impacts notwithstanding, the role of nature in shaping culture remained a key question. Around the turn of the twentieth century geographers answered it with environmental determinism, the idea that the physical environment, particularly climate, determined the essential traits of a population's culture. Modern environmental determinism, the roots of which can be found in the writings of Greek antiquity, is usually associated with British geographer Halford Mackinder and two North American geographers, Ellen Semple and Elsworth Huntington. Writing initially in the years preceding World War I, Semple's and Huntington's theorizing expressed a distinct confidence in the superiority of 'Western' civilization and its environment. Two brief quotes will illustrate the general character of environmental determinism. Semple wrote, 'The southerners of the sub-tropical Mediterranean basin are easy-going, improvident except under pressing necessity, gay, emotional, imaginative, all qualities which among the Negroes of the equatorial belt degenerate into grave racial faults' (1911: 620). For Huntington, climate was the key explanatory variable: 'The climate of many countries seems to be one of the great reasons why idleness, dishonesty, immorality, stupidity, and weakness of will prevail' (1915: 294). Written at the pinnacle of European empire, descriptions of non-European cultures such as these can be viewed in hindsight as serving to explain and justify imperialism. Moreover, environmentalist writings on cultural hierarchies appear now as overly racialized, indeed racist, indicating the affinities of environmental determinism with the cotemporaneous fields of social Darwinism and eugenics.

From the late nineteenth century to the early twentieth century environmental determinism, or environmentalism as it was also known, was the leading framework in geography for understanding human–environment relations. The limitations of some of its more simplistic and cruder generalizations and its scientifically unsound methodology, however, soon came under attack, most notably from North American geographer Carl Sauer (1924). Sauer sought to shift geographic inquiry away from environmentalism and toward the role of humans in transforming the natural landscape, and developed an historical and evolutionary approach in tracing the influence of 'culture groups' through time. Sauer's interest in the agency of culture groups eventually translated to an increasing concern with human impacts on natural ecosystems (see Thomas et al., 1956). Recalling the third fundamental question investigated by Glacken regarding the role of humans in altering their environments, Sauer can be viewed historically as developing the line of inquiry that Marsh pioneered in the mid-nineteenth century. In focusing on anthropogenic landscape change, Sauer was not particularly concerned with the ecological interactions between human society and its environment. Others, including students he had influenced, were, and they moved the investigation of human–environment relations in new directions, inspired by advances in the study of ecosystems.

Cultural ecology

For social scientists in various disciplines, biological ecology, and the ecosystems concept specifically, have long held promise as models or metaphors for understanding human social systems. In 1922, for example, Harlan Barrows, in his Presidential Address to the Association of American Geographers, called for a reconceptualization of geography as 'human ecology' (Barrows, 1923). Barrows likely borrowed the term from his colleagues at the University of Chicago where a group of sociologists, led by Robert Park, employed it for their method of studying urban society. Barrows' idea was to develop geography as a social science for the study of 'the adjustments of man to … elements of the natural environment' (1923: 4). His concept of 'adjustments' was fundamentally materialist, declaring that most forms of human–environment relationships are established from society's primary efforts to make a living from the earth. Though echoes of Barrows' suggestions reverberate in later developments in natural hazards research and economic geography, his conceptualization of geography as human ecology was not widely adopted. North American cultural geography, especially as it developed under Sauer at the University of California at Berkeley, was perhaps a more important ancestor in cultural ecology's intellectual lineage. Many practitioners of this brand of cultural geography, however, were not preoccupied with ecological relationships *per se*, but landscape transformations and questions of the geographic origin and diffusion of crops, ideas and technologies. Sauer did, nonetheless, have an influence on anthropologist Julian Steward, whose writings are widely viewed as providing the most direct inspiration for cultural ecology (Butzer, 1989).

Steward, who had studied at Berkeley with both Sauer and anthropologist Alfred Kroeber, argued that explaining variation, change and adaptation was of key importance for understanding human–environment relations (Steward, 1955). He was interested in using concepts of biological ecology to understand the effects of environment on culture. Specifically, he sought to give culture the role in human society that genetics plays for non-human species in evolution and adaptation to the environment. For Steward, and the cultural ecologists who followed him, 'the concept of environmental adaptation underlies all cultural ecology' (ibid.: 39). He was concerned, in part, with recovering the importance of the natural environment in shaping cultures, a research focus that had been abandoned by anthropologists reacting against environmental determinism. Steward stressed that the environment does not determine culture, nor is it simply a passive set of conditions that enable or constrain human activities. Human societies and the natural environment are in constant flux and interplay and the creative behavioural responses (i.e., adaptations) to environmental conditions provide an important key to explaining cultural change.

The cultural ecologists that followed Steward found great methodological potential in the ecosystem as the basic unit of analysis. The ecosystem concept was first fully articulated by the plant ecologist, A.G. Tansley, who reasoned that all the parts of an ecosystem, 'organic and inorganic, biome and habitat – may be regarded as interacting factors which, in a mature ecosystem, are in approximate equilibrium' (1946: 207). A key assumption was that ecosystems are characterized by homeostasis and equilibrium. Homeostatic systems are self-maintained and self-regulated through complex control mechanisms, energy pathways and feedback loops in a way that resists change and results in a stable equilibrium state. This concept of self-regulating systems held great appeal to anthropologists and geographers interested in demonstrating that cultural adaptation was the key to understanding complex human–environment interactions. The idea of the ecosystem – consisting of identifiable components and variables in constant flux through interdependent interactions – as the primary unit of analysis provided cultural ecologists with the methodological tools for in-depth field studies of the role of culture in mediating human–environment relations in agrarian communities. Ecosystem concepts such as environmental thresholds, carrying capacity, negative and positive feedback loops and, especially, adaptation, became the lingua franca of cultural ecology.

This functional adaptation/systems approach to analyzing culture in human–environment relations reached its apogee in American anthropologist Roy Rappaport's study of the ecological role of ritual among the Tsembaga Maring of New Guinea's central highlands (Rappaport, 1968). In his methodology, 'populations' and 'ecosystems' served as the primary units of analysis and ritual as the 'mechanism' that regulates their relationship. The population was comprised of 204 Tsembaga engaged in subsistence swidden farming using simple technology: digging sticks, steel axes and bushknives. The ecosystem was analogous to the 3.2 square miles of primary and secondary tropical forest that they occupied and utilized for subsistence. The ritual that Rappaport identified as the regulating mechanism centred on the uprooting of the *rumbim* plant (*Cordyline fruticosa*), a small tree that held great symbolic importance for Tsembaga group identity and coherence. Ritual uprooting of the *rumbim* among the Tsembaga, he argued, 'helps maintain an undegraded environment ... adjusts man–land ratios, facilitates trade, distributes local surpluses of pig in the form of pork ... and assures people of high-quality protein when they most need it' (ibid.: 224). The ritual therefore operated like a thermostat, according to Rappaport, functioning to regulate the relationship of Tsembaga population and their ecosystem and thus produce a stable equilibrium state over the long term. Like a thermostat, the ritual signals that the system has reached a certain state and that formally proscribed activities (i.e., local taboos) could now take place in order to readjust the relationship of key variables.

It is difficult to do justice here to the depth and nuance of Rappaport's work and there is a danger of caricature in such a brief summary. The study had an enormous impact on the development of cultural ecology and *Pigs for the Ancestors* was for years required reading for anthropology, sociology and geography graduate students. The painstaking measurements, detailed observations, and intellectual scope of the study set a benchmark toward which other cultural ecologists would strive. Moreover, *Pigs for the Ancestors* can be viewed as the archetypical cultural ecology study – grounded in ethnographic fieldwork and empirical data collection in a small, remote, Third World community that employed simple technology in a subsistence-oriented economy. Finally, and most importantly for the task at hand, Rappaport's work clearly illustrates one branch of political ecology's intellectual lineage. Several geographers whose research and writing have been critical to the early formulation of political ecology (explored later in this chapter) shared research interests with Rappaport. Harold Brookfield, and later William Clarke, and then Lawrence Grossman, all associated with the Department of Human Geography at the Australian National University, conducted fieldwork in New Guinea that was, in part, in dialogue with Rappaport's and other Columbia University anthropologists' research there. Michael Watts, as a doctoral student in the Department of Geography at the University of Michigan, was a student of Rappaport's when he taught in the Department of Anthropology there and later became one the most challenging critics of his formulation of cultural ecology.

Though Rappaport's influence is undeniable, the limitations of systems analysis for studying human–environment relations became increasingly apparent. Even the most 'primitive' tribes and 'isolated' communities have become participants in a global circulation of commodities and labour. This is not even a particularly new phenomenon, a fact that has sometimes produced methodological difficulties for anthropologists wanting to study autarkic groups. Take, for example, the so-called 'Bushman' of Africa's Kalahari Desert, often characterized in popular media and, until very recently, anthropological writing, as Stone Age primitives living untouched by the currents of human history. Gordon (1992) pointed out how, in the 1970s, anthropologists conducting fieldwork among the Bushmen had to wilfully overlook evidence of their unfortunate involvement with the forces of capitalist trade. Indeed, examining the historical record, Gordon finds that the Bushmen, far from being isolated and untouched hunter–gatherers, had been active participants in the global circulation of commodities since the mid-nineteenth century. Cultural ecologists faced a dilemma. If the Kalahari Bushmen, the quintessential prehistoric hunter–gatherer culture, had been reduced to an impoverished rural proletariat, where could researchers turn to find bounded, self-subsisting cultures? The concept of the autarkic, self-regulating human ecosystem as a unit of analysis became increasingly difficult to reconcile with the reality of labour migrations, commodity production, market participation and the rapid introduction of new technologies, any one of which will fundamentally alter human–environment relations. The critical methodological challenge this posed for cultural ecologists translated into new problems in theorizing human–environment relations.

In the 1970s and 1980s, researchers began to shift the focus of cultural ecology towards an analysis of how Third World communities dealt with the social and ecological demands of an external capitalist economy. Two brief examples of geography research from Central America (Nietschmann, 1973; 1979) and Melanesia

(Grossman, 1984), will serve to illustrate the shift in focus from local cultural beliefs and practices to external economic relations. On the Caribbean coast of Nicaragua, Miskito Indian communities had developed a subsistence production system founded on both land-based gardening and marine resource extraction. Employing a broad range of ecological and ethnographic methods, geographer Bernard Nietschmann sought to understand how the pressures of external market demand for resources altered human–environment relations and affected the long-term viability of local cultural practices, social structures and the biotic environment. As an illustration, the case history of the sea turtle demonstrates how the Miskito's increasing involvement in market relations led to ecological degradation as well as a decline in the subsistence production and eventually to a process of proletarianization among the Miskito. The meaning and economic value of turtles changed when turtle processing companies arrived in the area and began offering cash and extending credit so that the Miskito could harvest turtles year-round instead of seasonally. Subsistence production suffered as labour was directed to harvest turtles, turtles became scarcer and more labour time was required to hunt them in a desperate effort to pay debts and buy food. Ultimately, the turtle population was decimated and increasing numbers of Miskito had to resort to wage labour migration in pursuit of cash, further reducing the possibilities for the recovery of the former subsistence production system.

The second example comes from research in the highlands of Papua New Guinea. Geographer Lawrence Grossman studied the effects of introducing rural commodity production on the cultural ecology of a community's subsistence system. He concluded from his study that smallholder production of agricultural commodities for external markets – in this case, coffee and beef cattle – conflicts with subsistence production, even when land and labour are in absolute surplus. Among the factors producing conflict he identified: (1) the displacement of subsistence production further from settlement; (2) a disruption of the linkages between subsistence production and the local ecology; and (3) the diversion of labour away from subsistence production, contributing to food shortages. Among the study's important contributions was a demonstration of how the socio-economic stratification of rural communities that accompanied increasing commodity production and market integration produced marked differences in individuals' and families' abilities to respond to ecological perturbations. This finding, then, explicitly links the concerns of political economy – socio-economic differentiation, class formation and agrarian transformation – with the concerns of cultural ecology. To summarize the message of these studies, the transition from autarky to involvement in commodity production and market relations means that for many remote communities 'economic risk is added to natural risk' (Clarke, 1977: 384).

While these and other rural Third World studies tried to reconcile the realities of an expanding and deepening global capitalist economy with concepts of self-regulating homeostasis and cultural adaptation, geographer Michael Watts took a wrecking ball to cultural ecology's epistemological foundations (1983a; 1983b). Particularly targeted for demolition were the concept of adaptation and, more generally, the philosophical basis of systems theory. In theorizing the relationship between drought and famine among Hausa peasants in northern Nigeria, Watts identified serious flaws in the assumptions and philosophical underpinnings of cultural ecology and environmental hazards research (a related field discussed later in this chapter). To begin, cultural ecology adopted an unexamined distinction between 'human' and 'environment', treating each as discrete objects subject to observation. Watts criticized this as naïvely positivist and empiricist and pointed out that this understanding of society and nature is traceable to a seventeenth-century Newtonian–Cartesian mechanistic view of the world. Furthermore, by relying on concepts inherited from biology and cybernetics, the varied and complex social character of human relations is reduced in cultural ecology to interactions between atomized individuals. These individuals are characterized as 'rational actors' making informed choices in response to environmental change. Human behaviour, reframed as 'adaptation', thus becomes crudely functionalist and teleological. An alternative, he suggested, is to conceptualize a dialectical unity of society and nature and to give greater attention to the social and historical contingencies of knowledge and political economic structure. In a nutshell, Watts argued against using biological and systems theories or metaphors for exploring human–environment relations, and instead emphasized the need to engage with social theory, particularly Marxist political economy. At this point it would be useful to look at the historical and intellectual context for this turn to Marxist political economy and then take a closer look at the main target of Watts' critique, natural hazards research.

The critique of natural hazards

The broader context for geographers' engagement with Marxist thought was a renewed interest among North and South American and Western European social scientists in the 1960s and 1970s in the analytical and explanatory potential of Karl Marx's nineteenth-century theory of capitalist societies. In geography this interest in Marxist political economy first emerged in the early 1970s, partly in reaction against efforts to define the discipline as a 'spatial science' and against the philosophy of positivism more generally. Spatial science was formulated during the quantitative revolution in geography. Proponents of the quantitative revolution sought to use statistical formulations to reinvent geography as an autonomous science based on predictive, generalizable, and quantifiable models of spatial phenomena. In other words, the 'revolution' was concerned with transforming geography from an idiographic (i.e., preoccupied with the unique and particular) to a nomothetic discipline (i.e., concerned with theorizing and abstraction) known as spatial science. By the late 1960s, the quantitative revolution had begun to run out of steam. Events outside of academia, including new social movements formed around issues of decolonization, civil rights, the environment and women's rights and general social unrest stemming from racism, poverty, and the Vietnam War conspired to accelerate its decline. To paraphrase David Harvey (1973), first a leading practitioner and then prominent critic of the quantitative approach in geography, the mechanistic and statistically driven theories had little to say about the leading social issues of the day and a new theoretical framework was needed. Marxist political economy would provide the method and theoretical concepts to reconstruct a more socially relevant human geography.

It was within the broad context of this historical shift in human geography towards social theory and away from the naïve empiricism and positivist underpinnings of spatial science that Watts formulated his critique of cultural ecology and its cognate field, natural (or environmental) hazards. Hazards research focuses on how and why people are exposed to extreme natural events and how they responded when exposed. Within geography, a distinct school of hazards research originated with the 1950s' work of Gilbert White on floodplain hazards in the United States. Through collaborations with other investigators in the 1960s and 1970s, particularly Robert Kates and Ian Burton, a set of methods and assumptions were applied to a wide range of hazards and locations around the globe (see White, 1974, and Burton et al., 1978). In The Environment as Hazard, White and his collaborators sought to summarize the state of knowledge regarding how individuals and societies respond to extreme natural events such as droughts, floods, hurricanes and earthquakes (Burton et al., 1978). In the process they examined, among other questions, whether natural disasters were becoming more damaging and, if so, why? Their approach was founded on a Newtonian–Cartesian conceptualization of the environment as functioning 'largely independently of human activities' and as 'an object of scientific inquiry' (ibid.: 19). To investigate the question of how individuals and societies respond to natural hazards, they imported from cultural ecology the concept of cultural adaptation. To simplify, cultures that weathered natural hazards were adapted to their environments, cultures that did not were maladapted.

Despite the stature of White and his colleagues in geography and in policy circles, their two major works received scathing reviews (Waddell, 1977; Torry, 1979). Torry characterized *The Environment as Hazard* as 'flawed by lapses of scholarship, dominated by feeble typologies, and lacking any unifying theory' (1979: 368). Some of the criticism was directed at the questionable use of statistical quantification in hazards research and reflected the general criticisms of the quantitative revolution in human geography. Waddell (1977), for instance, criticized the studies in White's (1974) *Natural Hazards* for utilizing an inappropriate and overly scientistic methodological approach that produced 'the most banal results'. Moreover, when the approach was exported to Third World settings, the results became even less reliable and meaningful. Investigators failed to recognize locally rooted indigenous strategies for coping with hazards and instead adopted an unexamined model of development that dismissed non-Western societies as 'backward' and in need of 'modernization'. For Watts, one of the major shortcomings in this research was its reliance on a limited and intellectually suspect concept of rational behaviour to explain exposure and response to natural hazards. The White–Kates–Burton school of hazards research reduced exposure and response to hazards to a series of purposeful choices by rational individuals, with little reference to social structural constraints or historically contingent conditions.

To a great extent, Watts' *Silent Violence* and his related publications were an attempt to develop a new kind of human ecology/natural hazards research that rejected the focus on individual rationality and the cybernetic model of cultural adaptation and instead sought to locate and explain local responses historically, socially and politically. In outlining this new approach he wrote: 'I would like to suggest that the forces and social relations of production constitute the unique starting point for human adaptation which is the appropriation and transformation of nature into material means of social reproduction' (1983b: 242). This reorientation towards investigating the social relations of production was guided by a broadly Marxist body of scholarship in geography, social history, peasant studies and the transformation of nature (e.g., Marx, 1967; Schmidt, 1971; Thompson, 1971; Scott, 1976; Bernstein, 1978; Sayer, 1980). Watts' purpose was to show that the vulnerability of peasant societies to natural hazards – in his study, recurrent drought in northern Nigeria – was not due to irrationality, backwardness, or cultural maladaptation, but to the particular way that regional pre-capitalist modes of production were articulated with a global capitalist system under the aegis of the colonial state. Watts' study of drought and famine was a watershed in the development of contemporary political ecology and it is worthwhile presenting some of his methods and findings to close this section (see Extract 1).

extract 1

Silent Violence: on methods and findings

On methods
I have quite deliberately employed an eclectic array of sources including oral evidences and a local-level fieldwork (village) study of some duration ... The majority of this information was derived from extensive discussions with elders (dattawa)... Two other primary data sources were of special significance. First, I utilized journals, diaries and travelogues written by a handful of nineteenth-century explorers who in varying degrees resided in Kasar Hausa. The second source consists of a wealth of colonial archival materials located in Nigeria and Great Britain ... The distorted optic provided by a wholesale dependence on archival sources can, and I would argue must, be complemented by oral fieldwork ... During the village study in 1977–78 I collected field data using a variety of what I refer to with some trepidation as methodological techniques; sometimes they involved large-scale survey methods and on other occasions small, nonrandom samples of householders and farmers.
Source: Watts (1983a: 32–5)

On findings
Colonialism in northern Nigeria was a process of incorporation in which pre-capitalist modes of production were articulated with the colonial, and ultimately the global, economy. This articulation was principally affected through the colonial triad of taxation, export commodity production and monetisation ... To the extent that pre-capitalist elements in northern Nigeria were eroded by colonial integration, the adaptive capability of Hausa communities and the margin of subsistence security accordingly changed. In the process, peasant producers—particularly the rural poor—became less capable of responding to and coping with both drought and food shortage.
Source: Watts (1983b: 249)

25

It is quite clear that in northern Hausaland groundnuts were the principal tax-paying crop, which perhaps goes a long way to explaining the apparently 'irrational' behaviour of a peasantry which produced more groundnuts when the commodity price had actually fallen. More generally, of course, the 'groundnut revolution' meant a decrease in the area devoted to foodstuffs, increasing subjection to the vagaries of the world commodity market, and the ever-present threat of indebtedness at the hands of middlemen ... The point that I wish to emphasise is that colonialism broke the cycle of reproduction of peasant households ... In a very real sense, then, hazards <u>had been redefined by the transformation in the social relations of production.</u>
(Source: 1983b: 250–2, emphasis in the original)

For while all households are theoretically capable of coping with various forms of stress, in practice these responses are mediated by social and economic inequality ... Clearly, then, in peasant communities, where socioeconomic differentiation is so pronounced, poor farmers, shackled by their poverty, are largely powerless to effect the sorts of changes that might mitigate the debilitating consequences of environmental hazards. <u>Hazard response is thus contingent upon the social context of the responding units and upon their situation in the productive process.</u>
(Source: 1983b: 255–6, emphasis in the original)

Third World environmental degradation

While Watts' study in Nigeria was focused on theorizing and empirically documenting the relationship between drought and famine, other proto-political ecologists were investigating Third World 'environmental degradation', a catch-all term for a range of ecological problems such as desertification, soil erosion, deforestation and species loss. In the 1960s and 1970s, a number of books with provocatively apocalyptic titles such as *The Population Bomb* (Ehrlich, 1968) and *The Sinking Ark* (Myers, 1979), warned of unfolding ecological catastrophes in the developing countries of the South. These and similar writings linked the loss of forest cover, the spread of deserts and the decline in species numbers to misuse, over-use, and mismanagement by local populations (i.e., peasant farmers and pastoralists) in the Third World. Neo-Malthusianism – the idea that population growth is the primary or even the sole cause of environmental degradation – was the foundation of much environmentalist thinking and writing during this period (Adams, 2001). This led to a simplistic and reductionist formulation of environmental degradation;

over-grazing causes desertification, which is caused by too many livestock (over-stocking), which is caused by too many people (over-population). With little variation, neo-Malthusian thinkers applied this formula to every ecological problem imaginable and population control, especially in the global South, became the answer to environmental degradation.

Closely associated with neo-Malthusian writings are technocentric and managerial approaches to environmental degradation. These approaches can be traced to the post-World War II development agenda for the Third World that linked economic growth with environmental control and management (ibid.). Technocentrists accept that over-population is an environmental problem, but posit that technological solutions exist or can be developed to accommodate additional population while avoiding ecological damage. Introducing check dams and terraces and instructing local peasants on appropriate farming techniques, for example, are the primary solutions to the problem of soil erosion resulting from population increases. The related managerial approach begins with the assumption that environmental degradation results from the mismanagement of resources by local populations and concludes that the solution is to introduce rational planning by specialists (e.g., agronomists, range scientists, soil scientists). The classic example of this writing is Garrett Hardin's (1968) 'The tragedy of the commons', wherein the author posits that mismanagement is endemic to the common property regimes typical of many Third World communities. The piece was principally written as a polemic in favour of population control, particularly for the South. Much of the reaction to it, however, has focused on Hardin's argument concerning the over-stocking of the commons. Briefly, he argued that in cases where resources − in his example, pasturage − are held in common by a community, individuals will put increasing numbers of stock on the range to maximize their individual economic gain, while the ecological costs of that action are borne by the entire community. The solutions he offered were to privatize the resource (i.e., introduce the rationality of the market) or intervene with the coercive power and authority of the state in order introduce rational resource management practices. What was intended as an argument for population control was widely taken in policy and academic circles to be an argument against the local customary management of resources and in favour of privatization and outside intervention.

In a critical response to these and other such writings, a number of geographers, anthropologists and sociologists began to interrogate the empirical and ideological bases for their assumptions and conclusions (e.g., Franke and Chasin, 1980; Homewood and Rodgers, 1984; Redclift, 1984; Blaikie, 1985; Hecht, 1985). While the differences in disciplinary training provided nuances in method and analytical focus, these writings had two things in common. First, each contained a cogent refutation of 'mainstream' (see Adams, 2001) thinking about the causes of and cures for Third World environmental degradation. The point of these critiques was to expose neo-Malthusianism as simplistic, empirically unsubstantiated, and theoretically barren and to show that technocentrist and managerial solutions ignored the social relations, economic constraints and political power structures that shaped land and resource use. Second, each offered an alternative interpretation of the causes of degradation that was founded on the principles and concepts of political economy, including questions about wealth distribution, social patterns of accumulation, interclass relations, the role of the state, patterns of land ownership and control over access to natural resources. In sum, these alternative approaches began with the premise that ecological problems were at their core social and political problems, not technical or managerial, and that what was required was a theoretical foundation to address the complex social, economic and political relations in which environmental degradation is embedded. To better understand the development of political ecology it is worthwhile to review here some of these studies in greater detail.

An early example of this type of analysis is *Seeds of Famine*, an exploration by an anthropologist/sociologist duo of the links between desertification, famine and land use in the aftermath of the 1968–74 Sahel drought (Franke and Chasin, 1980). Subtitled *Ecological Destruction and the Development Dilemma in the West African Sahel*, their book challenged the prevailing diagnoses of development agencies that the Sahel was over-populated and that indigenous pastoralist societies were mismanaging and degrading their rangelands because they maintained 'backward' common property systems and made 'irrational' land use decisions. They amassed historical and contemporary evidence – including tax and debt burdens, dislocation from and reduction in customary pasturage, the geographic expansion of export cropping, and increasing and conflicting labour demands – that addressed the underlying rationale behind the rangeland management decisions of local pastoralists. Beyond questioning conventional wisdom on the causes of desertification, they suggested that the empirical evidence for its actual occurrence was limited and weak and that much of the concern over degradation seemed to be ideologically driven and derived from questionable colonial-era assessments. They offered what they termed a 'radical approach' that avoided simplistic and reductionist causal explanations. 'The radical approach uses history, climate data, social processes, and more specifically, the effects of the imposition of the colonial economy and its postcolonial dependency relationships between the Sahel nations and the international capitalist system' (ibid.: 129). In linking local land-use decisions to the constraints posed by national and international political economic structures and historically-embedded patterns of exploitation, Franke and Chasin anticipated some of the central concerns of what would in a few years become identified as political ecology.

As researchers increasingly recognized political economy as critical for under-standing human–environment relations and explaining degradation, they began to turn their attention to an analysis of the state. In trying to understand the seem-ingly economically irrational destruction of the Amazon rainforest, Hecht (1985) focused on the development policies of the Brazilian state. Methodologically, Hecht moved away from the micro-level analysis typical of cultural ecology to what she termed 'mid-level analysis', focusing not on individuals and isolated com-munities, but on state institutions and policies, the accumulation strategies of a domestic class of landowners and businessmen, and the lending policies of multi-lateral banks. Nevertheless, with its emphasis on the collection of extensive ecological data, her research adhered to another strong tradition within cultural ecology studies. Theoretically, she sought to demonstrate the failings of existing frameworks commonly employed to explain environmental degradation and to offer an alternative framework that focused on an analysis of the political economy of Amazonian development.

Using a complex and convincing set of economic, political and ecological data, Hecht demonstrated that the Brazilian state's development policies for the Amazon basin (supported by bilateral and multilateral aid agencies and banks) fuelled capital accumulation for a small domestic class of investors while destroy-ing the productivity of the land. Briefly, the state sought to promote the settle-ment and development of the Amazon through the establishment of a cattle ranching industry. Extraordinary subsidies were offered to investors, including 100 per cent tax exemptions, the relaxation of import duties on equipment, extremely cheap credit and other incentives. These incentives, combined with very high rates of inflation, made land subject to speculative investment. 'The exchange value of the land', Hecht explained, 'was far higher in this speculative context, than any commodities it could produce. Entrepreneurs depended for profits, *not on the annual productivity of the land, but on the rate of return to investment*' (1985: 678, emphasis in the original). The detailed data she gathered on changes in soil chem-istry following forest clearance and cattle grazing supported the conclusion that the ecological result was rapidly declining land productivity leading to abandonment and the further spread of deforestation (see Figure 2.1). Her study, in sum, successfully combined a Marxian analysis of class relations and the state's role in facilitating wealth accumulation among a small class of speculators with ecological field methods to show the limitations of neo-Malthusian approaches.

Figure 2.1 Many forests in the tropical Americas, Costa Rica in this case, have been converted to cattle pasture.

While Hecht was concerned with demonstrating the role of the state in promoting degradation, geographer Piers Blaikie (1985) asked why state programmes and policies intended to correct problems of environmental degradation more often than not fail. The book wherein he pursued this question, *The Political Economy of Soil Erosion in Developing Countries* (Blaikie, 1985), is now recognized as a foundational text in political ecology's development as a distinct field. Its status in political ecology's growing canon has much to do with the fact that the book explicitly was intended to provide a methodology for understanding environmental degradation's causes and cures in the Third World. It suggests the critical questions to ask, the appropriate units of analysis, and the theoretical concepts that should guide investigation. In short, it provides something of a roadmap for investigating the linkage of environmental degradation to political and economic structures and processes. The starting point for such investigations must be 'place-based' (ibid.: 5), that is, where degradation is taking place and with the individuals proximately responsible for land-use decisions. The analyses would then move beyond to 'non-place-based' (ibid.: 5) factors, that is, the social relations of production and the nature of the state. Tracing non-place-based factors moves the investigation beyond a fixation on proximate causation that constrains positivist approaches. Finally, the scope of degradation analyses should be enlarged to include an assessment of the perceptions and 'rationality' of not just the local land users, but also of the government officials, conservationists, and scientists.

At the core of Blaikie's analysis is a focus on the relationship between 'under-development' (a set of social and economic conditions that translate into rural poverty in the Third World) and environmental degradation. Specifically, he argued that environmental degradation is at once a symptom, result and cause of under-development. Building upon the work of geographers and economists (e.g., Wisner, 1976; Bernstein, 1979; de Janvry, 1981), Blaikie linked the economic mar-ginalization of land users to their ecological and spatial marginalization. For exam-ple, it is often the case in Third World countries that the most productive land has been appropriated by large-scale capitalist enterprises while poor peasant farmers (i.e., a socio-economically marginalized class) are relegated to less productive and more ecologically fragile (i.e., marginal) lands. Thus, if one wants to understand the underlying causes of environmental degradation, one must understand the under-lying causes of poverty and if one wants to understand the causes of poverty, one needs a theory of political economy. Here Blaikie was less explicit and systematic than Watts (1983a; 1983b), but does make clear that the analysis of poverty needs to focus on modes of surplus extraction at various geographic scales. He also made clear that the increased incorporation of Third World peasants into the market and into systems of wage labour is not, as mainstream development think-ing would have it, the solution to poverty and degradation, but all too frequently exacerbates poverty and degradation. Poverty and degradation are therefore closely linked to social and spatial patterns of wealth accumulation.

Though *The Political Economy of Soil Erosion* was not explicitly an attempt to the-orize human–environment relations, it did raise a number of theoretical questions that continue to be debated within political ecology and social theory in general. By insisting that the perceptions of policy-makers, government officials and scien-tists be scrutinized as closely as those of Third World peasants, he opened the door to questions of power, knowledge and ideology as they relate to claims about environmental degradation. In a sense, the book foreshadowed the incor-poration of feminist, postcolonialist, and postmodernist challenges to European Enlightenment notions of rationality and universal truths into the human–environment debates of the late 1980s and beyond (see Chapter 3). The book also stressed, without much theoretical elaboration, the need to conceptualize soil erosion (and degradation in general) as simultaneously a political, economic and ecological problem, requiring, somehow, that the epistemological and methodological differences between the social and natural sciences be bridged. Following the postmodernist turn in social theory, these differences and the debates surrounding their possible resolution have only intensified in subsequent years. Blaikie's book is now considered to be a 'classic' text in the development of political ecology (Adams, 2001: 251).

Political ecology takes shape

In retrospect, the works cited in the two preceding sections can be viewed as representative of an unfolding paradigm shift (Kuhn, 1970) in social scientists' conceptualizations of human–environment relations and the causes of and solutions to environmental degradation. There was much discussion in the 1970s of the need for a new integration of social and ecological methods and approaches in order to arrive at a fuller understanding of environmental degradation. By the mid-1980s, scholars from a variety of disciplines were increasingly adopting a critical, often radical, perspective in investigations of the relationship between environment and development. Their empirical studies tended to focus on tropical Third World 'lands at risk', such as rainforests, mountain slopes, and arid grasslands (Little and Horowitz, 1987). The more radical of these studies indicted prevailing economic development models and practices for their role in increasing poverty and environmental degradation in the Third World, linking the fuller integration of the non-European world into a system of global capitalism to a rash of ecological and social crises. Scholars gradually began to employ 'political ecology', as a term that could encapsulate a new, theoretically informed, critical perspective in environment and development research.

The term, political ecology, first appeared in the 1970s as a way for journalists and academics to stress that 'the environment' had become a highly politicized object (Wolf, 1972; Enzensberger, 1974; Cockburn and Ridgeway, 1979). These early usages of the term, however, were not accompanied by a set of theoretical or methodological suggestions for investigating the relationship of the political and the ecological. Later uses of the term by anthropologists more closely approximated the type of approach that has come to characterize the field of political ecology. Turshen (1984), in her book, *The Political Ecology of Disease in Tanzania*, linked European colonial conquest, the proletarianization of African labour, and the coerced introduction of cash cropping to ecological change and the spread of human and animal diseases. In their study of Amazonia, Schmink and Wood (1987) made an early effort to outline a political ecology approach, describing it as a way to analyse resource management 'from the perspective of political economy' (ibid.: 39), highlighting patterns of surplus production and appropriation and the role of the state in promoting accumulation in the private sector.

It is the geographers Piers Blaikie and Harold Brookfield, however, who are now widely recognized as making the first explicit and extended attempt to 'develop a methodology ... and basis for theory construction' for political ecology (Blaikie and Brookfield, 1987: xxi). In a concise and much-cited phrase, they defined political ecology as an interdisciplinary field that combined 'the concerns of ecology and a broadly defined political economy' (ibid.: 17). One key element in their formulation of political ecology was the idea of marginalization, a syndrome that geographers in critical development studies of the 1970s identified to describe a combination of ecological, political and economic circumstances that took communities and their environments down a path of mutual destruction (e.g., Wisner, 1976; Torry, 1979). To develop this idea as a fundamental building block for political ecology they defined and linked three different conceptualizations of marginality. First, they incorporated from Ricardo the neo-classical idea of the economic margin as the point at which the cost of bringing additional inferior land into production is just met, but not exceeded, by the income gained from that production. Second, from ecology they incorporated the idea of the biophysical limits to the geographic range of particular species. Third, from political economy they incorporated the idea that often in the course of economic development, certain social groups and entire regions are excluded from opportunities for employment, adequate housing and health services, social advancement, and political participation. They argue that the close relationships among these concepts of marginality mean that changes in the status of one can, and often do, bring about changes in the status of the others. 'Hence land degradation is both a result of *and* a cause of social marginalization' (Blaikie and Brookfield, 1987: 23) (see Extract 2).

extract 2

Regional political ecology

The complexity of these relationships demands an approach which can encompass interactive effects, the contribution of different geographical scales and hierarchies of socioeconomic organizations (e.g., person, household, village, *region, state, world) and the contradictions between social and environmental changes through time. Our approach can be described as <u>regional political ecology</u>. The adjective 'regional' is important because it is necessary to take account of environmental variability and the spatial variations in resilience and sensitivity of the land, as different demands are put on the land through time. The word 'regional' also implies the incorporation of environmental considerations into theories of regional growth and decline.*

The circumstances in which land managers operate in their decision-making over land use and management can be considered in the context of core–periphery relations. Location-specific studies of the settlement frontiers of Brazil, the United States and Southeast Asia, as well as of agricultural decision-making in economically declining areas, provide considerable evidence for suggesting that declining regional economies provide an important context for lack of initiative and investment of labour and capital in managing land ...

The phrase 'political ecology' combines the concerns of ecology and a broadly defined political economy. Together this encompasses the constantly shifting dialectic between society and land-based resources, and also within classes and groups within society itself.

We also derive from political economy a concern with the role of the state. The state commonly tends to lend its power to dominant groups and classes, and thus may reinforce the tendency for accumulation by these dominant groups and marginalization of the losers, through such actions as taxation, food policy, land tenure policy and the allocation of resources.
Source: Blaikie and Brookfield (1987: 17)

A second feature of what they labelled a 'regional political ecology' approach is an attention to spatial and temporal scales in seeking explanation and tracing the constantly shifting society–nature dialectic. They called this aspect of their approach, 'chains of explanation' (Blaikie and Brookfield, 1987: 27). The chain of explanation begins with the individual 'land manager' – the person with direct relations with the land that the authors appear to equate chiefly with Third World peasants (see ibid.: 74–8) – and then traces the social relations of production outward and upward to the local, national and, ultimately, the global scale. The social relations of production include, among other things, the control of land, labour, and inputs, patterns of surplus extraction, and decision-making authority for investments in land improvements, and are embedded in particular systems of property rights. Explanations of environmental degradation must also be traced in time, as ultimate causation may lie with historic events and decisions. The authors explain, 'we found it necessary to move not only "upward" from the land manager to the social and political system, but also backward in time to understand the antecedents of modern conditions' (ibid.: 100). Some degree of historical analysis, then, is critical in their formulation of political ecology.

Blaikie and Brookfield's effort to outline a political ecology approach suffered somewhat for being indeterminate and open-ended. Their chain of explanation has been criticized as a hierarchical structure that implies the 'conceptualization of scale as a series of pregiven sociospatial containers' and neglects consideration of how scale is socially produced (Zimmerer and Bassett, 2003b: 3). In their proposed approach, the list of circumstances and social factors that influence environmental degradation is so inclusive as to 'cast doubt on how far the approach represents a theoretical abstraction at all' (Black, 1990: 45; Neumann, 1992). These shortcomings aside, Blaikie and Brookfield put a name to a new field and helped to spark a dynamic, wide-ranging, and probing debate and body of research on ecological and social change. *Land Degradation* was published at a time of considerable ferment in policy and academic circles regarding the relationship between environment and development. The outcome of the ferment in policy circles was the mainstreaming of sustainable development, exemplified by the publication of the Bruntland Commission's report, *Our Common Future* (Bruntland, 1987), which linked poverty and environmental degradation. On the academic side, the result was the emergence of a series of research fields in traditional social science and humanities disciplines in which human–environment relations were the central focus (see Bryant and Bailey, 1997: 15–17). *Land Degradation* exemplified this trend, but stood out in its explicit attempt to develop a theoretical and methodological foundation for the study of human–environment relations. By doing so it provided scholars and researchers with a set of hypotheses, propositions and methodological agendas to test, challenge and extend through both inductive and deductive theory building.

A spate of studies in geography and anthropology guided by a political ecology 'approach' or 'perspective' soon followed the publication of *Land Degradation* (e.g., Bassett, 1988; Blaikie, 1989; Stonich, 1989; 1993; Black, 1990; Thrupp, 1990; Bryant, 1992; Neumann, 1992; Peluso, 1992a). Most of these to some degree attempted both to clarify the outlines of an emerging field and to explore the insights that a political ecology analysis could bring to specific cases. Bassett (1988), for example, employed a political ecology perspective to investigate conflicts between livestock herders and farmers in the Ivory Coast, focusing on the role of the state in promoting private accumulation. Stonich's (1989) study of land degradation in Honduras demonstrated that the historical processes of the concentration of land ownership and the expansion of capitalist agricultural production have forced poor farmers onto marginal lands and into ecologically destructive land use practices. Using a variety of ethnographic, survey, and documentary research methods, she connects the shifting emphasis on export crop production and livestock to the restructuring of agriculture to the detriment of poor farmers and the land (see Figure 2.2). Bassett and Stonich's research are examples of 'classic' political ecology case studies, combining an analysis of the state's role in fuelling accumulation, intensive ethnographic fieldwork, and an assessment of ecological change.

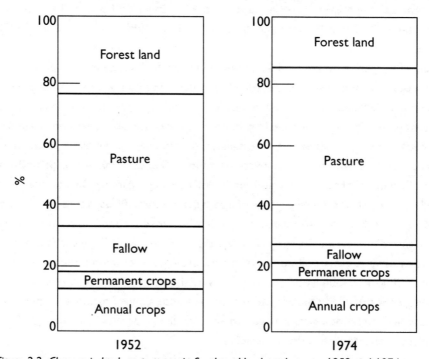

Figure 2.2 Changes in land-use patterns in Southern Honduras between 1952 and 1974.

In a follow-up to Land Degradation and Society, Blaikie (1989) elaborated on how a chain of explanation approach to land degradation could provide the understanding necessary to inform and change state policies. He presents a flow chart that attempts to show the links between biophysical and political-economic conditions by scaling up the analysis from the place-specific location of degradation to the regional, state and global scales (see Figure 2.3). Among the many challenges that Blaikie highlights is the fact that the explanatory links in such an analysis become more and more tenuous and difficult to confirm the further one moves from the site. We might also add that it is not at all clear from the chart how and when 'factors' become 'causes' (see Watts, 2000a). Furthermore, he presents an argument concerning the relationship of the chain of explanation and policy that is in the end inevitably self-contradicting. That is, he states that an effective soil and water conservation strategy must be founded on 'a comprehensive and accurate explanation of why degradation has occurred' (Blaikie, 1989: 23). Yet after describing and illustrating the various explanatory links in the chain, he acknowledges that the more radical – in terms of challenging existing social relations of production at various scales – the explanation becomes, the less likely it is that a politically feasible policy can be formulated. Since issues of land distribution, patterns of accumulation, national debt, north–south trade relations and so forth are part of the chain of explanation, it is difficult to imagine a 'non-radical' explanation. In this contradiction lies the source of one of the enduring criticisms levelled at political ecology, that it is long on critique and explanation and short on policy recommendations.

Bryant, building primarily on the work of Blaikie and Brookfield, sought to cast political ecology as 'an emerging research agenda in Third World studies' (1992: 12). He suggested that three areas of inquiry constitute a Third World political ecology framework. First, political ecology studies must include the contextual sources of environmental change, specifically state policies, interstate relations and global capitalism. The second area of inquiry focuses on land and resource access rights, local struggles and ecological transformation. Studies of agrarian change, peasant economies and politics, and changing property regimes – all of which imply an historical perspective – are relevant to this line of investigation. Finally, Third World political ecology should investigate the political ramifications of environmental change, particularly the inequitable distribution of the costs of degradation across socio-economic strata. By focusing on the Third World, Bryant correctly identified political ecology's roots in tropical ethnography and development studies while perhaps neglecting the possibilities for a more robust political ecology capable of overcoming the constructed divisions of urban–rural and First World–Third World.

Theoretically, then, early political ecologists treated 'political economy' as the touchstone for a new field. The emphasis on political economy, however, even if restricted to a Marxian version, can raise as many questions as it answers (Staniland, 1985). Considering the collective endeavours cited above, political

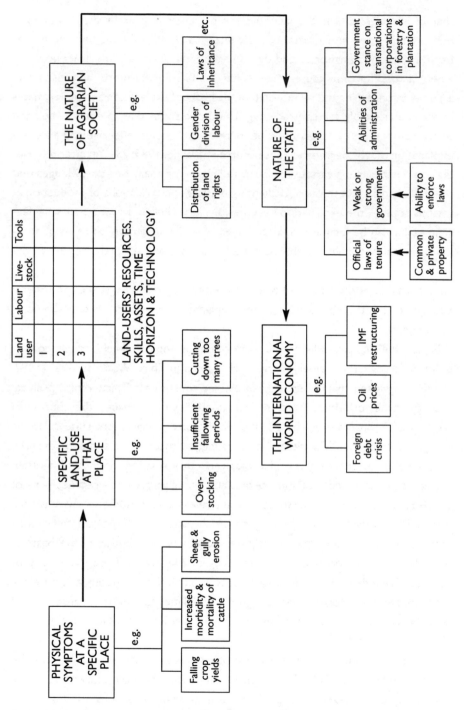

Figure 2.3 An explanation of causes of soil erosion: the chain of explanation.

economy is so broadly conceived that everything 'social' is potentially important to the analysis. Collins (1986: 1), for example, identified 'tenure, credit policies, titling and other institutional factors' as central to understanding degradation. Schmink and Wood (1987: 39) focused on the 'relationship between surplus production, social class, the function of the state in promoting private accumulation and the role of ideology in public discourse and development planning'. Blaikie and Brookfield (1987: 17) identified 'taxation, food policy, land tenure policy and the allocation of resources' as important state actions to include in their analysis. The *general* theoretical thrust is clear, but when it comes to conducting specific analyses, the list of potential 'factors' and 'causes' that one needs to address is less so.

I suggest here that these first attempts to engage and elaborate on a newly identified political ecology approach mark its transition to an established human geography field with its own internal debates, schools of thought and research agendas. I further suggest that the 1993 publication of two special issues of *Economic Geography* edited by Richard Peet and Michael Watts on 'environment and development' marks the completion of the transition and a branching out of the field into compelling new interactions with social and ecology theories. The special issue contributors moved the field beyond a mere correction to cultural ecology and hazards research and refutation of neo-Malthusian explanations of environmental degradation. Contributors, for example, brought the insights of feminist theory to bear on the politics of land and resource access, highlighting the importance of gender analysis to political ecology (Carney, 1993; Schroeder, 1993) (see Vignette 3). Theories of new social movements, identity politics, and cultural meanings were engaged to counter a static, homogenized vision of 'indigenous knowledge' and overly materialist interpretations of environmental conflict (Bebbington, 1993; Moore, 1993). The double special issue, later revised and published as *Liberation Ecologies* (Peet and Watts, 1996b; 2004), both demonstrated the diverse theoretical and geographical influences on the field and proposed a course for its further development. It is to the latter effort that I now turn to wrap up the current chapter and set the stage for the next.

extract 3

Gender and agrarian change

I examine forms of environmental change on the wetlands of The Gambia during the past 25 years. Irrigation schemes play a central role in government policies aimed at diversifying agricultural exports while improving self-sufficiency in food grains. But the intensification of household labor regimes to year-round cultivation is inducing unparalleled gender conflict as communities reorient the common property regime to the new economic emphasis on irrigated production.

An examination of contemporary changes in the Gambian wetlands illuminates the interplay of environmental transformation, accumulation strategies, and women's work to changing common property regimes. In the Gambian system land is managed for individual use but is not individually owned. A number of users enjoy independent rights of usage, which is to say, individual rights to the benefits of his or her labor. Community land access is regulated by households with rights to exclude non-members of that collectivity. This political ecological analysis, which examines labor and rights of access to resources, draws environmental attention to the relationship of Gambian women's protests against the changing forms of control exercised over community property systems in the wetlands.

In outlining the social and historical processes of changing land use strategies on the Gambian wetlands, this paper reveals that more than the environment is being transformed. So too are the social relations that mediate access to, and use of, land within rural households. As commodification transforms the use of wetland environments, the social relations that produce these environments are also restructured.
Source: Carney (1993: 329–30, 345).

In their introduction to the special issue, Peet and Watts (1993) suggest five themes in a heterogeneous assortment of scholarly projects that at the time were beginning to extend the frontiers of political ecology. First, they highlight efforts to refine political economy by bringing questions of the environment into a reformulation of Marxist theory, particularly the notion of a 'second' contradiction of capitalism (see M. O'Connor, 1994a). Second, they identify attempts to bring a broad notion of politics – everyday forms of resistance, livelihood movements, and gender relations – more centrally into political ecology. Third, they draw attention to the ways that theories of state–civil society relations – particularly pertaining to the conditions under which environmental movements develop and effectively (or not) challenge state predations – have informed political ecology studies. Fourth, they identify an emerging concern for social constructions of knowledge, especially with regard to the natural sciences and to popular ideas of nature and the environment. Fifth, and finally, they suggest that political ecology relies on outdated theories of stable equilibrium models of ecology, and would benefit by incorporating 'new' ecology models of disequilibria. Underlying these themes is, of course, a diverse and sprawling body of twentieth-century scholarly works produced by – in no particular order and with no attempt at comprehensiveness – Antonio Gramsci, Michel Foucault, Donna Haraway and Anthony Giddens. In Chapter 3 we will explore the ideas of these and other scholars and their influence on the development trajectories of political ecology.

Conclusion

Nearly twenty years after its initial publication, Watts characterized his work, *Silent Violence*, as 'a sort of head-on collision with the magnificent work of Roy Rappaport ... and the cultural ecology of Barney Nietschmann' (2001a: 626). The seeming nihilism of the metaphor is probably unintended for the result of Watts' and related efforts was not merely wreckage. Rather, if I may return to my own metaphor of the wrecking ball, the epistemological foundation of cultural ecology had to be cleared before a new foundation for understanding human–environment relations could be constructed. At the risk of over-extending the metaphor, one can observe that many of the methodological building blocks of cultural ecology, such as an intensive focus on small, rural communities and ethnography combined with ecological data collection, were recycled to construct political ecology. The 1970s' ferment within geography and related disciplines produced a creative intellectual outburst that spawned a number of studies in the early 1980s that began the construction effort. They did not carry the label 'political ecology' but in retrospect have come to be viewed as the foundation of a new field. The works cited above heralded a shift away from an interest in self-sustaining and ecologically stable human ecosystems towards questions about the causes of and solutions to environmental degradation and risk.

A pattern in the purpose and content of these proto-political ecology studies emerges. To one degree or another, a primary purpose was to demonstrate that neo-Malthusian formulations, neo-classical economic models emphasizing the individual rational actor and technocentric approaches, are ideological, overly simplistic, focused on proximate phenomena, and thus limited in their explanatory power. One can also detect a pattern in the way researchers went about 'doing' political ecology. Moving the analysis of environmental change beyond proximate causation dictates a number of methodological adjustments. First, historical analysis is crucial, both to understand the extent and nature of environmental change and to explain how current geographical, social and political relations and conditions came to be. Second, it is necessary to conduct the analysis on several geographical scales as a way of linking place-specific conditions to regional, national and global patterns and processes. Finally, ethnographic fieldwork, broadly conceived, is important to address questions of rationality and to understand the roots of conflict in the differing meanings attached to the environment. Ethnographic analysis is not limited to studies of the exotic 'other', but is equally focused on institutions and organizations: governmental, non-governmental, and multilateral.

In theoretical terms, the strongest influence on the early development of the field was Marxist political economy, with the most direct contributions coming from peasant studies, dependency theory, and world systems theory (e.g., Shanin, 1971; Frank, 1967; Wallerstein, 1974). This translated in political ecology to a focus on the role of the state, particularly in fuelling accumulation among dominant classes and in structuring land and resource access through laws and policies. It implied a focus on conflict and struggle over the environment and questions about the relationship between social and geographic patterns of poverty and the occurrence of environmental degradation. The influence of world systems, dependency, under-development theory and the like meant giving attention to the way specific locations and communities were incorporated into the global capitalist economy. Marxist political economy also meant that our understanding of nature–society relations must be conceptualized as a dialectical unity, rather than a set of 'interactions' between two distinct objects. The social relations of production and environmental change are mutually constitutive.

There has been a great deal of change in the world at large in the past decade or more that has shifted the context of the field's development and affects the kinds of questions political ecologists ask and how they ask them. New technologies have grown more sophisticated, both in their potential to affect human–environment relations and to monitor those effects. Innovations in biotechnology, culminating in the mapping of the human genome and successful experiments in the cloning of livestock, will increasingly challenge our ideas of nature and the place of humans in it. New international agreements, such as the 1992 Convention on Biological Diversity, attempt to clarify proprietary claims to genetic resources and in the process raise new debates and ignite new struggles over ownership and access to land and resources. Decades of monitoring and new computer modelling techniques have produced a near scientific consensus that anthropogenic climate change is well underway, creating new questions regarding the causes of and the exposure and response to environmental risk. 'Sustainable development' has been mainstreamed and the World Bank, once the poster institution for ecologically destructive global capitalism, has reinvented itself as global environmental manager through the establishment of the Global Environmental Facility. The Berlin Wall came down, existing socialisms across the world faded away, neoliberalism rules the day, civil society and the market are in, and the state is out. The 11 September, 2001, terrorist attacks on the World Trade Center and the Pentagon have only accelerated a well-advanced movement to redefine the environment as a security issue. These are just a few of the major events and trends that shape political ecology in the twenty-first century.

In the academy, recent advances in social theory have produced new branches of political ecology. The structural and deterministic aspects of Marxist political economy have been challenged by feminism, postcolonialism, constructivism, post-structuralism and postmodernism. Political ecologists, in an evolving effort to engage social theory, have grappled with their implications for analysing human–environment relations and environmental change. Equilibrium assumptions in biological ecology have also been challenged by theories of non-linear change and system disequilibria. These shifts in biological ecology also have important consequences for the conduct of political ecology research. In the next chapter we will examine some of the major shifts in social theory and biological ecology and show how geographers and others have borrowed from and built upon their insights to produce a vibrant and multifaceted new field.

3
NATURE AND SOCIETY

Early political ecology, it should now be clear, demonstrated that 'the environment' was not simply a problem for science and technology to solve, but was fundamentally and thoroughly social and political. Nature–society relations, it was argued, should be regarded as a dialectical unity (Watts, 1983b). Environmental problems should be treated as simultaneously political-economic and ecological in character (Blaikie, 1985). If we take seriously the necessity of integrating the biophysical and social worlds in our analyses of environmental problems, we are immediately presented with a series of methodological and philosophical challenges. How do we reconcile epistemological differences between the biophysical and social sciences in order to reach some mutual understanding of the causes of and solutions to environmental problems? How, for example, do social scientists demonstrate causal proof to natural scientists when the 'chain of explanation' of soil loss includes 'oil prices', 'abilities of administration', and 'laws of inheritance' (Blaikie, 1989)? How do we reconcile a poststructuralist position that treats environmental conservation as the production of 'fourth order of simulacra' (Bartram and Shobrook, 2000) with a conservation biologist's response that characterizes social theory as a 'covert assault' on science (Soulé, 1995)? What sort of dialogues are commenced or curtailed by a feminist theoretical stance that treats science as a masculinist discourse or a postcolonial theoretical stance that treats it as a colonizing enterprise?

The answer, at least to some of the above quandaries, is that reconciliation is not possible. A profound postmodernist position that rejects the privileging of any single truth claim, for instance, can never be made compatible with the epistemology of logical positivism. On the other hand, plenty of space remains in the middle ground between social and ecological theory to create exciting new synergies between the humanities, social sciences, and biophysical sciences. Political ecology, perhaps more than any other field, is particularly suited to positing an interdisciplinary understanding of nature–society relations. This chapter will explore some of these possibilities, beginning with a look at how political ecology has incorporated and helped advance the important developments in social theory in the final quarter of the twentieth century. The chapter then shifts to examine environmental history, a field distinct from political ecology, but overlapping and in dialogue with it. Environmental history has gone through its own maturation process as it both responded and contributed to new developments in social and ecological theory. The profound transformation of ecology from a science governed by a paradigm of stable equilibrium to one governed by a paradigm of non-equilibrium complexity is tackled next. The final section details the most recent efforts in political ecology to seize on the tectonic shifts in the philosophical bedrock of the social and ecological sciences as an opportunity to create a new interdisciplinary understanding of nature–society relations.

Social theory

Social theory is a term so frequently and unreflectively tossed about in academic writing as to inevitably produce confusion and frustration among the uninitiated, particularly for those trained in the positivist/empiricist philosophy of the biophysical sciences. This confusion and frustration, I suggest, are a significant source of the difficulties arising in interdisciplinary efforts to link politics and ecology. It is crucial, therefore, to begin by clarifying what is meant and implied by the term 'social theory' and its post-prefixed subsets. First, social theory is an ambitiously broad and encompassing concept that necessarily transgresses the established disciplinary boundaries of the academy. The work of Michel Foucault, to take a prominent example, could be read as sociology, history, political economy or philosophy. Similar conventionally unclassifiable work, such as that of Anthony Giddens (1984), has been referred to as an effort to establish a body of 'grand theory' that is not based in any single academic discipline (Onuf, 1989). Some have characterized social theory as a 'post-disciplinary' endeavour (Sayer, 2000: 7) and thus not really 'theory' in the classical sense of creating the distinctive framework and *raison d'être* of a particular discipline (Onuf, 1989). Second, because it is ambitiously broad and encompassing, the meaning of social theory is ambiguous and controversial, containing many opposing ontological and epistemological positions. There is no need to tackle the controversies and contradictions here, but merely to point out that there is no easy way to categorize social theory.

In the interests of moving this discussion forward, I will adopt Gregory's (1994) conceptualization of social theory. Gregory treats social theory

> as a series of overlapping, contending and contradictory discourses that seek, in various ways and for various purposes, to reflect explicitly and more or less systematically on the constitution of social life, to make social practices intelligible and to intervene in their conduct and consequences.

> (1994: 79)

Contained within this over-arching idea of social theory are the various permutations of Marxism, structuration, feminism, postmodernism, poststructuralism, and postcolonialism. Each of these are in turn constructed of their own overlapping, contending and contradictory discourses and I will make no attempt to investigate their complexities here. Rather, I propose to concentrate on the way political ecology has adopted, challenged or been altered by social theory, focusing particularly on differing conceptualizations of nature and ecological change.

The social construction of nature

Social theory, in its various forms and to varying degrees, problematizes positivist science's claim to possess 'objective' knowledge that reflects the reality of nature, positing instead that nature is socially produced or socially constructed. But what exactly does it mean to say that nature is socially constructed or socially produced, and do they mean the same thing? To answer the second part of the question first, while there is a great deal of overlap in meaning and the phrases frequently seem to be used interchangeably, they have distinct theoretical origins. The idea of the production of nature can be traced to efforts to overcome the conceptual duality of nature and society as discrete objects through an engagement with Marxist historical materialism (Smith, 1984; 1996; Harvey, 1993; Swyngedouw, 1999). Smith (1984) built his argument for the social production of nature on Marx's idea of the dialectical unity of nature and society – nature is shaped by human labour, and the labourer is in turn shaped through this encounter. He presented two concepts, 'first nature', that materiality which is unaltered by humans, and 'second nature', which is comprised of the institutions of society, the market, the state and so forth. First nature, through capitalist production, is incorporated into second nature and in the process is transformed into another commodity.

While all societies may be said to produce nature on one scale or another, under industrial capitalism, nature is produced on a global scale. Using climate change as an illustration, Smith points out, 'increasingly first nature is produced from within and as part of second nature' (1996: 50). That is, globally organized industrial production systems have altered biotic, atmospheric, and hydrologic systems on a global scale with the result that there is no 'first nature' left that is not socially produced. This is not to say that nature is 'not real'. The concept of socially produced nature is fundamentally a materialist one and accepts that biophysical things and processes exist, but that they exist as a dialectical unity of nature–society.

The idea of social construction (sometimes cultural construction) of nature is a term commonly employed to stress the role of representation, discourse and imagery in defining and framing our knowledge of nature and the natural. This approach has been characterized as 'certain radical forms of "postmodern deconstructivism"' that 'asserts that all we ever perceive about the world are shadows' and thus denies the external existence of nature (Soulé and Lease, 1995: xv). While bordering on caricature, this can be accepted as a fair enough assessment of strong anti-realist positions held by some postmodernists (see Sayer, 2000). For example, in offering an 'open poststructuralist critique' of attempts to defend the reality of nature through the relational dialectics described above, Bartram and Shobrook argue that this approach only perpetuates 'nature's endless duplication' (2000: 378). Their point, based on Baudrillard's notion of scientific and technological simulation, is that environmental conservation in the twenty-first century is an illusion produced by 'endless duplications of nature' (ibid.: 393), a process 'that only confirms its irrevocable loss' (ibid.: 377) rather than recovering its reality.

Neither this 'open poststructuralist critique' nor Soulé and Lease's characterization, however, are reflective of the conceptualization of the social construction of nature in political ecology. Political ecology rejects the 'defeatism' that abandons 'all hope of distinguishing better from worse explanations' (Sayer, 2000: 30) implied by strong postmodernist positions, while at the same time sharing poststructuralist concerns of the importance of discourse, representation, and imagery in structuring knowledge of the world (Blaikie, 1996; Peet and Watts, 1996a). Smith and others have stressed that the social production of nature 'incorporates material with conceptual construction' (1996: 50; Harvey, 1996; Castree and Braun, 1998; Neumann, 1998; Swyngedouw, 1999). To elaborate, Castree and Braun argue that 'discursive relations and representational practices are constitutive of the very ways that nature is made available to forms of economic and political calculation and the ways in which our interventions in nature are socially organized' (1998: 16). Insisting that nature is social and historical does not 'require its transformation *tout court* into discourse, and the exclusion of natural "agency"' (Smith, 1998: 274). The central point to take from this summary is that our models of nature can neither be naïvely accepted as objective reality divorced from social and power relations, nor as merely an illusion produced through discourse (see also Chapter 4). It should be clear from this brief discussion that while ideas of the social construction of nature and social production of nature have different lineages in social theory and can imply different and distinct positions on the reality of nature, they are often used interchangeably.

Feminist critiques of science

One more important source for the constructivist approaches to nature, feminist theory, particularly in its critique of the biological sciences, must be considered here. Feminist theory relating to ecology and the environment is extremely diverse, containing many ongoing debates on the 'essential' qualities of women and their association with nature (e.g., Shiva, 1989; Jackson, 1993) and there have been several attempts to categorize the breadth of feminist approaches (Merchant, 1992; Keller, 1996; Rocheleau et al., 1996a). In the context of this discussion I want to focus on the work of a group that Rocheleau et al. – in their effort to establish a feminist political ecology – have labelled 'feminist poststructuralists' (1996a: 4). Feminist poststructuralists, of whom Donna Haraway is perhaps the most prominent, present a critique that challenges the 'very assumptions of objectivity and rationality that underlie the scientific enterprise' (Keller, 1996: 30). Feminists' rejection of the prevailing concept of objectivity in science is based on a strong scepticism of scientists' claims that gender, politics, sexuality, history, class, ethnicity and every other situational characteristic could be overcome in scientific observation. That is, they are sceptical of the idea that scientists' observations can somehow be disembodied (removed from all context) to produce an objective and universal empirical truth. The problem this position presents for feminist science is this. How does one recognize the subjectivity of all observation, while at the same time maintain a commitment to accurate accounts of the 'real' world (Haraway, 1988)? Haraway's answer is 'situated knowledges', the idea that all observation is located, embodied and partial, and that by recognizing and accepting this partiality science can be better positioned to understand the limits (and limitations) of knowledge claims. In making her argument, Haraway rejects both the view from everywhere (the totalization of vision) and the view from nowhere (relativism) and substitutes the view from somewhere (situated knowledge) (ibid.).

Feminist (as well as other) constructivist critiques of science have been misunderstood and stereotyped as suggesting the impossibility of judging one set of 'facts' as a more accurate reflection of reality than another, thus consigning us to a world in which all truth claims are relatively valid. This is not what feminist poststructuralists are proposing. The argument is not that all knowledge is subjective and therefore nothing remains but relativism and a gross politicization of truth claims. Rather, it is that paying careful attention to the history and social context in which scientific knowledge is generated will 'require and generate stronger standards of objectivity' (Harding, 1996: 237). In short, the idea of situated knowledge does not reject the practice of science, but offers a path to improve it and its knowledge product.

Social constructivism brings critical insights into political ecology. By emphasizing the importance of discourse, representation and imagery to identify and frame the causes and solutions to environmental problems and by insisting on the need to situate and contextualize knowledge claims, constructivism provides the conceptual tools to critically evaluate, as Blaikie (1985) urged, the perceptions and 'rationality' of not just the local land users, but also of the government officials, conservationists, and scientists. At the end of the day, the challenges that feminism, postmodernism and poststructuralism present to political ecology revolve around the nature of reality and the reality of nature. Social theory has destabilized 'nature' as constant, material reality from which we can derive moral values and lessons for society (see Harvey, 1996).

Critical realism

One of the principal objections to social constructionist approaches to nature is political. As Hayles poses the question, 'If nature is only a social and discursive construction, why fight hard to preserve it?' (1995: 47). Soulé (1995) closes his essay criticizing constructivist approaches by arguing that they play into the hands of anti-environmental political initiatives. For Worster, the exploration of the history and sociology of science 'can only lead either to complete cynicism or to the acceptance of any set of ideas or any environment that humans have created as legitimate. Disneyland, by the theory of historical relativism, is as legitimate as Yellowstone National Park' (1995: 78). Some of these objections appear more as attempts to kill the messenger, rather than as critical responses to relativism. Disney Corporation, among other vacation/entertainment enterprises, has worked hard in its advertising and product packaging to make their theme parks equivalent to national parks on a menu of family holiday destinations, constructing, for example, their 'Wilderness Lodge' resort at Walt Disney World as, according to their advertising, 'a majestic monument to the National Park lodges of the great Northwest'. Disneyland and Yellowstone *may be* equally legitimate for many affluent consumers, but the blame for this cannot be placed at the feet of poststructural social theory, but rather on confusion within modern society over what is and is not nature or natural (see Williams, 1976).

Within political ecology, a prominent response to the challenges of postmodernism has been to seek a way out of the impasse – variously labelled 'constrained constructivism' (Hayles, 1995), 'artifactual constructivism' (Demeritt, 1998), and a 'third position' (Proctor, 1998) – that accepts the existence of a material world independent of human consciousness and sensory perception while at the same time recognizes that our knowledge of that world is always situated, contingent, and mediated. Implicitly and explicitly, these 'middle path' attempts to link the insights of social constructivist concerns with a scientific understanding of nature have adopted a philosophical position known as 'critical realism' (Bhaskar, 1975; Sayer, 2000). Critical realism starts from the premise that the world exists independently of our knowledge of it and that its very independence means that human knowledge is not 'reality', but a representation of it. Thus, nature exists 'out there' as a reality, but scientific efforts to describe or give order to it should not be confused with that reality (Willems-Braun, 1997; Castree and Braun, 1998). When the theory of an Earth-centred universe was overturned, for instance, it shook humanity's notion of its place in the natural order, but it did not have the effect of rearranging the reality of the cosmos.

Critical realism, then, provides a 'third way' for scientific theory and method between empiricism and positivism, on the one hand, and extreme relativism, on the other (Sayer, 2000). Beyond simply proclaiming the existence of an independent world, social theorists and political ecologists have adopted Bhaskar's (1975) schema of the real, the actual and the empirical as a means of exploring how scientific inquiry orders knowledge (Sayer, 2000; Forsyth, 2003). The 'real' refers to things, natural or social, that have particular qualities, powers, susceptibilities, and relationships with other things, whether we recognize them or not. The 'actual' refers to the actuation of the power of things and the resulting effects that occur through their relationship with other things. The 'empirical' refers to what we can observe and measure of the actual and the real. Furthermore, the world is constantly emerging as new phenomena and things come into being through the conjuncture of two or more features of reality. These concepts of 'stratified ontology' (Sayer, 2000: 12) – the independence of the real and the actual from the empirical

– and emergence have numerous implications for the relationship between scientific knowledge and reality. Among these are the fact that the 'real' is not limited to what is empirically observable and that causation is not defined by how many times some series of events has been empirically observed. For political ecology, the appeal of critical realism is 'that it advances a powerful framework for understanding how environmental explanations may emerge as the result of partial empirical research and lead to fixed models of causality that do not reflect more complex underlying causes of change' (Forsyth, 2003: 71).

Hayles (1995), approaching the issue of the relationship between nature and our knowledge of it from a feminist theory perspective, advocates 'constrained constructivism', a concept that shares some common ground with critical realism. She starts from the assumption that the world exists independently of our knowledge of it, which she labels the 'unmediated flux'. Our understanding of that flux is structured by interactivity and positionality; that is, our knowledge of the world is conditioned by our interaction with it and this interaction is mediated by our position, culturally, historically, socially and geographically. For Hayles, the world becomes real for us 'through self-organizing, transformative processes that include sensory, contextual, and cognitive components. These processes I will call the cusp' (Hayles, 1995: 49, see Extract 4). Thus, we can never 'objectively' know reality unmediated by our own interaction with it. Like critical realism, constrained constructivism rejects both positivism and extreme relativism and therefore opens one possibility for a political ecology that engages social constructivism while maintaining the ability to judge the relative validity of various representations of nature by the degree to which they are consistent with 'our interactions with the flux' (ibid.: 53).

extract 4

'Constrained constructivism': the middle ground

For humans, the cusp is constituted through modalities peculiar to our physiology, including binocular vision, vertical posture, bilateral symmetry, apprehension of that portion of the electromagnetic spectrum we call light, and so forth. The cusp is also constituted through individual history and cultural expectations. Research by Christine Skarda and Walter Freeman, for example, has shown that for many species, including humans, previous experience influences how sensory data are processed, even before they are consciously apprehended. To illustrate

our complete dependence on the cusp for our understanding of the world, I have speculated elsewhere on how Newton's three laws might look to a frog. Drawing on the famous article by J .Y. Lettvin and colleagues, 'What the Frog's Eye Tells the Frog's Brain,' I argued that a frog gifted with Newton's reasoning power but with a consciousness constituted through a frog's sensory equipment would have drawn very different conclusions than Newton did from being hit on the head with an apple. Of course, such an idea is a playful oxymoron, because my argument implies that cognitive abilities are intimately bound up with the sensorium that helps to constitute them. To be a frog is to think like a frog, no less than to be a human is to think like a human. As Humberto Maturana (one of the investigators who did the pioneering work on the frog sensorium) was fond of pointing out, there can be no observation without an observer, including this observation itself. The reflexivity inherent in this situation suggests that Newton's laws (and any other scientific generalizations) are not true in any absolute or transcendent sense removed from a human context. Rather, they are consistent with the experiences of species-specific, culturally formed, and historically positioned actors.
Source: Hayles (1995: 49–50)

Some of the questions raised by social constructionist approaches to nature can be addressed through careful historical analysis that explores the relationship of ideas about nature to the materiality of biophysical processes. The new field of environmental history has been founded on just such an exploration, which demonstrates that the production of nature is at once material and discursive. Let us turn to examine some of the key insights on nature–society relations derived from environmental history.

Environmental history

The field that has come to be known as 'environmental history' emerged in the 1970s from an eclectic mix of regional and theoretical perspectives in history, geography and anthropology (Beinart, 2000; Rothman, 2002). Under influences as disparate as American Studies, African Studies and the French *Annales* historians, the field has sought to reinsert nature as an agent in human history and to bring historical analysis to bear on questions of the direction and cause of ecological change. These goals have necessarily resulted in a strong degree of overlap with the concerns of political ecology, not the least of which is the problem at hand, the formulation of a theoretical understanding of nature–society relations. More so than political ecology, however, early environmental history readily accepted prevailing scientific models of nature more or less without question. Particularly in North American environmental history, this meant that the ideas that pristine nature (wilderness) was in balance before the destructive arrival of humans, and that ecological change took place in a series of predictable stages towards a stable equilibrium, prevailed. By the late 1980s, environmental historians had begun to seriously challenge both the idea that nature equalled wilderness and that stable equilibrium was the 'normal' state of ecosystems. Moreover, the influences of feminist and poststructuralist social theory began to seep into historians' writings and cast doubt on the wisdom of accepting science's models uncritically. As one environmental historian argued, 'scientific knowledge should not be regarded as a *representation* of nature, but rather a socially constructed interpretation of an already socially constructed natural-technical object of inquiry' (Bird, 1987: 255, emphasis in the original).

As the new history took shape, North American environmental historians were compelled by developments in both social theory and empirical studies to debate the problem of nature–society interactions. Worster (1990) proposed that the new history proceed in its analysis on three levels, presenting a theoretical hierarchy wherein nature forms the *base*, the mode of production constitutes the *structure* and ideology the *superstructure*. The task of environmental history would be to focus on the relationships among these levels to uncover the 'lines of historical causality' (1990: 1091). Such a hierarchy is open to criticism for advocating a form of vulgar Marxism that promotes simple deterministic relationships between levels and also encourages the conceptual separation of material production from ideology (Cronon, 1990; White, 1990). Moreover, building a structure with some sort of pristine and taken-for-granted nature at its base is highly problematic (Cronon, 1990). While historians have had to rely on ecological scientists' models of nature, Worster acknowledged that this left environmental history 'in a very awkward position' (1990: 1092) when established models of balance and stability in nature became increasingly challenged (see discussion in following section). Ironically, environmental history, by uncovering the temporal dynamism of ecosystems and demonstrating that human activities have long been shaping so-called natural systems, had helped to undermine the scientific models that they had initially used to evaluate history (White, 1990). In short, Worster's proposed structural hierarchy was built on an unstable foundation that environmental history had itself worked to dismantle.

Despite the theoretical differences among environmental historians over the question of the nature–society interaction, the field is united in its fundamental materialism. Historians have been forced, nevertheless, to come to terms with the challenges that postmodernism posed for claims of truth and objectivity in the production of scientific knowledge. For Worster, the danger that postmodernism poses is the 'degenerate worldview' of historical relativism (1995: 78). If ecological change is inevitable and unpredictable and if harmony and balance in nature are figments of the Western imagination, then how can we say anything definitive about nature–society relations? Is one environment as good as the next, one environmental history as true as the next? Worster answers by arguing forcefully that we need not resort to historical relativism, that we can objectively view some representations of reality as truer than others, and that we can continue to draw lessons for society from nature. Worster's (1995) denunciation of historical relativism, however, did not address how, exactly, environmental history could respond to postmodernism's challenges. For that we turn to two influential essays by William Cronon.

Narrating environmental change

In the first essay, Cronon (1992) observes that while environmental historians have used the models of the natural sciences in attempting to understand ecological change, narrative (or storytelling) remains central to their explanations. That is, environmental historians create plots to order their explanations of ecological change, and in doing so 'move well beyond nature into the intensely human realm of value' (Cronon, 1992: 1349). Cronon recognizes that environmental history's reliance on storytelling lays the field open to the challenges that postmodernism presents to the narrative form. In an extended reflection on several narratives of the history of the North American Great Plains, he takes up the challenge of postmodernism (ibid.). He uses the conflicting explanations and conclusions of the various Great Plains historical narratives to demonstrate that as much as environmental historians might try to tell the story of nature, they ultimately produce stories about people and their values. Thus, historians can agree on the central facts and events of a narrative, but come to wildly different conclusions about causes and effects. What can environmental historians confidently and reliably tell us about nature, how it has changed, and why? Ultimately, Cronon argues that while historical narratives may be contested, that does not mean that any story told about ecological change is as equally valid as the next. Nature has a material reality that cannot simply be fabricated to fit the needs of narrative (see Extract 5).

Cronon's position, then, brings him in close alignment with those of critical realism and related constructivist approaches reviewed previously.

extract 5

Stories of environmental change

This vision of history as an endless struggle among competing narratives and values may not seem very reassuring. How, for instance, are we to choose among the infinite stories that our different values seem capable of generating? This is the question that lurks so threateningly at the intersections of the different Great Plains histories we have encountered ... If our choice of narratives reflects only our power to impose our preferred version of reality on a past that cannot resist us, then what is left of history?

The stories we tell about the past do not exist in a vacuum, and our storytelling practice is bounded in at least three ways that limit its power. First, our stories cannot contravene known facts about the past ... At the most basic level, we judge a work bad history if it contradicts evidence we know to be accurate and true. Good history does not knowingly lie. A history of the Great Plains that narrated a story of continuous progress without once mentioning the Dust Bowl would instantly be suspect, as would a history of the Nazi treatment of Jews that failed to mention the concentration camps ...

Environmental historians embrace a second set of narrative constraints: given our faith that the natural world ultimately transcends our narrative power, our stories must make ecological sense. You can't put dust in the air – or tell stories about putting dust in the air – if the dust isn't there. Even though environmental histories transform ecosystems into the scenes of human narratives, the biological and geological processes of the earth set fundamental limits to what constitutes a plausible narrative. The dust storms of the 1930s are not just historical facts but natural ones: they reflect the complex response of an entire ecosystem – its soils, its vegetation, its animals, its climate – to human actions. Insofar as we can know them, to exclude or obscure these natural 'facts' would be another kind of false silence, another kind of lying ... Nature is unlike most other historical subjects in lacking a clear voice of its own. The very fact that Great Plains historians can ascribe to the same landscape such different meanings is one consequence of this lack of voice. Still, nature is hardly silent. No matter what people do, their actions have real consequences in nature, just as natural events have real consequences for people. In narrating those consequences, we inevitably interpret their meaning according to human values – but the consequences themselves are as much nature's choice as our own ...

Finally, historical narratives are constrained in a third important way as well. Historians do not tell stories by themselves. We write as members of communities, and we cannot help but take those communities into account as we do our work ... The stories we write, in other words, are judged not just as narratives, but as nonfictions. We construct them knowing that scholars will evaluate their accuracy, and knowing too that many other people and communities – those who have a present stake in the way the past is described – will also judge the fairness and truth of what we say.
Source: Cronon (1992: 1370–3)

In the second essay, Cronon (1995) tackles the notion of untouched wilderness as synonymous with a Western conceptualization of nature. Wilderness, as it has come to be understood in Western thought, is a human creation, he argues, that North American conservationists in particular have loaded with core cultural values. In this line of thought, nature is idealized as a peopleless wilderness, clearly placing human society and nature in separate spheres and leading to the inevitable conclusion that a human presence alone is enough to degrade nature. This dualistic vision of nature–society relations is for Cronon 'the trouble with wilderness' (ibid.: 69). His cultural constructionist approach suggests two fundamental empirical and theoretical limitations of the wilderness model of nature. First, acceptance of this model would require that we ignore the conclusions from the empirical findings of cultural geographers, environmental historians, and archaeologists that people have manipulated and shaped nature 'for as long as we have a record of their passing' (ibid.: 83). In short, the physical actuality of nature as a peopleless wilderness is not supported by geo-historical research. Second, the wilderness–humanity duality leaves no room for considering other, less environmentally destructive theories of human history and society. As Cronon explains the core paradox of wilderness, 'if nature dies because we enter it, then the only way to save nature is to kill ourselves' (ibid.: 83). Recognizing wilderness as a cultural construction is thus for Cronon not equivalent to denying the material reality of nature, but a first step toward a more clear-eyed vision of the past and less constrained possibilities for more ecologically sustainable consumption and production practices in the future.

Wilderness as nature is a powerful metaphor in struggles over the control and use of natural resources, one that reflects and reinforces deep-rooted political and cultural agendas. In the history of European colonization of the Third World, for instance, a recurring theme in Western scientific discourse was that the land and resource use practices of non-Western peoples were inherently environmentally destructive. Thus the mere presence of native peoples could be read as an indication of environmental degradation. The portrait of non-Westerners as environmentally destructive provided European colonial states (and, later, postcolonial states) with the moral and scientific authority to seize control of land and natural resources. It also justified every manner of state intervention to control the lives, land uses and settlement patterns of colonized subjects.

Challenging degradation discourses

In a path-breaking study that has 'rapidly achieved paradigmatic status' in African environmental history (Beinart, 2000: 276), Fairhead and Leach (1996) inverted the widely accepted scientific thinking on non-Western land and resource use. The location of their study is the West African savanna–rainforest transition zone where outsiders' (notably colonial and postcolonial natural scientists) understanding of ecological change has been structured largely by the wilderness model of nature. Outside scientists and resource managers have assumed that local peoples' land uses in the transition zone were ecologically degrading. Specifically, outsiders have 'read' the savanna–forest landscape mosaic of the transition zone as an area that was once covered by a stable climax forest community prior to the invasion of human populations. The forest islands that distinguish the mosaic landscape thus have been characterized as remnants of a once undisturbed wilderness that is disappearing as a result of human occupation. Fairhead and Leach's research suggests, however, that 'human settlement has generally been responsible for forming forest islands' (1996: 79, emphasis in the original). Using a variety of data sources, they convincingly demonstrate that the establishment of new villages in the transition zone is historically associated with the creation of forest islands. In short, outside experts, guided by the wilderness model of nature and negative preconceptions about African land uses, have 'misread' the African landscape.

The results of Fairhead and Leach's study offer strong support for a social constructionist approach to analyzing the direction and causes of ecological change. They argued that the landscape history of the savanna–forest transition zone is told through multiple, sometimes contradictory narratives about nature and society that must be critically evaluated through attention to the social and political contexts within which they are generated. Like Cronon and others, Fairhead and Leach emphasized that treating interpretations of ecological change as socially constructed does not 'negate the fact that certain readings can be demonstrated as false' (1996: 3). Their methodological solution to the problems presented by a social constructionist approach is both instructive and revealing. By combining ethnographic techniques with archival research, the findings of scientific studies, and the analysis of remotely sensed imagery, they were able to 'accumulate multiple sources, multiple perspectives, on any given issue, comparing them for their mutual support or inconsistencies' (ibid.: 16). Thus, they are able to express a degree of confidence in assessing the relative validity of alternate narratives of ecological change. Some stories fit the empirical evidence better than others. Revealed in their methodological choices is an underlying, albeit unstated, commitment to a critical realist understanding of nature–society relations.

Fairhead and Leach's study suggests the importance of an interdisciplinary approach to nature–society research that includes not only the theories and methods of the social sciences, but also those of the natural sciences, particularly ecology. The materiality at the heart of environmental history means that scientific models of nature are at once the foundation upon which to construct a history of ecological change and the subject of critical analysis. For Fairhead and Leach, this meant demonstrating that the scientific model of nature that predicts forest communities at stable equilibrium was not supported by the evidence and that new scientific models of non-equilibrium ecology were more appropriate to their results (see the discussion in the following section). It also meant giving attention to the agency of nature in historical patterns of human occupation and ecological change. That is, not all the ecological consequences of settlement were intended, but resulted from a dynamic interaction between natural processes and human society. In sum, what we see in environmental history is a critical engagement with ecological science, simultaneous with an effort to reinsert the role of nature and natural process in shaping human affairs.

Linking environmental and imperial histories

To a significant degree, political ecology and environmental history have developed parallel interests in new models of non-equilibrium ecology and the agency of nature in human history. This confluence of interests is perhaps best exemplified by Mike Davis's recent 'political ecology of famine', *Late Victorian Holocausts* (2001:

15). Influenced by Watts's (1983a) germinal work on famine, *Silent Violence*, Davis adopts the perspective of 'environmental history and Marxist political economy' (2001: 15), thus bringing us full circle to one of political ecology's foundational studies. His methods, however, are not ethnographic, as were Watts's, but world historical. His aim is to document the role of a series of global droughts in initiating Third World under-development at the end of the nineteenth century. Davis's study details the horrific spectacles of mass famines in the tropics that marked the end of the nineteenth century and links them to three 'implacable cogwheels of modern history': the late nineteenth-century world economy, climatic extremes triggered by the El Niño–Southern Oscillation (ENSO), and European imperialism (ibid.: 12). In the process he provides a scathing critique of the market idolatry and Malthusianism of colonial overlords, international grain merchants, and global financiers that allowed tens of millions of famine deaths. His argument is that these famine holocausts were modern phenomena. Pre-modern societies and empires in Asia and Africa, he explains, had complex and flexible social and political institutions with which to deal with climate instabilities and avoid mass starvation.

Among the important contributions of Davis's study to political ecology is the way he enlists the latest empirical and theoretical advances in climate studies to help explain the impoverishment of tropical empires as they were incorporated into the nineteenth-century world economy. The scientific discovery of ENSO and subsequent research on its influences on global weather suggest that the climates of many tropical regions are inherently unstable and subject to periodic, but unpredictable, extremes in precipitation. Davis emphasizes the role of ENSO in the historical creation of the contemporary Third World, arguing that there is 'an extraordinary amount of hitherto unnoticed environmental instability in modern history' (ibid.: 280). For Davis, giving nature its due in world history does not mean falling into the old trap of environmental determinism. Rather, research on the historic role of ENSO and its associated climate extremes has worked to 'demolish orientalist stereotypes of immutable poverty and overpopulation' as the preconditions for famine (ibid.: 288).

To summarize, what we have witnessed in the maturation of the field of environmental history is a move away from a search for the balance of nature to new models of nature in flux, ecological instabilities, and non-linear change. In Fairhead and Leach's study, the emphasis is on the need to rethink ecological theories of stable forest climax communities in West Africa. In Davis, the focus is on the way late nineteenth-century responses to recurrent but non-linear and unpredictable shifts in global climate helped to create the 'Third World'. There is, then, a certain confluence between the shift in scientific models of ecological change and post-structural social theory around questions of universality, predictability and uncertainty. Therefore, it is important that we understand developments in ecological science and how these are being incorporated into political ecological thought and research. It is to an examination of equilibrium and non-equilibrium models in ecological science that we now turn.

Equilibrium and non-equilibrium ecology

The idea that balance, order, and permanence characterize nature has long held sway in ecological science. The roots of this view can be located at least as early as classical Greek civilization, where by the time of Aristotle's death in the fourth century BC, ideas of orderliness and purpose in nature had been firmly established (Glacken, 1967). As Glacken observed of the works of Plato, Aristotle, and others:

> In these earlier writings, however, references to the terrestrial order were not elaborated upon although it was conceived of as a balanced and harmonious creation of which man was a part; it is in this conception that we should seek the origins of the modern ideas of a balance in nature, so important in the history of biology and ecology, with the significant difference that in the modern idea human activities have often been regarded as interferences – often destructive – in this balance.
>
> (ibid.: 49)

The 'modern ideas' to which Glacken referred were first most fully articulated by George Perkins Marsh in his 1864 classic *Man and Nature*, a work which influenced early state forest and soil conservation policies in the USA and elsewhere and inspired scholarly research for over a century. Marsh believed that nature produced ecological communities of 'almost unchanging permanence of form, outline, and proportion' (1965 [1864]: 29), which human activities had a tendency to disrupt and destroy. He put forth a concept of a natural order in which the biotic and abiotic components of a landscape interact to create a stable harmony:

> The organic and the inorganic world are, as I have remarked, bound together by such mutual relations and adaptations as secure, if not the absolute permanence and equilibrium of both, a long continuance of the established conditions of each at any given time and place, or at least, a very slow and gradual succession of changes in those conditions.
>
> (ibid.: 36)

For Marsh, then, change in nature occurred so gradually that ecological conditions could, for all intents and purposes, be considered permanent.

By the early twentieth century these ancient ideas of harmony, balance, and stability were firmly embedded in the new science of ecology as fundamental assumptions. In a sense, the early theoretical development of ecology constitutes a sophisticated elaboration on Marsh's ideas of a nature that, while changeable in the long term, is ultimately constant and predictable. Frederick Clements's (1916) work on plant community succession, for example, was concerned with explaining and modelling observable changes in natural systems. Clements believed that assemblages of plant communities were analogous to living organisms and that they changed through a linear series of stages, which ultimately culminated in a final, stable climax stage. Clements's idea that plant communities underwent linear, predictable change towards a stable climax prevailed in ecological science throughout most of the twentieth century. Ecology textbooks built upon Clements's writings and taught undergraduates that in an area where climate dictated a forest climax, there could be many communities in various stages of succession, but ultimately they 'will all end in forests' (Whittaker, R.H. 1975: 182). Even in landscapes that appeared as ecological mosaics, students were taught to look for 'a central or most extensive (steady-state, undisturbed) community-type that comprises the largest share of climax stands in the area' (ibid.: 183). Change and spatial heterogeneity were thus recognized in late twentieth-century orthodox ecology, but were explained without challenging the basic assumptions of stability, equilibrium, and predictability.

Equilibrium in island biogeography theory

Islands, because they are discrete and relatively easily measurable systems, became sort of living laboratories where scientists could develop and test equilibrium ideas in ecology. The most influential and debated theory for island ecology over the past three-plus decades is the equilibrium model developed by MacArthur and Wilson (1967). MacArthur and Wilson's theory of island biogeography can best be summarized as a set of three principles. First, there is an orderly positive relationship between the size of an island and the number of species it contains. In general, as size increases, the number of species it can hold increases. Second, the number of species on an island is a dynamic equilibrium between immigration and extinction rates. If immigration is decreased or extinction increased, the island will equilibrate at fewer species. This will occur where the degree of isolation from a species' genetic source is increased or the area of the island is decreased. Third, there is a negative relationship between the distance of an island from its propagule source and the number of species it contains. In general, as distance increases, the number of species decreases. This principle is closely linked to the concept of equilibrium and the effect of increased isolation on species numbers. MacArthur and Wilson's equilibrium theory of island biogeography (ETIB) quickly became the dominant theory of island ecology and has also come to serve as a model in applied fields of resource management.

Indeed, managers and applied scientists have built a number of important models for resource management upon the fundamental assumption that ecosystems develop in a linear, predictable fashion to reach a final 'climax' stage of stable equilibrium (Ellis et al., 1993; Scoones, 1999). These management concepts include maximum sustained yield (MSY), carrying capacity, and various protected area designations for nature preservation (e.g., national parks as island analogues, see Chapter 5). The concept of MSY has guided forestry and fisheries planning for well over a century. The implementation of MSY management requires that the ('normal', stable) rate of productivity of a given species in a community be ascertained and then a harvesting schedule devised so that extraction rates are equal to replacement rates. Closely associated with MSY is the concept of carrying capacity. Scientists first developed the carrying capacity idea studying cultured microorganisms in the nineteenth century and it was subsequently used to guide range management for wildlife and livestock. Again, the generalized assumption was that the productivity of any given range, pasture, or plant community was in a steady state over the long term. The amount of productivity that could be extracted without endangering the long-term stability of a system determines the maximum number of wildlife, livestock, or people (in human ecology) that could be supported. Finally, the idea that climax communities remain in stable equilibrium unless disturbed by human activities underlies the philosophy of nature preservation in national parks and wilderness areas promoted by state policies of exclusion (see Chapter 5). National parks and wilderness areas are assumed to be in a stable, natural condition at the time of their designation and ecological change has traditionally been viewed as a threat to be controlled through management. More specifically, conservation biologists have used ETIB to explore optimal protected area designs that will preserve equilibrium conditions (e.g., Diamond, 1975; Abele and Connor, 1976; Miller, 1978; Simberloff and Gotelli, 1984).

Beyond equilibrium: flux, instability, and uncertainty in the environment
In the final three decades of the twentieth century, the equilibrium view of ecology came under increasing scrutiny as more and more empirical findings contradicted

it. Ecological scientists attempted to explain the lack of stability in observed ecological communities as cyclical equilibria or multiple equilibria in an attempt to fit findings to the dominant paradigm of balance and stability (Moore et al., 1996). By the mid-1980s, ecologists who had been trained to see stability in nature but failed to find it wrote of the 'albatross of equilibrium that weighs heavily about the necks of community ecologists' (Schaffer, 1985: 103). Noting that ecologists whose findings did not support the equilibrium view resorted to ad hoc explanations rather than refutation, Wiens, following Kuhn (1970) suggested that this was 'characteristic of attempts to preserve a prevailing paradigm' (1984: 448). Even more fundamentally, growing disillusionment with equilibrium ecology challenged the Newtonian–Cartesian view of nature as a highly ordered and predictable machine.

A 'new ecology' – non-equilibrium ecology as opposed to equilibrium ecology – has subsequently emerged that suggests that stability is not the norm for many natural communities and that revised, if not revolutionary, models of nature are required (Botkin, 1990). The new ecology replaces assumptions of equilibrium, predictability and permanence with instability, disequilibria, chaotic fluctuation and dynamism. Holling, for example, suggested a view of communities that 'emphasizes variability, spatial heterogeneity, and nonlinear causation' (1986: 295). He explores this view through the explication of two key concepts in ecology – stability and resiliency – the former referring to a system's propensity to reach and maintain equilibrium and the latter to its ability to 'maintain its structure and patterns of behavior in the face of disturbance' (ibid.: 296). This concept of resilience, it should be noted, differs from the traditional view that a system's resilience is measured by how fast it is able to return to equilibrium. Thus, in Holling's model, disturbance is no longer considered anomalous, or an event from which a system 'recovers', but rather is considered to be integral to the system's functioning. Fires, infestations, disease and storms, can happen with such frequency that species can become adapted to disturbance to the degree that they trigger and maintain disturbance. In short, many systems that are unstable (in the equilibrium ecology sense) are actually highly resilient. Holling's view reflects ecologist's findings from the early 1970s onwards that natural disturbance was so common and frequent as to render moot the idea that the 'normal' state of nature is equilibrium (Sprugel, 1991).

The development of chaos theory has also influenced the introduction of the notion of non-linear change in ecology. Among the contributions of chaos theory to non-equilibrium ecology is the idea that complex, dynamic systems can be specified with equations, yet they are seldom predictable (Schaffer, 1985;

Malanson *et al.*, 1990). An emphasis on complexity recognizes that chance – or more correctly, an event that is the result of a *series* of chances each dependent on many different factors – is inherent in natural systems (Botkin, 1990). Chaos theory, then, suggests that what appears as chaotic change is actually ordered, though not linear or predictable. Furthermore, chaos theory demonstrates that many systems display high sensitivity to initial conditions. That is, small differences in initial conditions magnify into great differences in final conditions (Holling, 1986; Malanson *et al.*, 1990). The invention of computers has been key to the introduction of these ideas into a new science of ecology, serving as both a metaphor for natural systems and as a tool for understanding complex stochastic processes in nature. As Botkin explained, 'Because of the ease with which computer programs can be made to mimic chance events, computers reinforce this metaphor and offer in themselves a new basis for the metaphor of nature as a set of probabilities' (1990: 124) (see Extract 6).

extract 6

Chaos, non-linearity and the 'new' ecology

Assumptions have a tendency to slowly bury themselves in our unconscious, becoming in effect myths; the computer relentlessly confronts us with these assumptions and their implications. When we make nature act like a machine in a computer program, it does so exactly and the results are quite unnatural; when we follow the knowledge and long experience of an ecologist ..., add to it information gained in laboratory studies of photosynthesis and the growth of trees done by many scientists, and then translate these data carefully into computer code, the model works ... Such models help us avoid two traps of the past that I have emphasized repeatedly in this book; continuing to believe in myths about nature even when they are clearly contradicted by facts, and believing two contradictory ideas about nature at the same time (such as nature is constant and nature is not constant). At the practical level, these models help us synthesize what is too complex for our minds to combine working alone.

The profound philosophical arguments that arose from the development of quantum theory in the 1920s opened up the possibility of a very different perception of the physical universe: the universe as fundamentally stochastic to some degree. With this as a background, it may be easier for us to accept the idea of chance in our perception of biological nature. Because of the ease with which computer programs can be made to mimic chance events, computers reinforce this metaphor and offer in themselves a new basis for the metaphor of nature as a set of probabilities.

Making predictions that involve chance requires not only techniques but also a change in our myths about nature ... Until the advent of modern computers, it was not possible to make extensive projections that involve stochastic processes. The acceptance of the idea that we might benefit by viewing nature as characterized by chance and randomness is a deep and unsettling change.

Although this nature of chance may seem less comforting than a clockwork world, it is the way that we find nature with our means of modern observation, and therefore it is the way that we must accept nature and approach the management of resources. Managing from the comfort of a deterministic world when one lives in a world of chance is like following the beam of a flashlight at night ... what appears in the beam is very clear, but one is likely to stumble and fall over the roots and rocks that lie just outside one's vision. Once we accept the idea that we can deal with these complexities of nature, we begin to discover that the world of chance is not so bad, that it is interesting and even intriguing now that we understand that chance is not chaos ... Thus we must accept nature for what we are able to observe it to be, not for what we might wish it to be.
Source: Botkin (1990: 120, 124, 129, 130)

A final feature to emphasize in non-equilibrium ecology is the importance of spatial and temporal scale in the analysis of ecological change. First, a linear or regular relationship between the intensity of ecological impact and distance in time or space cannot be assumed (see Figure 3.1). That is, impacts do not necessarily diminish with distance from an activity or event, particularly when biophysical systems are coupled with social and economic systems (Holling, 1978). Second, non-equilibrium ecology raises the question of how large a spatial scale is necessary before we can confidently identify a system in balance. Third, it further suggests that in complex natural systems, different rates of change, propelled by different abiotic and biotic processes, are occurring simultaneously at different spatial and temporal scales (Holling, 1986; Botkin, 1990). Small-scale events can cascade upward to create large-scale change. Additionally, global abiotic processes influence local ecosystems, but 'are mediated through strong biological interactions within the ecosystems' (Holling, 1986: 297), which produce complex interactions. An important focus, then, is the coupling of subsystems operating under different periodicities and at different spatial scales.

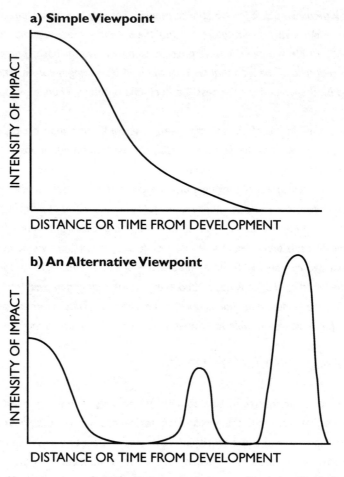

Figure 3.1 *Alternative views of relationship between distance and intensity of ecological impact.*

Developments in non-equilibrium ecology have both influenced and been influenced by empirical and theoretical advances in island biogeography. Ecologists and biogeographers have tested MacArthur and Wilson's equilibrium model on both actual islands and analogous isolated mainland habitat islands numerous times for more than three decades. At the risk of over-simplifying a large, complicated and occasionally contradictory set of findings, the general conclusion has been that the equilibrium model is not supported. In a recent special issue of the journal, *Global Ecology and Biogeography,* that reviewed the status of ETIB, Brown and Lomolino concluded that research results have produced 'too many complications, exceptions, and violated assumptions to ignore' (2000: 89). Contributors to the issue suggested that equilibrium conditions in species richness are rare occurrences and that a 'new paradigm' for island biogeography is needed (Heaney, 2000; Lomolino, 2000). One of the central problems identified in the equilibrium model is that it lacks a sense of geography, in that it treats space as a homogeneous plane (Lomolino, 2000; see also Stoddart, 1986). In addition, researchers noted that species richness is highly sensitive to scale, both temporal and spatial, and suggest that one of ETIB's key variables, area, is relatively less important than other biogeographic variables (Lomolino, 2000; Whittaker, R.J., 2000). A new paradigm would have to account for these variables as well as the role of frequent disturbances and the complex interdependent interactions among species across scales of time and space.

The preceding discussion suggests that the long-standing view of nature in balance has been turned on its head by empirical and theoretical advances in ecology and island biogeography. While this is true to a degree, it is important to recognize that not all ecologists and biogeographers are prepared to reject the idea of steady-state natural systems altogether (see Illius and O'Connor, 1999). There are systems that appear to be at stable equilibrium, but they are much rarer than once was thought and certainly they can no longer be generalized as the 'normal' state of nature. Ecologists have begun to think in terms of systems of multiple equilibria (Holling, 1986), systems characterized by conditions of non-equilibrium (Wiens, 1984), or systems of dynamic disequilibrium (Heaney, 2000). Some have proposed that it is useful to think in terms of a continuum of states, including dynamic equilibrium, dynamic non-equilibrium, static equilibrium and static non-equilibrium (Whittaker, R.J., 2000). Others of a self-described 'more radical disposition', call for the 'complete ditching of equilibrium theory once and for all' (Stott, 1997: 208). At the very least, the empirical and theoretical advances of the new ecology mean that ecologists and biogeographers cannot simply assume that equilibrium conditions prevail in the absence of supporting evidence.

Natural resources law and policy implications

In terms of the interests of political ecology, one of the most important aspects of the rise of non-equilibrium ecology is what it implies for both the applied sciences of resource management and development policies. Range, forest, fisheries and wildlife management sciences were all founded on the assumptions of equilibrium ecology, as were most of the national laws and international agreements governing resource use (Botkin, 1990; Ellis *et al.*, 1993). We can consider these management strategies as experiments to test the equilibrium view of ecology (Holling, 1986). Since the 1970s, resource scientists have increasingly questioned the validity of basic management concepts derived from equilibrium assumptions, such as MSY and carrying capacity, yet they often continue to provide the framework for sustainable development policies (McEvoy, 1988; Botkin, 1990; Zimmerer, 1994; Neumann, 2000). For example, in the case of the now-extinct California sardine fisheries, MSY was set at a point based on the assumption that population was in a state of dynamic equilibrium. In reality, the population was highly sensitive to frequent, irregular changes in the ocean environment. When harvesting levels based on MSY interacted with sudden ecological change, the sardine fishery was destroyed, producing a management disaster that contributed to the reduction of MSY models in fisheries science (McAvoy, 1988).

Similar to MSY, the carrying capacity concept has come under increasing scrutiny, particularly in applied range science. The essential problem is this. In systems characterized by frequent and irregularly occurring disturbance, such as the arid and semi-arid environments of Africa, range carrying capacity is nearly impossible to determine (Bartels *et al.*, 1993; Behnke and Scoones, 1993; Turner, 1993). In a careful examination of the carrying capacity concept, Bartels *et al.* (1993) reviewed over a dozen published definitions of the term and suggested that there are two fundamental views. In economic carrying capacity, a concept developed for beef production in temperate region commercial ranching, the objective is to maximize net income by producing the greatest amount of meat from a circumscribed range. In ecological carrying capacity, a concept with roots in Malthus's hypothesized relationship between population and food supply, the main measure is the number of individuals of a population that can survive to reproduce. That is, it is the maximum population size given available resources. Both definitions, it should be noted, are based on assumed equilibrium conditions, though economic carrying capacity is more obviously structured by subjective human judgements.

The relevance of these two different views of carrying capacity can be illustrated by looking at political ecology research on African pastoral systems in arid and semi-arid environments (Abel and Blaikie, 1990; Homewood and Rogers, 1991; Behnke *et al.*, 1993; Turner, 1993; Little, 1996; Brockington and Homewood, 2001). The dominant scientific view of these environments has been that they are potential steady-state systems that have been destabilized by African herding practices (Ellis and Swift, 1988). The 'ecological principle behind this view is that stocking rates are crucial to plant dynamics' (Brockington and Homewood, 2001: 452). That is, since the systems are assumed to be potentially at equilibrium, density-dependent biotic forces such as livestock grazing are the main cause of ecological change. National government and international development interventions therefore almost exclusively have focused on controlling livestock grazing pressure through policies of destocking and the transformation of land tenure systems. The rationale for these policies is based on the idea of economic carrying capacity, where commercial ranchers attempt to maximize income on individually owned privatized ranges.

Political ecology research has challenged the equilibrium view of African pastoral ecosystems and the explanation for ecological change and intervention policies that follow from it. First, rainfall in the arid and semi-arid zones of Africa is extremely erratic and subject to frequent, irregular droughts, leading to a system in which range productivity comes in erratic pulses (Ellis and Swift, 1988; Behnke and Scoones, 1993; Brockington and Homewood, 2001). The variability in rainfall and vegetation productivity is so great as to make the idea of a system in equilibrium meaningless and irrelevant. Moreover, the extreme fluctuations in climate conditions have produced arid and semi-arid systems that are highly resilient, rather than highly fragile as suggested by equilibrium models (Abel and Blaikie, 1990). Second, these environments are characterized by a great degree of landscape heterogeneity and spatial variability in productivity. Some assessments of carrying capacity in African pastoral systems completely disregard or downplay the importance of spatial variability and thus fail to include key resources (Behnke and Scoones, 1993; Little, 1996) (see Extract 7).

extract 7

Ecological disequilibrium and African pastoralism

The disequilibrium approach is more consistent with African models of environment and biodiversity, which have never excluded anthropogenic disturbance nor pursued ecological equilibrium as an objective. For example, the herd management strategies of East African pastoralists – which have always been the bane of conservationists – assume drought, some degree of range degradation, and fire (burning) as norms, and have never tried to pursue ideas of carrying capacity or equilibrium. The ecology of disequilibrium perspective also adds considerably to our understanding of the 'overgrazing' or desertification debate, another global issue that is centered on African pastoralism and savanna land-scapes. It suggests that we know far less about what degraded or overgrazed rangeland looks like − in terms of plant cover − than earlier work has led us to believe. According to this new line of thinking, a degraded or desertified parcel of land may have little to do with many of the standard vegetation indicators that have been previously used.

I suggest that fundamental misunderstanding of key resources (in this case, wetlands) and their importance to local social and economic systems has misdi-rected arguments about land degradation and human mismanagement in pas-toral savanna areas. By focusing on a region of northern Kenya − the Lake Baringo basin of Baringo District − where global discourse and concern about biodiversity loss and 'desertification' are both strongly voiced the article suggests that the causal connection with or relevance of local social practice to either phenomenon has been vastly exaggerated. In the case of Baringo it will show (1) how the value of the basin's swamps is constantly understated and misunder-stood by the state and other outside interests, to the detriment both of local herders and of the area's biological resources, and (2) how the perceived role of African herding in creating environment degradation ('desertification') contra-dicts the recent acknowledgement of pastoralism's positive contribution to main-taining biodiversity.

Source: Little (1996: 38−9)

Given these findings, political ecologists have argued that non-equilibrium condi-tions prevail in arid and semi-arid Africa and that density-independent factors (climate and physical features) are far more important in determining vegetation dynamics than density-dependent factors (livestock grazing). Furthermore, a vari-ety of studies have demonstrated that African systems of land tenure relations and pasture and livestock management strategies are rational responses to an erratic and unpredictable environment (Ellis and Swift, 1988; Behnke and Scoones, 1993; Little, 1996; Brockington and Homewood, 2001). What these findings demon-strate is 'a convergence between pastoral techniques of range exploitation and recent developments in scientific range ecology' (Behnke and Scoones, 1993: 28). The most important of pastoral strategies is mobility, which allows pastoralists to take fullest advantage of vegetation productivity that is highly variable in time and space. We can think of carrying capacity in non-equilibrium environments as a constantly moving target that pastoralists pursue through transhumance, nomadism and other forms of mobility. Thus, the basis for African pastoralism is closer to the idea of ecological carrying capacity than to economic carrying capacity.

The ecological and political ecological research on African pastoral systems concludes that current environmental intervention policies are clearly misguided. At the heart of the error are the assumptions of equilibrium conditions and destructive pastoralist stocking practices, which the empirical evidence does not support (cf. Illius and O'Connor, 1999). Given the prevalence of non-equilibrium conditions and the relative unimportance of stocking densities for vegetation dynamics, conventional intervention policies are precisely the opposite of what they should be. Policies designed to reduce density-dependent effects through destocking are unlikely to improve range conditions shaped by density-independent forces and are likely to be devastating to pastoral economies. Stott suggests that in Africa, the forcing of equilibrium models onto a non-equilibrium system through policies of destocking, sedentarization, and land tenure change 'could even be regarded as a criminal act' (1998: 2). Policies can be redesigned in recognition of the instability of African environments and the opportunist logic of pastoralists' management strategies. That is, interventions should be designed to facilitate pastoralist strategies of mobility, range stocking, and tenure relations (Ellis and Swift, 1988; Behnke and Scoones, 1993).

A key point to be taken from the preceding discussion is that non-equilibrium thinking has yet to penetrate national and international environmental planning to a significant extent. Political ecologists have suggested that many policies for international development and biodiversity conservation continue to be guided by a view of nature in balance and attempt to force the idea of equilibrium onto non-equilibrium systems (Zimmerer, 1994; Sullivan, 1996; Stott, 1998). One reason is that the design and functioning of modern management systems are fundamentally incompatible with natural systems that are characterized by dynamism, spatial heterogeneity, and multiple equilibria (Holling, 1986; Holling and Sanderson, 1996), leaving some to conclude that management and control of non-equilibrium systems 'are unlikely, if not impossible' (Scoones, 1999: 490). The incompatibility of natural systems and modern resource management is exemplified in the historical development of scientific forestry in early nineteenth-century Germany. Rather than adjust management to the functioning of a complex, heterogeneous and dynamic forest system, modern scientific forestry was designed to simplify the system and create 'a forest that was easier for state foresters to count, manipulate, measure, and assess' (Scott, 1998: 15). Moreover, the forest that scientific forestry created reflected a narrow set of economic interests within modern society, resulting in a forest that is politically, rather than ecologically defined (Scott, 1998; Peluso and Vandergeest, 2001; see Chapter 5).

The example of scientific forestry's origins brings us to another reason that non-equilibrium theory is slow to take hold in the design of environmental planning in arid Africa. In a word, it is politics. Claims of environmental degradation and theories of causation are embedded in relations of political power interacting at multiple scales: global, regional, national and local. The question must be asked, whose interests are served by which views of nature and degradation? In the case of Africa, the primary moral justification for European colonization was the mission to 'civilize' and 'improve' the lives of its people and to prevent them from destroying their environment by their own 'irrationality'. Hence it has long been the mainstream view of Northern range specialists that 'whatever pastoralists are doing is inappropriate' (Ellis and Swift, 1988: 452) and efforts to 'improve' pastoralists' lives have focused on stopping them from doing it. Advances in non-equilibrium ecology and studies of African pastoralism show these claims to be based less on science and empirical evidence than on ideology and political interests (Sullivan, 2000; Brockington and Homewood, 2001). Ideas about equilibrium nature and the pastoralists' role in destroying it hardly disappeared with colonialism. Northern views of nature in balance and African pastoralists' role in destroying it remain hegemonic, with disastrous results for both Southern livelihoods and ecology (Stott, 1998).

Towards synthesis in political ecology

Political ecology emerged and matured as a distinct field in a period of revolutionary theoretical shifts in both the biophysical and social sciences, which challenged many widely accepted ideas of human–environment interactions. As an interdisciplinary field, political ecology has been at the forefront of attempts to integrate the advances in non-equilibrium ecology with new social theory in nature–society research. We find in these efforts that non-equilibrium ecology 'often meets on the same terrain as critical social science or political ecology studies' (Watts, 2000b: 35). That is, political ecology studies that explore local meanings and practices in land use have confirmed 'what the new "nonequilibrium" posits, namely that climax models of ecological stasis are unhelpful' (ibid.). Thus, both critical social science and non-equilibrium ecology call for greater attention to local perceptions and knowledge, a central preoccupation of political ecology since its inception. It should come as no surprise, then, that political ecologists – whether arguing the need for more politics (Stott and Sullivan, 2000; Forsyth, 2003) or more ecology (Peterson, 2000; Zimmerer and Bassett, 2003b; Little, 2004) – have seized upon non-equilibrium ecology as key for advancing the field.

In the wake of these developments, there have been a number of attempts to identify convergences in non-equilibrium ecology and social science that can provide the basis for something like a theoretical synthesis in political ecology (Zimmerer, 1994; 2000; Scoones, 1999; Stott and Sullivan, 2000; Forsyth, 2003; Zimmerer and Bassett, 2003b; Little, 2004). Among these overt efforts at synthesis, there are four themes that emerge repeatedly, though not necessarily with equal emphasis in each and every formulation. The first concerns the production and utilization of environmental knowledge in conventional science. Much of this work focuses on the critical evaluation of taken-for-granted scientific claims about the direction and causes of environmental change. Researchers are combining the lessons of non-equilibrium ecology and critical social theory to demonstrate the weakness, or in some cases, the complete absence, of scientific evidence to support claims about human–environment interactions. For instance, a recent collection of political ecology studies focuses on the discrepancies between generalized and increasingly globalized environmental narratives and the knowledge and practices of more local actors (Stott and Sullivan, 2000). Stott and Sullivan 'consider that many knowledges about "the environment" are mythologized as scientifically correct while being based on very little "science" indeed' (ibid.: 7). The editors' intent is not to blindly privilege the local and reject scientific method and the pursuit of objectivity, but rather to point out that too much of what passes for scientific fact about the environment can be traced historically to assumptions and hypothesized human–environment relationships that have never been tested. Their origins forgotten, environmental narratives become 'hegemonic myths' accepted as scientific fact (ibid.: 7). The work of Fairhead and Leach (1996), discussed previously, and Bassett and Koli Bi (2000), discussed in Chapter 4, are cases in point. Stott and Sullivan's position calls for an interdisciplinary political ecology that brings together the new advances in ecological theory with such social theoretical concepts as discourse, power and narrative.

In a similar vein, Forsyth (2003) refers to unsubstantiated claims of degradation as 'environmental orthodoxies' (see also Leach and Mearns, 1996).

> Environmental orthodoxies are generalized statements referring to environmental
> degradation or causes of environmental change that are often accepted as fact, but
> have been shown by field research to be both biophysically inaccurate and also

73

leading to environmental policies that restrict socio-economic activities of people living in affected zones.

(Forsyth, 2003: 38)

Examples of environmental orthodoxies are the claims of global trends in desertification, deforestation and rangeland degradation emanating from the environmental sciences. Forsyth calls for a 'critical' political ecology that combines critical realism and poststructural discourse analysis with new models of non-equilibrium ecology. Analysing and testing the validity of environmental orthodoxies in specific places and particular historical moments, Forsyth rather successfully demonstrates how this synthesis helps us to understand how certain narratives, unsupported by scientific evidence, become accepted orthodoxies.

It is worth emphasizing that such critical evaluations of environmental narratives do not constitute a rejection of science and empiricism, but rather force us to recognize that scientific knowledge must be specified and contextualized geographically, historically, culturally and politically. Only through such an acknowledgement of the politics of the environment 'can current scientific and conservation thinking be literally brought down to earth' (Blaikie, 1995: 209). The disjunctures among empirical evidence, multiple subjective interpretations, and political power, become extreme when we jump from the scale of global discourses on biodiversity, deforestation and climate change to the scale of the local. Political ecologists do not deny the occurrence of human-caused environmental degradation but rather assert that we can neither simply assume its existence nor recklessly generalize about its causes. Non-equilibrium ecology and social theory both suggest that there is no single or straightforward nature–society relationship (Scoones, 1999). Multiple environmental perspectives will be generated not only from human societal diversity (class, race, gender, ethnicity), but also from a non-equilibrium theory of ecology in which the range of possible outcomes is large and unpredictable. Stress is thus placed on a more pluralist approach, creating an understanding of human–environment interactions through multiple perspectives, including locally produced environmental knowledge (Zimmerer, 1994; 2000).

A second theme emphasizes how incorporating the insights of non-equilibrium ecology can bring a renewed focus on nature's agency in shaping human-environment interactions. Recognizing nature's agency in human affairs requires a fundamentally materialist philosophical position, while at the same time acknowledging that our understanding of material reality is always situated and partial (Blaikie,

1995; Castree and Braun, 1998; Scoones, 1999). This, of course, is the 'third way' of critical realism. As Zimmerer and Bassett write:

> This philosophical embrace of the environment as having an ontological basis and a dynamic role as an agent in its own right, combined with our understanding of nature's agency as socially mediated, reflects a 'natural turn' in the social sciences that is known as 'critical realism'.
>
> (2003b: 3)

As related previously, this position resonates strongly with environmental history's paradigm within which 'plants, animals, soils, climates, and other nonhuman entities become the coactors and codeterminants of a history not just for people but of the earth itself' (Cronon, 1992: 1349).

For Forsyth (2003), a renewed attention to nature's agency in non-equilibrium ecology acts as a corrective to an overly reductionist approach in political ecology focused on capitalism as the cause of environmental degradation. This approach is reductionist 'because it does not refer to biophysical factors that exist independently of such conflicts [i.e., poverty, social justice] between economy and society' (ibid.: 117). While it is hard to argue that blaming environmental degradation on 'capitalism' is as reductionist and unenlightening as blaming it on 'over-population', Forsyth's treatment of biophysical factors as existing 'independently' of society appears to resurrect the duality of nature–society. Political ecology is nothing if not a rejection of the notion that our ideas about 'the environment' or what constitutes 'degradation' can be disassociated from the political-economic contexts in which they are generated. This does not mean that biophysical processes can be discounted in human history. Davis's (2001) study of the role of climate flux in late Victorian times, discussed previously, is an excellent example of understanding the role of biophysical processes in human history through a critique of capitalist expansion in what would become the tropical Third World.

A third theme highlights the importance of temporal and spatial scales in both non-equilibrium ecology and social theory (Scoones, 1999; Zimmerer and Bassett, 2003b; 2003c). Historical analysis has always been an important component of political ecology studies (Neumann, 1992) and the emergence of non-equilibrium ecology has reconfirmed its central role. The analysis of human–environment interactions on a temporal scale underscores the non-linear, non-cyclical and chaotic character of environmental change identified in non-equilibrium ecology. The critical evaluation of the production of knowledge on a temporal scale helps

elucidate the politics and relations of power from which environmental orthodoxies emerge and become entrenched as scientific truth. A non-equilibrium
understanding of ecological change through time thus unites with a historical
analysis of environmental science discourse in order to test both the validity of
environmental orthodoxies and the logic of local environmental knowledge.

Political ecologists have long considered spatial scale to be critical in efforts to
identify the occurrence and causes of environmental degradation. Blaikie's (1985)
'chain of explanation' (see Chapter 2) is precisely an attempt to build a conceptual
model that linked ecological change to political-economic forces operating across
scales ranging from the very local to the global. For ecologists, spatial scale has
also been a key concept for modelling biophysical systems as organized 'from the
interaction of structures and processes operating at different scales' (Peterson,
2000: 4). Advances in non-equilibrium ecology and poststructural social theory
have created an opening for new synergies centred on spatial scale. In this synthesis, the focus is on the 'contingent and dynamic nature of environmental change
and how this is intimately bound up with social and cultural processes' (Scoones,
1999: 493). Ideas of spatial heterogeneity, interscaler connectivity, and scale-
dependent processes in non-equilibrium ecology are combined with a social theoretical approach that treats scale as socially produced rather than ontologically
given. For Scoones, Giddens's (1984) structuration theory is particularly apt in formulating nature–society relations in terms of the interactions of 'structure and
agency across scales' (1999: 493). Yet attention to spatial scale in itself is insufficient to understand how the imposition of fixed scales and boundaries is central
to the politics of environmental conflict (Zimmerer and Bassett, 2003c). Scale in
political ecology, like space or nature, must not be accepted as ontologically fixed.
As Zimmerer and Bassett urge: 'One of the challenges facing political-ecological
scholarship is to break out of these pregiven, scalar containers (local, regional,
national, global) to examine human–environment dynamics that occur at other
socially produced and ecological scales' (ibid.: 288).

The fourth and final theme concerns the critical evaluation of the institutions,
policies and management practices in light of the advances in social theory and
non-equilibrium ecology. In these attempts at synthesis in political ecology, there
is a notable emphasis on pluralism, multiple perspectives and uncertainty of outcomes in environmental policies and practices. As Scoones explains, 'it is the interaction between these two perspectives – socially constructed perceptions and
representations and real processes of biophysical change and ecological dynamics
– that is key to policy and practice' (1999: 497). Allowing for multiple perspectives

in society and unpredictability and indeterminancy in nature has brought new appreciation of local management systems, demonstrating the roles of local institutional arrangements and cultural practices that emerge in an ecological context defined not by stability, but by extreme spatial and temporal variability (Scoones, 1999; Little, 2004). For instance, the institutions and cultural practices of livestock herders have been shown to be in dynamic interaction with a rangeland characterized by variability, complexity and non-linearity in biophysical processes (Behnke and Scoones, 1993; Turner, 2003; Little, 2004). Political ecology studies have also identified mismatches between the spatial scale of human institutions and ecological processes, such as the case of the rigid and static bounding of conservation territories. The perspectives and rights of local progressive social organizations could be linked with concepts of non-equilibrium ecology to create a more dynamic and flexible conservation model (Zimmerer, 2000).

The fusion of critical social theory and non-equilibrium ecology is both potentially liberating and immobilizing with regard to general environmental policies and specific environmental interventions. On the one hand, it is liberating in the sense that the possibilities for multiple perspectives on nature and ecological change can lead to more socially just and culturally relevant environmental interventions, such as in the case of conservation territories (Zimmerer, 2000). It can loosen the constraints produced by the association of nature with a stable, undisturbed wilderness ideal that underpins the policies and practices of many scientific and conservation organizations (Botkin, 1990; Cronon, 1992). Multiple perspectives on the specific environmental issues will be generated both from the diversity within society (locality, class, race, gender, ethnicity) but also from a non-equilibrium theory of ecology in which the range of possible outcomes is large and unpredictable. Environmental degradation narratives that condemn local land-use practices out of hand are less and less defensible as empirically rich political ecology studies reveal that too often ideology and powerful political interests, rather than sound science, are the sources of the orthodoxies. Contrary to the concerns of many conservation biologists and environmental scientists, these critical, social constructivist approaches do not place human interests over nature, but rather insist that the domination or liberation of either cannot be treated separately (Harvey, 1993; Haraway, 1996; Peet and Watts, 1996a; Smith; 1996).

On the other hand, this fusion is potentially immobilizing in the sense that environmental management, planning and policy-making become increasingly difficult as certainty and predictability decrease. Management and planning institutions as currently structured are ill suited for ecosystems characterized by complexity, flux, and non-linear change. Perhaps more troubling, a critical and pluralist social theoretical stance makes problematic an unquestioned acceptance of the new ecological model of non-equilibrium. As Beinart articulates the challenge, if the new 'ecological science can so quickly turn the old on its head, should we not be skeptical about it?' (2000: 295). The answer is, yes, we *should* be sceptical, as ideally all investigation of human–environment interactions should proceed with scepticism towards orthodoxies and untested hypotheses. Non-equilibrium ecology is a work in progress and its assumptions should and will be tested. The key point is that

> much environmental debate and explanation in political debates today is conducted on the basis of alleged frameworks of environmental causality and structure that have been widely criticized from debates in philosophy and sociology of science [and] from within new approaches to ecology.
>
> (Forsyth, 2003: 2)

The challenges associated with trying to understand the direction and causes of environmental change lie not with excessive scepticism, but with excessive credulity in regard to the notion of nature in stable harmony.

The model of nature as a system in harmony and balance has exhibited remarkable strength and resiliency over time (Glacken, 1967; Botkin, 1990). What critical social theory and non-equilibrium ecology have achieved, separately and collectively, is a momentous challenge to the balance of nature concept that has been deeply embedded in and foundational to the institutions of Western science and natural resource management. For George Perkins Marsh and the conservationists and environmental scientists who have drawn inspiration from his great nineteenth-century treatise, *Man and Nature*, human society could only disturb a nature that was in perfect balance. No clearer illustration of this perspective can be found than the original title he had proposed for his masterpiece, 'Man the Disturber of Nature's Harmonies' (Lowenthal, 1965: xxiii). This view of nature has held sway in environmental science well into the late twentieth century and continues to structure prevailing models of resource management and conservation. Critical social theory and non-equilibrium ecology have initiated a revolution in the way we conceive of nature and society's interactions with it that throws into question much of what environmental managers and scientists have taken for granted. Some have urged that we need a whole new way to verbalize ideas about nature–society interactions, a 'metalanguage' that would replace the vocabulary of 'equilibrium', 'stability', and 'balance' with 'movement', 'flexibility', and 'resilience' (Stott, 1998). Something along these lines may already be occurring in political ecology as scholars incorporate and contribute to the theoretical advances in social science and ecology.

ENVIRONMENT AND DEVELOPMENT

4

With development comes destruction. This, according to Marshall Berman, is a key message in Goethe's early nineteenth-century classic *Faust*, 'the first, and still the best, *tragedy of development*' (Berman, 1982: 40, emphasis in the original). Goethe's Faust experiences a personal triumph in his role as developer, but his achievement is tempered by his knowledge of what is lost in the process of development, and of the costs to humanity and nature. Berman relates how towards the end of the story Faust had managed to transform the whole region around him with the exception of a small piece of ground in the midst of the new landscape.

> This is occupied by Philemon and Baucis, a sweet old couple who have been there from time out of mind. They have a little cottage on the dunes, a chapel with a little bell, a garden full of linden trees. They offer aid and hospitality to shipwrecked sailors and wanderers.
>
> (ibid.: 67)

Faust insists they must make way so that he may complete his development plan, but they refuse to leave. Faust is obsessed with their presence and asks for the help of Mephisto and his henchmen in removing them. 'Mephisto and his special unit return in "deep night" with the good news that all has been taken care of. Faust ... learns that their house has been burned to the ground and they have been killed' and is overcome by the realization of the destruction he has set in motion (ibid.: 67–8).

Goethe's tragic vision of modernity remains relevant today as we try to make sense of the geographic and social patterns that link wealth accumulation, poverty and ecological change. Compare Berman's exegesis with Susan Stonich's political ecological analysis of industrial shrimp farming in the Gulf of Fonseca in Honduras (Stonich and Vandergeest, 2001). Stonich explains that during a visit to the region, activists from a grassroots NGO took her

> to witness the attempted removal of an elderly couple from their home by the owner of a new shrimp farm. For more than forty years, Andina and Fausto had lived in a house built of mangroves and thatched with palm fronds located at the mouth of an estuary that fed the gulf.
>
> (ibid.: 263)

The couple's livelihood centred on fishing the bay and gathering wood and honey from the surrounding lands. The central government of Honduras, however, had given the politically connected new owner a highly subsidised concession to establish on that spot a commercial farm to raise shrimp for export and he wanted them out. 'By the time of my visit, the elderly couple's home and boat were completely isolated – an islet surrounded by a shrimp pond – completely cutting off access to the sea.' Supporters of the couple, rallied by a local NGO, had arrived to face off against 'a group of hired thugs and a few soldiers dressed in uniform' that the new owner had hired to intimidate the resisters. After holding out for several hours, the old couple out of 'fear and desperation' finally left quietly (ibid.: 263).

Development, among other connotations, means transformation, embracing a new way of being and thinking and leaving the old ways behind. The tragedy of development includes people who do not fit with the new, who, along with the environments that sustain them, are in the way. In his version of Faust, Goethe invented a new literary category 'people who are in the way – in the way of history, of progress, of development' (Berman, 1982: 67). In the Honduras case, Andina and Fausto and the small-scale artisanal fishing economy upon which their livelihoods were based were in the way of a state development plan, formulated with the support of the World Bank and the United States Agency for International Development. The plan seeks to address a national economic crisis by generating foreign currency through the production and export of 'non-traditional' crops, including shrimp. The campaign to promote export growth through industrial shrimp farming has resulted in the forced removal of long-time residents, the enclosure of large tracts of seashore by a handful of commercial producers, declining water quality in the gulf and the destruction of thousands of hectares of mangrove forest (Stonich and Vandergeest, 2001).

Together, these two tales, one an allegorical fiction written some two centuries ago and the other all too real and recent, suggest many of the questions and issues regarding the modern development project that political ecology research addresses. What are the costs, socially and ecologically, of development? Are there parallels and patterns in the political ecology of development that can be discovered through historical comparisons or across the constructed divide of the First and Third Worlds? What role does violence play and what forms does it take in patterns of economic development and environmental degradation? Could a more ecologically sustainable and socially just alternative development be derived from the bottom up, building upon local institutions, knowledge and practices? What is the relationship between property rights, development and environmental degradation? What role do local NGOs and new social movements play in redefining and reorganizing development? In this chapter we will explore how political ecology has analysed and debated some of these questions.

Sustainable development

Thinking about development as the unfolding of modernity in particular places at particular times gives us a deeper historical and broader geographical perspective on its meanings and practices. Deeper, that is, than thinking about it only in terms of the structuring of post-World War II political-economic relations between the global North and South. This perspective asserts that the 'age of development' began on January 20, 1949 when US President Harry S. Truman declared in his inauguration speech that the South was 'under-developed' (Sachs, 1992: 1-2). While Truman's speech indeed may have signalled the discovery of an under-developed hemisphere and the launching of the global post-war order of American hegemony, it did not mark the beginning of the North's attempts to carry development to the South. In the 1930s, Britain's search for a path of economic recovery and an answer to the social and political unrest in its empire resulted in a new plan for development, expressed through the 1940 Colonial Development and Welfare Act (CD&W). The roots of the CD&W can in turn be traced to the Labour Party's 1920s' vision of a socialist British Empire that would employ rational scientific planning to provide for greater social justice in land use and occupation (Neumann, 2002). Twenty years earlier still we find future British Prime Minister Winston Churchill (sounding altogether Faustian) surveying rural Uganda and challenging his readers to doubt that one day it 'will throb with the machinery of manufacture and electric production' (Churchill, [1908] 1990: 101).

If we continue moving backward in time, the geography of development shifts from the tropical realm to the home countries in Europe and North America. The globalized model for the commercial development of a territory's timber resources, to take one example among many, was first developed in the Saxony region of Western Europe in the late eighteenth century. This model of scientific forest management has been imposed worldwide, requiring now, as it did two centuries ago, the displacement of customary access rights and the biological simplification of the forest ecosystem (Peluso, 1992b; Neumann, 1997; Scott, 1998). By the start of the nineteenth century, 'development had become a linear theory of progress, bound up with capitalism and Western cultural hegemony' (Adams, 2001: 6). In the United States, the westward movement of European migration – and the deforestation, biodiversity loss and displacement of the continent's indigenous peoples that accompanied it – was characterized as 'manifest destiny'; the inevitable march of progress and triumph of Western civilization. Development, in this historical and geographical context, is imagined as a civilizing mission, the replacement of backward or savage conditions, with modern prosperity. We need not, however, confine our search for parallel development experiences in the First and Third Worlds to a comparative analysis of past and present. Indeed, McCarthy (2002) suggests that the main difference between analyses of contemporary environmental conflicts in the First and Third Worlds is merely their geographic location. Many of the same questions about development addressed in Third World political ecology – the struggles between local communities, the state and capitalist enterprises over livelihoods, the structure of control over access to land and resources and the importance of local knowledge and perceptions of the environment – may be just as relevant in First World analyses.

All of this is not to imply that the meaning of development has been unchanged for 300 years. Quite to the contrary, the concept of development has undergone a series of transformations defined by shifting ideas about the relative roles of the state, civil society, and the market (Peet and Watts, 1996a). A significant change in international development thinking occurred in the 1970s when First World bureaucrats and managers discovered the importance of 'the environment' for planning national economies. This discovery resulted in the latest and current permutation, sustainable development, an appealing if imprecise term universally embraced by multinational energy companies, grassroots NGOs, conservationists and international lending institutions. Cambridge geographer William Adams (2001) has produced arguably the most comprehensive and carefully researched history of the idea of sustainable development. The capsule summary that follows is based on Adams' study and critique of the 'greening' of development.

The history of sustainable development can be traced to the second half of the nineteenth century when the environmental costs of 'taming' the North American landscape and the decline of wildlife in Europe's tropical colonies from overhunting became apparent. Throughout the first half of the twentieth century, scientific study and applied research on resource management were increasingly viewed as indispensable for development planning in the colonial territories. Following World War II, global population rise became the focus of the newly created agencies of the United Nations and international scientific organizations, driven by neo-Malthusian arguments about environmental limits to growth. By the end of the 1960s, when the colonial territories were transformed into 'under-developed' countries, First World scientists and managers were imagining the management of natural resources on a global scale. The 1972 United Nations Conference on the Human Environment held in Stockholm was a key event that brought together ideas of rational natural resource management, hopes for Third World economic growth and neo-Malthusian concerns of global over-population. The organizers and participants of the Stockholm Conference never used the term, sustainable development, but the idea that environment and development must be treated as an integrated whole underlay much of the proceedings.

In 1980, the World Conservation Strategy (WCS), a joint effort of the International Union for the Conservation of Nature, the United Nations Environment Programme and the World Wildlife Fund, became the first attempt to codify sustainable development. Though driven primarily by wildlife conservation interests and dismissed for its political naïveté, the WCS laid the foundation for sustainable development thinking for the 1990s and beyond. It was left to the World Commission on Environment and Development, widely known as the Bruntland Commission, to bring sustainable development into the political mainstream through the publication of its report, *Our Common Future* (Bruntland, 1987). The report presented what remains the most frequently cited definition of sustainable development: 'development that meets the needs of the present without compromising the ability of future generations to meet their own needs' (ibid.: 43). *Our Common Future* identified poverty as a fundamental cause of environmental degradation. If global managers are going to reduce environmental degradation, they will therefore need to reduce poverty, and the way to reduce poverty is to promote economic development. So runs the logic of sustainable development. Its appeal to mainstream development institutions, such as the World Bank, is plain to see. The dominant model of expansionist industrial capitalism as the path to national economic growth is not only left unchallenged, but also is now championed as the cure for both poverty and environmental degradation.

To a significant degree political ecology has operated as a critique of the discourse and practice of mainstream sustainable development. In the pages that follow, I will explore some of the central debates within political ecology concerning the relationship of environment and development. The first section looks at ideas about the role of civil society in creating a more socially just, economically equitable, and ecologically sustainable development strategy. Next, I take an extended look at the impact of poststructuralism and postmodernism on theories of development, focusing on the idea of development as discourse. The third section tackles the relevance of property regimes and the control over access to land and resources for development. In the final section, I will examine studies that push political ecology beyond its historic preoccupation with the rural Third World and suggest the need to deconstruct the analytical separation of North from South and rural from urban.

States bad, communities good?

Political ecology came into its own as a distinct field at a particular moment in the history of development thinking when the development populism of the 1970s collided with the neoliberalism of the 1980s. Development populism, perhaps best captured by the slogan, 'small is beautiful' (Schumacher, 1973), emphasizes the local, the rural and the small-scale in directing efforts to improve the lives of Third World peoples. Development populism was at once a critique and a rejection of modernization theory as scholars, activists and development practitioners sought 'alternative' paths to progressive improvement of social and economic conditions. One can see how this thinking influenced political ecology if we examine the writings of geographers Ben Wisner, Phil O'Keefe and Paul Richards on environment and development in Sub-Saharan Africa (see Richards, 1975a) or the parallel work by anthropologists (e.g., Brokensha et al., 1980). Richards (1975b), for example, critiqued development initiatives by questioning the superiority of Western scientific knowledge over other forms of knowledge and challenged restrictive Western notions of 'rationality'. He blended a dizzying theoretical cocktail of Marxist communalism, cultural relativism and small-is-beautiful thinking to suggest an alternative to mainstream modernization models, one based on local knowledge and perceptions of the environment. At the heart of his alternative was the conviction that the culture of the ordinary people together with the experience they have gained coping with the day-to-day problems of contemporary economic and social change contain ideas and techniques which could be of immediate value in the struggle to improve agricultural yields and farm incomes.

(ibid.: 105)

The neo-liberalism of the 1980s reformulated the development paradigm by framing the state as an obstacle to progress, stressing instead the role of the market and rational individual decision-making within civil society as the most efficient means of distributing resources for development. In the context of this reformulation, the state is bypassed and new developmental roles are ceded to indigenous, grassroots and other assorted non-governmental organizations (Thomas-Slayter, 1994). Soon, every bilateral and multilateral development institution, from the US Agency for International Development to the World Bank, began touting the centrality of communities, NGOs and other local entities to conduct the business of development. In the context of the IMF structural adjustment and the forced reduction of state expenditures, designating local people as development experts made for good fiscal policy. While political ecology has to a large degree operated as a critique neoliberalism, it has nonetheless shared a common interest in the 'local'. Blaikie's 'bottom-up' approach (1985: 11) and Watts's (1983a) Hausa ethnography, in their distinct ways, emphasized local peoples' knowledge, skill and perceptions with regard to 'rational' responses to environmental change and risk. The point I wish to make is that by the time that Blaikie and Brookfield (1987) formulated their idea of regional political ecology, critiques of the state from both the neo-liberalist right and neo-Marxist left – along with a new vocabulary of 'the local', 'the indigenous' and 'the community' – were in wide circulation in development discourse. This focus on local knowledge and community-oriented land and resource management, for better or worse, remains central to much political ecology today, even as it has expanded to incorporate analyses of rural development in the First World (Sayre, 1999; McCarthy, 2001; Walker, 2003; Hollander, 2004).

Indigenous technical knowledge

Much of the interest in local perceptions and practices falls under the rubric of indigenous technical knowledge (ITK), a concept that emerged in the 1970s and 1980s in efforts to conceptualize alternative development strategies (Brokensha, 1980; Chambers, 1983; Richards, 1985). An early and persistent current of thought within political ecology has presented ITK as a counter to overly general-ized claims of ecological degradation and as the foundation for a development model that would replace the ineffective and inappropriate technological fixes inherent in modernization theory. For example, Richards (1983) argued that Western ideas of environmentally destructive indigenous land use practices were based on evolutionary models of development that dismissed local land uses as culturally and technologically backward. A careful examination of localized prac-tices in specific and particular geo-historical contexts led him to be sceptical of Western scientists' claims and to counter with 'an optimistic assessment of the ecological and technological skills of peasants and proletarians' (ibid.: 2). In a similar vein, Hecht sought to demonstrate the possibilities for indigenous soil management techniques to 'serve as the foundation for sustainable agricultural models for small scale farmers in Amazonia' (1990: 154). Her reasons for endorsing ITK included the poor ecological record of temperate zone agricultural practices in tropical Amazonia and the institutional and economic conditions that constrain their usefulness for many of the region's indigenous peoples.

The role of ITK in environmental management and regional development has been widely debated within political ecology. Some have criticized proponents of ITK and champions of the 'local' for simply replacing one hegemonic discourse, modernism, with another, neo-populism (Blaikie, 1996). Blaikie pointed out how social science researchers seem to perennially rediscover ITK and mocked their 'surprise and enthusiasm how local people know so much about their own envi-ronment' (1996: 84). His point is that 'neo-populist developmentalism' – develop-ment critiques that replace Eurocentric and technocentric generalizations with the local and the particular – is another meta-narrative in postmodern disguise, privileging the local perspective without clarifying a role for Western science and state and international institutions. Similarly, Bebbington (1996) suggests that much of the ITK literature misleadingly generalizes that technological moderniza-tion is always and everywhere destructive of local economies and environments and that ITK is a necessary and sufficient foundation to improve the livelihoods of poor farmers. He argues that many champions of ITK overlook the fact that locally generated 'development alternatives' may include demands for increased access to modern technologies as 'a means of cultural survival' (ibid.: 101, emphasis in the original).

The argument that ITK should provide the basis for development 'from below' depended on a fairly limited conceptualization of knowledge. ITK has been con-structed as a self-contained body of knowledge separate from Western scientific knowledge, a distinction that is difficult to maintain for both epistemological and historical reasons (Agrawal, 1995). Furthermore, ITK is obsessively focused on detailed knowledge of local environmental conditions. What is overlooked are the other types of knowledge that peasant producers may not possess, such as market conditions, price variability and distant institutional constraints, that may be necessary for the improvement of local livelihoods. Social and economic forces operating in locations far distant from the point of production may undermine the most rational and most ecologically sensitive local knowledge. It is often the case that resource allocation decisions are made by centralized political authorities with little input from local peasant organizations. Some political ecologists would therefore insist that efforts to enhance local sustainable agricultural practices cannot stop with championing ITK, but must also include the reorientation of power in decision-making in such a way as to promote input from local peasant organizations (Bebbington, 1990).

Critiques of ITK suggest that ideas of localism and indigenism in contemporary development discourse may have kinship with earlier, romanticized visions of the rural community. In these visions, rurality represents an idealized social condition of harmony and stability and a relationship to the land that balances human welfare with ecological care taking. The idyllic rural community is almost always counterposed as an alternative to modern development. It may be located in the distant past or in a distant country, but it is always someplace else, in some 'other' society (Williams, 1973; Torgovnick, 1990). Political ecologists and others have criticized the community-oriented development planning and projects of the 1980s and 1990s for conjuring an idealized 'local community' that is socially and culturally homogeneous and has a vast reservoir of detailed knowledge about the local environment (Alcorn, 1994; Neumann, 1997). While local knowledge *is* often extensive, it is distributed unevenly within communities. Political ecology studies have shown local knowledge to be a realm of contestation, not only within communities, but also within individual households (Carney and Watts, 1990; Carney, 1993; Rocheleau et al., 1996a; Schroeder, 1999). Possession of ITK is thus, as often as not, fragmentary, contested and reflective of social divisions within communities rather than unified and collectively held.

Representing indigeneity and the environment
These critiques notwithstanding, the notion of ITK as a foundation for development has 'served the purpose of keeping alternative possibilities alive, at least in the imagination' (Li, 1996: 503). The romanticized and idealized images that

political ecologists have so convincingly deconstructed may operate as powerful imagery that indigenous peasant communities can strategically deploy to defend land rights and customary resource access against external assaults. Li explains that the language of 'community', 'tribal' or 'indigenous' rights, however invented or imagined, can provide local actors with a 'vocabulary of legitimation' (ibid.: 509). By this she means that the wide circulation of ITK and related terminology among international aid donors and international NGOs has created a space for local people to negotiate with the state and other powerful agents in defence of their livelihoods and control over land and resources. Similarly, Tsing (1999) argues that a focus on representations and the social construction of nature and culture may lead scholars to dismiss new social movements that have the potential to shape alternative development paths. She suggests, rather than choosing one represen-tation as more correct than the other or dismissing all representations of 'indige-nous' or 'tribals' as simplifications of complex reality, it is more fruitful, both theoretically and politically, to analyse the meanings given to certain representa-tional categories in particular situations. Using a case from the Meratus Dayak region of Kalimanatan, she shows how the boundaries of various categories of nature and culture are blurred and destabilized as 'tribals' engage with urban envi-ronmentalists over possibilities for sustainable development. This engagement, while producing confusion and ambiguities in representations of cultural identity, offers the possibility of an open and democratic debate about the path of development.

Tsing cautions, however, that strategic representations of indigenous knowledge and identity have a way of slipping into 'unexpected transformations and collabo-rations' (1999: 198). As a powerful illustration, international conservationists and environmental NGOs have seized upon the idea of indigenous knowledge of medicinal uses of wild plants as a strategy to promote sustainable development for tropical rainforests. In environmentalist discourse, the concept of ITK as a body of location-specific, utilitarian knowledge is transformed into the ancient wisdom and spirituality of tribal peoples living within nature. Brosius (1997) describes such a transformation in a case from Sarawak, Malaysia, where conservationists have rep-resented Penan foragers as possessing vast knowledge of medicinal plants that forms one of the pillars of their system of spiritual beliefs. Brosius cogently demonstrates that this representation of Penan knowledge has little to do with Penan ideas and everything to do with a tradition of Western romanticism. Not only that, but he also shows how environmentalist discourse is picked up by Penan informants and then reflected back to environmentalists as 'indigenous' commentary on their relationship to the forest. The effect is 'a kind of ethno-graphic hall of mirrors' where ideas and rhetoric circulate back and forth between indigenous peoples and environmentalists (Brosius 1997: 63) (see Extract 8). Also, alliances among indigenous peoples, the state and international environmentalists may take unexpected twists and reversals. In the Brazilian Amazon, to take one example, the political alliances of some indigenous peoples have shifted. Indigenous activists initially employed the rhetoric of secret knowledge of botani-cal medicines to gain the support of international environmentalists in their fight to defend their land and resource rights against state claims on the forests. More recently they have forged a new alliance with the state, repositioning themselves as defenders of national patrimony against the 'biopiracy' of foreign multinational corporations (Conklin, 2002).

extract 8

Indigenous knowledge and Western discourses

As noted, [indigenous knowledge] is transformed into wisdom, spiritual insight, or some other such quality. This transformation serves a certain purpose. In describing peoples such as the Penan, the problem for environmentalists and indigenous rights activists is twofold. First, how does one make a society narrat-able? That is, what must one do to be able to talk about it? However one defines indigenous knowledge, it is not easily accessible. It is not something that can be picked up in a few short weeks, particularly for individuals lacking linguistic com-petence. The problem for environmentalists is how, nevertheless, to create texts about peoples such as the Penan, and how to talk about the knowledge which they hold to be so valuable without actually comprehending much about that knowledge. Second, how does one create value? Environmentalist and indigenous rights campaigns are generally concerned with peoples who are 'endangered' precisely because they, their institutions, and their systems of land-tenure are disvalued by national governments. The Malaysian government considers the Penan a national embarrassment, a people who represent precisely those things they are trying to overcome in their national development efforts. The goal of environmentalists then is axiological: to demonstrate both to the government and to Western audiences what is at stake if the forest, and the Penan, are destroyed.

By reducing Penan knowledge to the sacred or ineffable, the Penan are made *both narratable and valuable. In linking knowledge to the sacred, commentators acquire a way to construct meta-commentaries about the meaning of a body of knowledge, rather than about that knowledge itself. The danger, of course, is that such meanings may only be interpolated and may, in fact, be Western in origin.*

Thus the rich, if generally mundane, Penan knowledge of the forest landscape by being transformed into something that is sacred, valued, and thus to be saved, is constructed in terms of categories that are Western in origin. We see here a hall of mirrors of representation – simulacra – as Penan knowledge is transformed into something that it is not, and Western discourses are transported to Penan, who again convey them to Western interlocutors. The essential – and diverse – qualities of indigenous knowledge are lost along the way. As the future of the forests, other biomes, and indigenous peoples is negotiated in the years ahead in a plethora of post-Rio international fora, the issue of who talks for whom and who constructs representations of whom is critical.
Source: Brosins (1999: 64, 66)

The limits of local knowledge

It should now be clear that questions concerning the role of local knowledge and institutions and the scale at which to control and orchestrate the process of development continue to be very much a subject for debate in political ecology. There has been much discussion concerning the category, 'local people', and the nature of 'their' interests since the World Bank and other institutions and agencies began an uncritical promotion of NGOs, civil society, and community in development policy. Critical research on the effects of these policies have highlighted how various factions within communities compete to position themselves as *the* representatives of the local people, promoting some community members' interests while neglecting others. Community-based NGOs may marginalize major segments of a community or simply constitute another layer of bureaucracy between rural producers and their land and resource base. Ergo strengthening or encouraging the creation of locally based NGOs as part of development may have deleterious outcomes for some community members. In particular, the interests and knowledge of women are overlooked or undermined when their involvement in community-based organizations and institutions is restricted. Political ecology studies informed by feminist theory have revealed the gender divisions in interests and knowledge within communities. These will be examined later in this chapter.

For a range of normative reasons relating to social justice, democratization, and local self-determination, an argument can be made for securing community members' participation in the control over land and natural resources critical to sustaining local livelihoods. Correspondingly, a technical argument can be made that community participation is necessary in order to tap the detailed local environmental knowledge required to implement sustainable development. At the same time, however, promoting ITK is far from sufficient. Local social movements rarely successfully blaze alternative development paths without the support of outsiders, including sympathetic state agencies, international NGOs and scientists. Furthermore, populist initiatives that champion ITK, but fail to address the unequal distribution of power and authority within communities (among genders, age groups, ethnicities and classes) and between communities and outside actors (such as state agencies, international NGOs and global institutions) are unlikely to achieve any lasting or widespread improvement in local livelihoods. Communities are not homogeneous or monolithic entities. Development populism is therefore seriously limited by its inability to recognize and analyse internal community struggles over resource access and control or the ways in which power is distributed unevenly within communities.

Finally, there remains a larger question regarding the nature of the development project itself and the place of local communities within it. Development in the mainstream literature is conceptualized as the solution to rather than the cause of backwardness, poverty and environmental degradation in rural Third World communities. For some political ecologists, however, the post-World War II project of Third World development is an exercise in domination – of the North over the South and the state over local communities – and therefore should be abandoned. Decades of development interventions, it is argued, have failed to relieve either poverty or environmental degradation while succeeding in strengthening the power and authority of the state and international actors over local communities. For these scholars, development is conceptualized as a discourse, constructed not to liberate Third World people from poverty, but to subjugate extensive regions in the global South to the needs of a northern-based capitalist world economy. We turn now to examine some of the key works in this area and the critical responses to them.

Development as discourse

One of the most provocative debates within political ecology concerns the treatment of development as discourse. Following the theoretical lead of Michel

Foucault, particularly in *Discipline and Punish* (1979) and *Power/Knowledge* (1980), scholars began in the late 1980s to examine the discursive aspects of the West's post-World War II efforts to develop the Third World. One of the earliest, and arguably the most significant, discursive analyses of development is James Ferguson's *The Anti-politics Machine* (1990). Ferguson focused his analysis on the West's development planning for the tiny African country of Lesotho, arguing that development institutions generate their own discourse that 'constructs Lesotho as a particular kind of object of knowledge' (ibid.: xiv). Through a methodical and thorough deconstruction of development documents, he convincingly demonstrates how the discursive construction of Lesotho has little relation to the historical experience and political-economic status of the territory and everything to do with the need for major development institutions to create a suitable 'object' for development. Summarizing his analysis of a World Bank report on the development of Lesotho, he wrote:

> At the end of this involved process of theoretical construction, Lesotho can be represented in 'development' discourse as a nation of farmers, not wage laborers; a country with a geography, but no history; with people, but no classes; values, but no structures; administrators, but no rulers; bureaucracy, but no politics. Political and structural causes of poverty in Lesotho are systematically erased and replaced with technical ones, and the 'modern,' capitalist, industrialized nature of the society is systematically understated or concealed.
>
> (ibid.: 66)

His point is not that this construction is silly or false (e.g., only 6 per cent of this 'nation of farmers' worked in agriculture), but rather that the object (Lesotho) is constructed to fit the existing machinery of development institutions and that there are real and far-reaching consequences for peoples' lives resulting from the implementation of such a plan, though these may be far different from the stated mission of 'developing' Lesotho.

Before proceeding further with this discussion, it might be fruitful to elaborate on the theoretical meaning of the term, discourse, particularly in human geography and political ecology. Discourses are formed by bodies of texts – scholarly, popular, journalistic or literary – that together produce not only an internally consistent knowledge field, but also the 'very reality they appear to describe' (Said, 1978: 94). Various definitions of discourses stress the way desires, imaginaries, ideologies and metaphors work to produce textual products that both reflect and shape relations of power. 'Discourses express human thought, fantasy, and desire. They are also institutionally based, materially constrained, experientially grounded manifestations of social and power relations' (Harvey, 1996: 80). A discourse is a framework that embraces 'particular combinations of narratives, concepts, ideologies and signifying practices' (Barnes and Duncan, 1992: 8) and 'emphasizes some concepts at the expense of others' (Peet and Watts, 1996a: 14). Peet and Watts theorize relations between geographical groups of people in terms of 'regional discursive formations' wherein 'modes of thought, logics, themes, styles of expression, and typical metaphors run through the discursive history of a region, appearing in a variety of forms, disappearing occasionally, only to reappear with even greater intensity in new guises' (ibid.: 16). In short, discourse analysis plays close attention to the role of language in constructing social reality as a complex system of signification.

Anthropologist Arturo Escobar (1995; 1996; 1999) has been a leading proponent of discursive analysis and a broad social constructionist perspective on environment and development as the basis for a 'poststructural political ecology'. One of Escobar's starting points for poststructural political ecology is the Foucauldian position that there can be no materialist analysis of development that is not, simultaneously and correspondingly, a discursive analysis. Building on Said's (1978) treatment of Western 'orientalist' knowledge as a discursive field, he similarly treats development as a discursive field. More specifically, he argues that 'global poverty', 'underdevelopment' and, indeed, the 'Third World' were produced in the post-war development discourse as objects to be treated by the application of modern technological and managerial practices introduced from the 'First World'. Within development discourse, the control of the vast areas of the global South by the global North is accomplished not through *repression*, but through the *normalization* of an endless variety of interventions into the daily lives of people living within the Third World. Lest he lay himself open to the criticisms levelled at Said for over-emphasizing the unidirectionality of colonial power in shaping orientalist discourse, Escobar takes pains to stress the agency of Third World peoples. That is, he sought to demonstrate that, however one-sided the production of development discourses may be, they may at the same time 'create conditions for resistance' (Escobar, 1995: 155). Alternatives to development, according to Escobar, will not be forged by re-imagining the development project as, say, sustainable development, but through the expression and nurturing of cultural difference in specific locations.

Another important point of departure in Escobar's poststructural political ecology is the field of ecological Marxism, which, among other inquiries, examines the question of the sustainability of capitalism as a global economic system (M. O'Connor, 1994a). Specifically, Escobar is interested in the political ecological significance of what James O'Connor calls the 'second contradiction' of capitalism wherein the costs of environmental destruction and the resulting political responses create a crisis for capitalist development (1994: 154). Where J. O'Connor is sceptical of capital's capacity to surmount this challenge, Escobar (1996) argues that capital has already moved into an 'ecological phase', expressed in the discourses of sustainable development and biodiversity conservation. Here he is building on Martin O'Connor's insights on the discursive incorporation of nature as capital. According to M. O'Connor:

> The image is no longer Marx's (or the classical economists') of human beings acting on external nature to produce value. Rather, the image is of the diverse elements of nature (including human nature) themselves codified as capital. Nature is capital, or, rather, nature is conceived in the image of capital.
>
> (1994b: 55)

A prime example of capitalized nature is rainforest biodiversity, which, under capitalism's ecological phase, is to be conserved as a potential source for future accumulation. Escobar thus seeks to understand the 'articulations established by capital between natural and social systems' in both forms of capital; 'exploitative and conservationist, modern and postmodern' (1996: 47–8).

Escobar's discursive analysis of 'sustainable development' points to a number of shifts in the conceptualization of the relations between nature and society, including the foregrounding of the Third World poor in explanations of degradation and the absence of any historical critique of the development process. More fundamentally, 'nature' is transformed into 'environment' in sustainable development discourse. That is, nature loses its agency as an independent entity and its spiritual and romantic connotations as it is reconstructed as a collection of resources vital to the global economic system. 'As the term is used today, "environment" includes a view of nature from the perspective of the urban-industrial system. Everything that is relevant to the functioning of this system becomes part of the environment' (Escobar, 1996: 52). He later extended this analysis of historical transformations of the meaning of nature to explore cultural and geographical differences in discursive and material constructions of nature (Escobar, 1999). He proposed an 'anti-essentialist' perspective on nature that identifies multiple natures, which he labelled organic, capitalist and techno-natures. His argument is that there is no *essential* nature, but rather *natures* that are hybrid and multiform. At the heart of this exploration is an effort to theorize political ecology 'as the study of manifold articulations of history and biology and the cultural mediations through which such articulations are necessarily established' (ibid.: 3).

Critical responses to discursive perspectives

Escobar's poststructuralist political ecology has not been without its critics and there is a lively, ongoing debate concerning the treatment of development as discourse and the nature of local encounters with development. Presenting a Gramscian analysis of the local politics of development in Zimbabwe in contrast to the discursive analyses of Ferguson and Escobar, Moore (2000) identifies a lack of historical depth in the former's treatment of post-World War II development institutions. Moore also suggests that there is an element of 'discursive determinism' in this work that overlooks the role that local cultural politics of identity, history, community and territory play in shaping development discourse, producing 'a sort of contraflow to globalizing influences' (ibid.: 257). Building on Gramsci's (1971) insights on culture and politics, Moore demonstrates that local resistance politics in Zimbabwe are not constructed simply in opposition to development, but as culturally embedded demands for development as a right or entitlement from the state. Similarly, several political ecologists have argued that in many cases, local social movements are concerned with managing modernization processes, gaining 'access to development, and forcing the state to assume greater responsibility in addressing problems of uneven regional development and social equity' (Little and Painter, 1995; Bebbington, 1996; Rangan, 1996: 206). Stonich (1999) points out that Escobar's anti-essentialist perspective on nature over-emphasizes an idealist position on culturally constructed nature at the expense of a productive engagement with new ecological models of non-equilibrium and complexity. She concludes that Escobar's theorization of hybrid natures is tangential to the current trajectory of political ecology, much of which is already anti-essentialist in character and has long been fully engaged with social constructivist approaches to nature (see Chapter 3).

Geographer Anthony Bebbington (1996; 2000) has been one of the most persistent critics of Escobar's poststructuralist critique of development. He argues that it is insufficient to urge, as Escobar does, the creation of decentred autonomous spaces for the formation of alternatives to development. 'In the final instance, alternative strategies are only worthwhile if they make concrete difference' (Bebbington, 1996: 87). In other words, promoting cultural difference and local resistance to the state and its international development allies is not enough to ensure that viable livelihoods will be secured. In what amounts to an empirically grounded refutation of Escobar's poststructuralist critique, Bebbington (2000) seeks to demonstrate how indigenous Quichua populations in the Ecuadorian Andes have managed to forge locally meaningful engagements with modernizing institutions and practices (see Extract 9). In the cases he presents from the Andes, *campesino* organizations have mobilized, not simply to resist development, but to try to gain access to and control over the development process. Along the way, these locally based social movements have gained support from collaborations with state agencies, the Catholic Church and NGOs. These cases suggest that development interventions are not merely exercises in cultural domination, but may also contribute to the restructuring of local power relations and access to resources in a way that is beneficial for subaltern groups. Individual agency is critical in terms of the way state modernizing policies are implemented as well as the ultimate effects on local peoples' ability to influence their collective destiny and reassert their cultural identity. Generalized discursive critiques of development as domination, concludes Bebbington, are not supported by place-based empirical studies.

extract 9

Poststructural critiques and development theory

Yet in this sense, poststructural positions are troublesome. By finding so little that is recoverable within the practice of development, by failing to address in any detail the economic dimensions of alternatives, and above all, by not exploring the diversity of development processes and outcomes, they fail to develop the empirical bases of a possible counternarrative. Furthermore, when subjected to empirical interrogation, the categorical assertions of such positions appear overstated, in turn suggesting theoretical weaknesses. As a result, and however unintentionally, they cede ground to neoliberal interpretations and the types of programs that might derive from them.

That poststructural critiques give little attention to alternatives and leave so little space for a continuing dialogue with the development experience to date is largely a consequence of their emphasis on discursive critique. Interpretations of

development, and its alternatives, might differ if they were based on ethno-graphic and historical analyses of the ways in which development interventions and market transactions become part of a longer, sedimented history of a place and its linkages with the wider world. Indeed, if we look at histories of places, rather than of discourses, and trace actual processes of livelihood and landscape transformation and the institutional interventions that have accompanied them, it becomes easier to identify elements of feasible development alternatives. Germs of these alternatives have already been elaborated at the intersection of popular practices and external interventions, albeit in quite unanticipated ways. In this sense, I will use discussions of regional transformations in highland Ecuador to point to problems (as well as strengths) in the normative positions and analytical tools of both neoliberal and poststructural interpretations. These observations will provide a basis for building theory that draws on insights of each type of interpretation, and that helps identify ways forward for a far more geographical theory of development revolving around notions of place and liveli-hood. Indeed, the implication is that a more comprehensive development theory has to be built at the interface of geography and history.
Source: Bebbington (2000: 496)

The persistence of hegemonic discourses

While the criticisms of Escobar's treatment of development as discourse highlight important limitations, his writings have helped to demonstrate the critical role of discourse analysis in political ecology. We need not accept the existence of a 'master development narrative that has erased alternative paths' that Escobar's work suggests (A. Ferguson and Derman, 2000: 121) in order to recognize that development does operate discursively to construct possibilities, constraints, categories and knowledge. J. Ferguson made this clear in his deconstruction of the World Bank report, demonstrating how the body of knowledge on Lesotho produced by development institutions bore little resemblance to the knowledge produced by scientific and academic institutions. Lesotho was discursively constructed to conform to the operation of an international development apparatus. It is precisely such constructions, however, that are subject to contestation as local communities and social movements struggle for some level of control over their own livelihoods and for the better living standards that development promises. Contestation around the meaning of development has provided the framework for radical challenges to social injustice and economic inequality (Peet and Watts, 1996a; Moore, 2000; Peters, 2000). The geographical and temporal specificity of such struggles 'belies any single, totalizing development discourse' (Moore, 2000: 655), but does not, however, reduce the relevance of discursive analysis to political ecology.

Indeed, it is important to recognize that some discourses do become hegemonic and globalized and that the consequences, ecologically and socially, are not insignificant. Fairhead and Leach demonstrated how institutions concerned with environment and development in Guinea produced a 'savannisation discourse' (1996: 22; see discussion in Chapter 3) that identified a process of deforestation caused by the destructive land use practices of the local inhabitants. As their study showed, this discourse became hegemonic for over a century, even though photographic, historical and ethnographic evidence suggested the opposite process; the establishment of forest islands *as a consequence* of human occupation. More recently, Bassett and Koli Bi (2000) have productively engaged the concept of 'regional discursive formation' (Peet and Watts, 1996a: 15) in a study from northern Côte d'Ivoire that complements Fairhead and Leach's analysis (see Figure 4.1). In this case the researchers investigated why a 'desertification discourse' became the framework for numerous policy documents produced by national and international environment and development institutions, despite the fact that there was almost no empirical data on ecological change in the region. The newest documentary presentation of this discourse is the country's National Environmental Action Plan (NEAP), mandated by the World Bank as sort of green conditionality for further development loans and articulated in the discourse of sustainable development. The hegemonic desertification discourse fundamentally structured the NEAP. Using a variety of methods – including surveys, interviews, air photo analysis and GIS – Bassett and Koli Bi's study revealed that the preoccupation with desertification is completely misguided. They found no evidence for desertification, but convincing evidence of bush and woodland expansion at the expense of livestock rangelands and a significant degree of geographic variability in the quality of ecological change (see Extract 10).

extract 10

The consequences of the 'desertification discourse'

A major finding of this comparative research on land-cover changes in the Katiali and Tagbanga areas is that, contrary to received wisdom, the savanna has become more wooded over the past thirty years. This finding runs counter to the

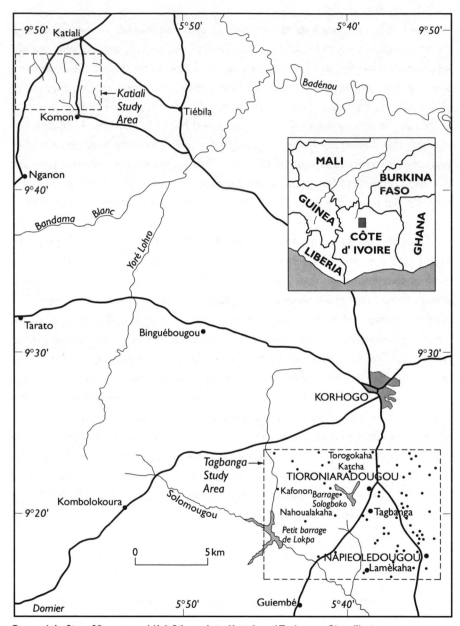

Figure 4.1 Site of Bassett and Koli Bi's study in Katiali and Tagbanga, Côte d'Ivoire.

dominant narrative, which assumes that the savanna has become less wooded and increasingly dominated by grass savannas. It also extends, both geographically and analytically, the findings of Fairhead and Leach on the expansion of wooded landscapes in the forest-savanna transition zone of Guinea (Fairhead and Leach 1996) to the sudanian savanna.

A second finding points to the diversity of savanna vegetation communities in the Korhogo region. The similarities and differences in the transformation of the Tagbanga and Katiali savanna areas underscore the importance of temporal and spatial variations in environmental change. This finding conforms to the scientific literature on savanna ecology that points to a wide range of plant communities, which are commonly distributed in mosaic form across the landscape. The most important factors influencing the nature and direction of vegetation change are farming systems, grazing pressure, population density, and changing fire regimes. These factors, which are themselves linked to changing political and economic processes extending beyond the region (e.g., cotton-development policies, immigration of Fulbe herders, or farmer-herder conflicts), interact with a host of biophysical factors such as soil type, slope, and rainfall to create temporally and locationally specific outcomes.

A third finding of this research is its relevance to environmental planning. Despite its problematic scientific status, the desertification narrative currently guides environmental policy. For example, NEAP-CI recommendations to combat the assumed reduction in tree cover include the regulation of bush fires through a range of increasingly coercive measures, restrictions on wood cutting, and the promotion of village-level tree planting. In light of the findings of this case study, such policy recommendations can be seen as misconceived and a waste of limited resources. The disjuncture between national and global environmental discourses and actual vegetation-change patterns is alarming. Our findings show that although desertification is not taking place, heavy grazing and early fires have significantly reduced the quality of the savanna for livestock raising. Tree and shrub invasion and a highly degraded herbaceous layer were evident in both the Katiali and Tagbanga study areas. Since livestock development is a priority of the Ministry of Agriculture, one would think that rangeland rehabilitation would be a centerpiece of the Côte d'Ivoire NEAP.
Source: Bassett and Koli Bi (2000: 89–90)

To summarize, the role of discourse theory and discourse analysis in political ecology is still very much under discussion. On the one hand, critical reactions to

Escobar and other poststructuralists indicate some of the limitations of a strong social constructivism that stresses idealist abstractions while neglecting materialist analyses. Recalling the discussions in Chapter 3, understanding the agency of nature in human history – the force of nature's *materiality* – and integrating new models of non-equilibrium ecology into political ecology are central to the development of the field. A political ecology that treats nature as mere representation and simulacra and the politics of development as hegemonic discourse is fundamentally barren. On the other hand, attention to discursive constructions of environment and development have been and will remain critical in analyses of the rationale for and consequences of state and international interventions to alter local land and resource uses. In fact, empirically based studies such as those of Bassett and Koli Bi and Fairhead and Leach remind us how consequential discourses can be, both in terms of understanding and addressing ecological change and for livelihoods in the rural Third World. Discursive constructions of environmental degradation justify and rationalize all manner of interventions into people's daily lives in the name of 'development' or 'environmental conservation'. One of the most powerful and pervasive, indeed, globalized, interventions over the past two decades has been in the area of property rights and land tenure. We turn now to examine some of the key political ecology research on the nature of the relationships among property rights, environmental change and economic development.

Development, tenure and environmental change

A key concern of political ecology has been to analyse the ways in which the structure of property rights at various scales (e.g., the state, community and household) influences access to resources and land. Of particular interest is how property rights are defined, negotiated and struggled over among different social groups, be they class, gender or ethnic groupings, and how this helps to explain patterns of development and environmental conservation and degradation. The question of who controls access is a critical one in analysing who participates in, gains from, or is excluded from the process of development. Particular attention has been paid to the spatial aspects of land rights in this question. This includes the way that ownership and rights vary by land type, land use, resource type and location, the notion of territoriality in relation to access control, and the importance of political-economic context in specific locales. Also included is an interest in the way that trees and tree planting or removal can operate to shift the meaning, control and ownership of territory, sometimes strengthening the security of land claims, sometimes geographically constraining access for certain individuals or groups, and very often constituting the focus of struggle and negotiation in the ongoing process of defining property rights. Finally – in the political ecology tradition of tracing outcomes in specific locales through causal linkages across scales and to non-place-based forces – there is a strong interest in the ways that global policy shifts in bilateral and multilateral development institutions translate on the ground to changes in property rights and the conduct of environmental management.

Apropos of the final point, part of the broader context for political ecologists' interest in tenure and property rights has been the rise of neo-liberal economic theory in the policies and practices of international development institutions from the 1980s and beyond. Privatization is a key word in the neo-liberal economic thinking that drove international development policies in the 1980s and continues today (Watts, 1994). The World Bank and other major players in international development have made land tenure reform a centrepiece of their privatization strategy for Third World economic growth. The World Bank has funded land survey and titling projects across the Third World under the assumption that the privatization of land is a first step in creating the sense of tenure security necessary to stimulate investments in land and increase productivity. Privatization, so the reasoning goes, would make individual owners secure enough to make long-term investments in the land, thereby leading to better husbandry and resource-conserving practices. The idea that privatization leads to greater economic efficiencies and improved land husbandry is appealing to international development planners and conservationists alike, helping to explain the wide popularity of and support for land titling in the rural Third World and the central role that tenure reform has played in sustainable development thinking. These policies, political ecology studies have shown, have had important unintended consequences for access to land, social justice, and environmental change. It is therefore critical that we examine the assumptions and logic that drive them.

In property theory, the concept of tenure encompasses both the notion of ownership and a corresponding bundle of rights (Bruce and Fortmann, 1988). A commonly used classification of tenure systems defines four ideal types of ownership: state, private, communal and open-access, and four categories of rights: use, transfer, exclusion and enforcement. The current logic for transforming communal to private ownership is embedded in an evolutionary model of tenure that positions private individual ownership as the 'highest' form of property (see Figure 4.2). In the evolutionary model, communal tenure systems are associated with 'inefficient' or 'traditional' agrarian economies, while private individual tenure is associated with 'efficient' or 'modern' economies (McCay and Acheson, 1987; Bassett, 1993). Hardin's (1968) 'Tragedy of the commons' is the best-known representation of the evolutionary model (see Chapter 1). His solutions to the purported inefficiencies of the commons are either to privatize it or subject it to state ownership and regulation. According to the logic of the model, 'privatization internalizes costs and benefits, reduces uncertainty, and thereby increases individual responsibility for the environment and the rational use of its resources' (McCay and Acheson, 1987: 5).

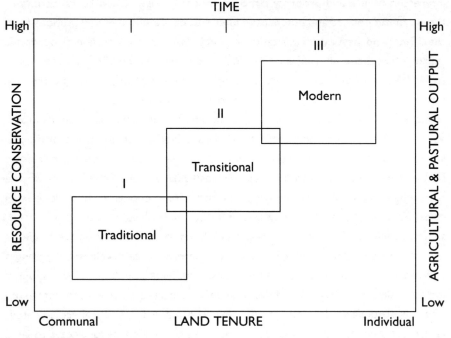

Figure 4.2 The modernization model of tenure change, environmental conservation, and agricultural growth.

Common property theory

A substantial body of literature, falling under the general rubric of common property theory, has risen as a critical response to the tragedy of the commons argument and the evolutionary model of tenure in which it is embedded. In their analyses of development, political ecologists have borrowed from and made important contributions to the common property literature and our understanding of tenure relations more generally. In political ecology, property rights are viewed as an expression of the social relations of production, forged in specific places in specific political-economic contexts and embedded in locally generated meanings of land

and resources (Blaikie and Brookfield, 1987; Watts, 1993). Development interventions intended to alter local property systems will therefore necessarily also entail restructuring social relations within and between producer units (e.g., farming households). Thus, development projects that raise questions of ownership, control and management of land and resources also raise questions regarding labour, production and surplus appropriation and vice versa (Carney and Watts, 1990; Schroeder, 1999). Furthermore, property types are rarely discrete and unequivocal categories. Rights to a particular area of land or resource may be overlapping and multiple and include both group (such as a village or lineage) and individual claims (Peluso, 1992c; Robbins, 1998). In many rural areas targeted for development, negotiations over rights and struggles over the power to ascribe meaning are ongoing and tenure relations are thus continually unfolding (Mackenzie, 1998).

In a word, political ecologists analyse land and resource tenure as a *political process* (e.g., Bassett, 1993; Mackenzie, 1993; Peluso, 1996). Several of these studies have demonstrated that – contra World Bank policy rationale – privatization is neither necessary nor sufficient for the promotion of development by increasing agricultural productivity (see Bassett and Crummey, 1993). In some instances, land titling has been demonstrated to threaten, rather than enhance, the security of producers (Roth, 1993; Vivian, 1994). Land titling can transform multiple and dynamic rights to resources and harvestable products to exclusive and rigidly circumscribed ownership in land, thereby curtailing access for a range of customary users (Peluso, 1996). What such studies and their findings demonstrate is that land tenure reform is often a highly charged politicized process that produces winners and losers. Rather than fixing universally agreed upon property rights in statutory law, titling and privatization often spark new controversies and political struggles over land access and meaning. In analysing the consequences of privatization and state appropriation of the commons, the fundamental question in political ecology studies has been, then, which rights are being secured for whom.

Territoriality has long been recognized in common property theory as key to institutions' capacities to effectively manage the commons and resist encroachment by outsiders, be they private enterprises or state bureaucracies (McCay and Acheson, 1987). Conversely, territorialization is also an important mechanism for the state to make claims and assert internal control over resources at the expense of common property institutions (CPI). For example, Vandergeest and Peluso (1995) developed a resource notion of territoriality to demonstrate the ways in which the state zones and demarcates areas within its boundaries as a way of asserting control over local commons. Recent political ecology studies use a similar notion of territoriality to argue that local CPIs have emerged as significant political actors opposing wholesale privatization or state appropriation. In Chiapas, Mexico, Zapatista organizers linked changes in the national land law to the implementation of the North American Free Trade Agreement (Stephen, 1998). Consequently one of the political goals of the Zapatista movement was to defend indigenous peasants' historical claims to access and control of communal lands as part of an overall rejection of neo-liberal reforms. In a study of struggles to control forest access in Guatemala, Reddy theorizes CPIs as political agents whose 'authority over a resource derives from a communal territorial claim to the resource rooted in a form of customary law' (2002: 272). Her study shows how the power of CPIs to maintain territorial control in the face of competing state claims depends on differences in the strength of community identity, the specific structure of CPIs, and the state's strategies of control.

As noted earlier, there has been a tendency in some development critiques to take an overly romantic view of local communities' social cohesion and to over-emphasize the extent and potential of indigenous knowledge for environmental management and economic development. Robbins (1998) suggests that common-property theory literature similarly reflects a romanticized vision of the local, dodging the difficult questions of class, gender and other social divisions within communities and of how differing and competing community interests might affect the ecological condition of community lands. He points out that studies that sys-tematically analyse the actual ecological outcomes under different property regimes or that provide an empirical basis for determining at what scale the con-trol over resources and land access should be located are rare. Robbins's (1998) rich, fine-grained study of community lands in Rajasthan, India (see Figure 4.3), links the political ecology debates over the respective roles of the state and the local community in guiding sustainable development – addressed previously in this chapter – with debates about how different tenure regimes affect ecological out-comes. His study did not focus simply on different forms of land ownership, how-ever, but on how different forms of authority to control access and use are embedded in unique systems of meaning. For Robbins, the precise location of insti-tutional control or ownership – local or state-centred – is less important than the legitimacy of the authority deployed in the enforcement of rules of access and use.

To demonstrate the links between institutional forms and ecological outcomes, Robbins compared four different types of resource management institutions: *gochers*, which are state-managed pastures; privately held community fallow pastures; state Forest Department enclosures; and *orans*, which are semi-sacred

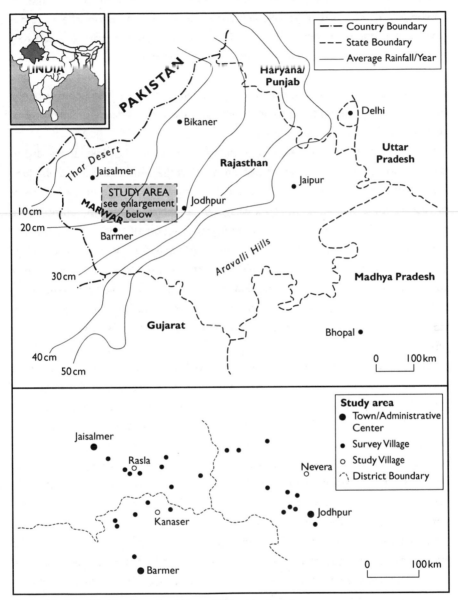

Figure 4.3 Site of Robbins's study in Western Rajasthan, India.

village forests. These four offer a complex combination of management types, allowing for the comparison of two land uses under two types of institutional control, the state in the cases of forest enclosures and state-managed pastures and the community in the cases of *gochers* and *orans*. He employed historical and ethnographic methods to understand the political and economic history that led to a situation of legal pluralism in the Rajasthan communities and the responses of rural producers to the authority of contemporary resource management institutions. Using vegetation transects, he then compared the landscape and ecology of the four types of community lands in order to assess the effects of institutional authority and producer responses.

Figure 4.4 summarizes the results of the comparison, but it is instructive also to consider some of the nuances of Robbins's culturally and historically embedded analysis of power and authority in resource management institutions. His analysis of *gochers*, for example, identified a village-wide ambiguity over the authority to manage these lands, reinforced by a gendered division of labour and gendered access to decision-making in the community. Women, feeling shut out of village institutions responsible for governing the *gocher* lands, do not recognize their authority and tend to disregard their edicts. Consequently, these lands experience higher levels of cutting and sparser tree cover. In contrast, village women cooperate with Forest Department rules for forest enclosures because the department offers access to high-paying planting and maintenance jobs and because its officers receive a degree of deference for their 'superior' knowledge. 'Forest Department enclosures operate, therefore, through a monopoly of interests in the village and through the deployment of a range of authority forms: coercive, economic, and expert' (Robbins, 1998: 423). Consequently, compliance with state rules is high. In *orans*, which have sacred meanings within local village cultures, the authority of traditional village councils combines with cautionary tales of divine punishment to keep the trees standing. Though both state forest enclosures and community-controlled *orans* have high levels of compliance, the ecological outcomes are different because management objectives differ.

Robbins's study advances political ecology in a number of ways. It points out the limitations of common-property theory's assumption of a homogeneous local community and suggests a synthesis of institutional theory to guide political-ecological analyses of struggles over land access. It provides compelling evidence that the debates over the most socially just and ecologically sustainable tenure regime must not be limited to the question of whether communal, private or state control is best. His approach effectively 'shifts analysis away from the somewhat

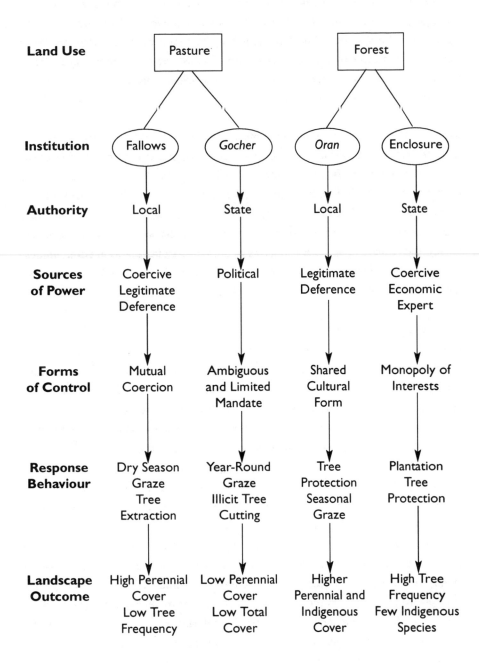

Figure 4.4 Institutions, control and landscape conditions in the desert grass and shrub lands of Rajasthan, India.

irrelevant issue of state and nonstate resource management to a more fundamental inquiry into the nature and effectiveness of social power deployed both through state and local systems of hegemony, domination, and control' (Robbins, 1998: 429). It points towards the need for greater sophistication in theorizing the relationship between land tenure regimes and ecological sustainability and throws into question blanket policy initiatives to devolve property rights to individuals or local communities and reduce the state's role. Perhaps most convincingly it offers an exemplar for something on the order of an experimental design to test the efficacy of state versus local resource management systems, one that combines qualitative methods of interpretive ethnography and political economy with the quantitative methods of ecological science. In this, Robbins's research follows one of the original premises of political ecology – that a full explanation of environmental problems requires the analytical tools of both the social and biophysical sciences. Finally, the research highlights gender as one of the key fault lines in communities' social tensions around access to and management of land-based resources, an issue that we will examine in greater detail next.

Gendered property rights

Gender has been an important focus in feminist political ecology research on the relationships among property rights, development interventions and environmental outcomes (Carney, 1993; Rocheleau et al., 1996b; Mackenzie, 1998; Jarosz, 1999; Schroeder, 1999). Women and men have different rights and responsibilities over land and resources and these differences are related in complex ways to their productive and reproductive roles in the household, community and larger society. Often gendered rights and responsibilities have a strong spatial dimension, such as the case where women and men are involved in different kinds of productive activities on different kinds of land with different agro-ecological potential. Land may be thus defined in relation to gendered knowledge about crop production and use rights. The integration of rural producers of the tropical regions into the world economy and the colonial state's role in structuring capitalist development have generally increased men's control over land access at the expense of women's. In colonial Kenya, for example, Kikuyu men – in their privileged roles as community informants – manipulated the official state inquiries into traditional land tenure to their advantage. Women's traditional rights to use land were subjugated by men's assertion and the state's acceptance of their authority to allocate land (Mackenzie, 1998).

A political ecology study of a Mandinka agricultural region in the Gambia provides a clear illustration of the complexities of gendered property rights and how development interventions aimed at increasing productivity can shift relations of power between men and women (Carney, 1993). In this case the expansion of irrigation led to greater labour demands on peasant households. By redefining the categories of land – and thus the nature of tenure and property rights – within the community, men were able to shift the burden of increased labour demands onto women while at the same time reducing women's control over the product of their labour. Not only are the environment and landscape of the Gambia basin altered by the development intervention, 'so too are the social relations that mediate access to, and use of, land within rural households' (ibid.: 345).

Ownership of and rights to economically valuable trees are an important, but poorly understood, aspect of gendered property rights, largely because there was little research conducted on this until fairly recently (Fortmann and Bruce, 1988). The emergence of feminist political ecology has helped to highlight the importance of gendered rights and responsibilities with regard to trees, in an understanding of the social and ecological consequences of sustainable development interventions (Schroeder, 1993; 1999; Rocheleau and Ross, 1995; Rocheleau et al., 1996a; Schroeder and Suryanata, 1996). These studies reveal the complex ways in which trees enter into material and ideological struggles and negotiations over the path of development, property rights of men and women, labour obligations within the household and community, and claims on production surpluses and other benefits. Often in contemporary agrarian societies men dominate the control of land access and allocation, a situation that severely limits women's ability to participate in and benefit from sustainable development programmes for tree planting and reforestation. Trees may also be used 'as an instrument of change to transform property rights and landscapes at the national, regional and household levels', with one common outcome being a reduction in women's access to land (Rocheleau and Ross, 1995: 417). That is, trees can be used to stake or reinforce claims to land and therefore produce social conflict and change far beyond anything intended or imagined by development planners.

One of the most meticulous and theoretically nuanced studies of the political ecology of gender, property rights and sustainable development is Schroeder's (1999) Shady Practices. Schroeder examined successive development interventions in a small town on the north bank of the Gambia River. He shows how shifts in the prevailing development ideologies – spurred by feminist and environmentalist critiques – translated on the ground into changes in the relative socio-economic status of men and women and corresponding intra- and inter-household struggles to control rights to land, labour and the profits from production. The first ideological shift took the form of 'women in development' (WID), which guided a series of projects in the early 1980s aimed at developing women's market gardening as a source of cash income. It coincided with a period of drought and the imposition of structural adjustment conditionalities in the Gambia, the combination of which greatly reduced men's income streams from dryland agriculture. The second ideological shift was the 'greening' of development in the late 1980s and early 1990s, with a new emphasis on sustainability and environmental stabilization. On the ground this took the form of new agroforestry projects designed to integrate a variety of tree crops into the irrigated garden plots.

Schroeder's study showed how the WID-inspired garden projects developed into an important income source for women and their households at the same time that men's incomes were shrinking dramatically. Two consequences followed. First, women took on greater responsibilities for their households and gained a certain degree of economic independence. Second, they also were able to increase control over access to plots of land that had been controlled by men under the customary land tenure system of lineage-based landholdings. When the prevailing development ideology shifted from concerns over women's livelihoods to concerns over environmental stabilization, men began to reassert claims on the land occupied by women's gardens by planting tree-crops in and around the garden plots. Through this tactic senior men were able both to reclaim lineage-based landholdings and to gain access to women's unpaid labour for irrigating and maintaining the new tree-crops (see Figure 4.5). Among this study's important contributions to political ecology, it shows how the rise of seemingly progressive development ideologies – improving women's livelihoods and stabilizing and reversing environmental degradation – played out on the ground as struggles between men and women over the control of access to land and corresponding claims on labour. In this case, the greening of development has had the effect in some locations of reversing the gains that women achieved during the market garden boom (see Extract 11).

extract 11

Gender, environment and development

Roughly a dozen garden/orchards were established in Kerewan between 1987 and 1995. Discussions with the landholders opening these perimeters revealed that they had adopted much stricter controls over land use than those in place

Figure 4.5 Unpaid women's labour was the key to male landholders' success in establishing fruit tree orchards in the Gambia.

in many of the community's older gardens. Kumakaa payments, for example, were eschewed altogether. In most cases, access to land was only granted under terms that required women to guarantee they would: (1) water the tree crop as long as they stayed in the perimeter; and (2) leave their plots as soon as the trees reached maturity. With a wary eye trained on the prospect of women mounting competing claims to land or trees on moral economic grounds, the male landholders either provided fences and wells on their own account or built them with the assistance of donors interested in promoting agroforestry, many of whom had sponsored garden projects on the same sites several years earlier. In one garden destined for conversion into an orchard, a contract was signed between the landholder, the donor agency, and a garden group stipulating a five-year limit to the women's vegetable-growing rights. In another, a project manager proposed a rule as a hedge against tenure erosion that would preclude anyone other than project participants and 'one small daughter per grower' (!) from working the plot. In a third site, garden gates were padlocked in recognition of full conversion to orchard production. Moreover, in 1991, the Kerewan town chief, fresh from an environmental sensitization training organized by an NGO, issued a proclamation that any gardeners responsible for starting a bush fire that destroyed trees would be fined the equivalent of $200. At least one woman was evicted from her plot when a fire she started accidentally destroyed just one of the landholder's trees.

By the late-1980s, therefore, firm consensus had formed among the Forestry Department, NGOs, voluntary agencies, and donors around the triple foci of (1) using the production of fruit commodities as the vehicle to promote agroforestry; (2) concentrating commodity-based tree-planting projects within gardens; and (3) managing the whole endeavor on the premise of being able to exploit a female labor reserve.

While the resulting mix of property and labor claims was not entirely without precedent in The Gambia, the heavy emphasis on female labor to carry out tree-planting objectives was striking. A UNDP official gave voice to the ideological basis for pinning the hopes of Gambian environmental stabilization efforts on women: 'Women are the sole conservators of the land ... the willingness of women to participate in natural resource management is greater than that of men. Women are always willing to work in groups and these groups can be formed for conservation purposes.'

In this context, trees grown by landholders represented a special threat. For with landholders becoming more deeply involved in tree crop production, the nature of the agroforestry system itself changed significantly. It was no longer a system that allowed the women to unilaterally diversify their crop selection and spread financial risk but a successional system deliberately designed to bring about a transfer of use rights and effective control from women gardeners to male orchard owners. The agroforestry system promoted by developers and adopted by landholders threatened to undermine the garden-based livelihood system, and gardeners consequently resisted it through aggressive tree trimming, 'accidental' damage to trees by fire, and malign neglect of watering responsibilities imposed upon them by landholders.

Source: Schroeder (1999: 102–3, 109, 122)

Beyond dualisms of North–South and urban–rural

This chapter opened with the juxtaposition of two tragic narratives of development, one from Goethe's *Faust* and the other from a recent political ecology study in Honduras. The purpose of this juxtaposition was to encourage us to think of development as the continuous unfolding of capitalist modernity in particular places at particular times. It was meant to distance the discussion somewhat from the more common alternative conceptualization; that development is an international programme composed of a set of economic policies and interventions and intended to improve the lives of Third World people through a fuller integration of their national economies into a world capitalist system. This conceptualization restricts the meaning of development to the post-World War II campaign managed by the IMF and the World Bank and its regional counterparts that is directed toward the postcolonial states of the South. It promotes the treatment of core and periphery or First World and Third World as discrete objects, rather than interrelated and uneven outcomes of a single process, the global expansion of capitalist social relations.

Political ecologists have been wrestling recently with just such conceptual vexations. Some have suggested that because the field has been dominated by research in rural, Third World settings that it has encouraged the notion that industrialized countries are inherently different (McCarthy, 2002; Walker, 2003). This tendency in political ecology, it is argued, has resulted in the theoretically suspect position that the First and Third World are distinct categories that demand separate analytics (Walker, 2003). They point out that many of the features of Third World political ecologies can be observed in the First World as well (McCarthy, 2002). In short, these authors suggest that struggles around environment and development are just as relevant (though not necessarily identical) in industrialized economies as they are in non-industrialized economies. They propose that we are witnessing 'the march of political ecology from the global South to the global North' (Walker, 2003: 11).

While these studies in urbanized, industrialized economies are important in their own right, some of the critiques of political ecology may be over-stated. We should not confuse an overwhelming preponderance of political ecology studies conducted in the rural regions of Third World countries with a theoretical claim for a distinct analysis for industrialized countries. Though initially few and far between, political ecology early on included studies from First World settings. Blaikie and Brookfield's foundational text, *Land Degradation and Society*, to cite one important example, extended political ecological analysis to the 'new conservation crisis in the "North"' (1987: 223). One of the earliest theoretical engagements with Blaikie and Brookfield's concept of regional political ecology was based on an empirical study conducted in present-day Western Europe (Black, 1990). It is nearly a decade since Rocheleau *et al.* (1996b) explicitly conceptualized feminist political ecology as transcending the dualisms of urban–rural, Third World–First World and industrial–agrarian. The point I wish to make here is that political ecology is not, nor should it be, narrowly defined as exclusively concerned with rural, land-based resource issues in developing countries. Environment and development, then, are conceived of in the broadest terms. Environment includes not only the forests and grasslands of rural communities in Nigeria or Nepal, but also the toxins-rich urban neighbourhoods of ethnic minorities in Los Angeles and the amenities-rich landscapes of the new rural gentry in the American West (Pulido, 2000; Walker, 2003). Development encompasses not only fuelwood projects in India and irrigated rice projects in the Gambia, but also Las Vegas urban sprawl and uranium mining and nuclear waste disposal on Native American lands (Kuletz, 2001; McCarthy, 2001).

This is not to suggest that fundamental differences between First and Third World national economies and the related social and environmental conditions do not exist. Rather it is to point out the necessity of theorizing political ecology beyond the dualisms of urban–rural, industrial–agrarian, and First World–Third World. The problems posed by these conceptual dualisms are of much greater significance than mere hairsplitting within the field. Indeed, these recent debates regarding the movement of political ecology northward echo long-standing debates in human geography. One debate related to the categorization of First World environmental movements as driven by consumption issues (environmental quality or amenities) and Third World movements driven by production issues (livelihood struggles) (Goodman and Redclift, 1991). Using the case of the Florida Everglades, Hollander (1995) demonstrated that such sharp distinctions are unwarranted and over-simplify the complexities of First World agroenvironmental conflicts that involve both production and consumption concerns. Another key debate addressed the theoretically inhibiting schisms within geography that separated the study of the city from the countryside, social nature from social space and core from periphery (Fitzsimmons, 1989). Fitzsimmons's answer was to approach the analysis of the geography of modern capitalism relationally: 'Urbanization is relational – a process which contains, constructs and conceptualizes both city and countryside' (1989: 110).

While continuing to recognize the distinctiveness of particular regional political ecologies, analyses must address *how they are produced* by interconnecting processes that link places around the globe through flows of commodities, knowledge, capital and labour, through time and across space. As Swyngedouw and Heynen recently asserted, 'In the emerging literature on political ecology ...

discussions about global environmental problems and the possibilities for a "sustainable" future customarily ignore the urban origin of many of the problems' (2003: 899). Their integrated and relational approach to urban political ecology, which stresses the ways in which interconnected social and biophysical processes produce highly uneven urban landscapes, offers valuable insights for the practice of political ecology research more generally. In a nutshell, political ecology needs to be framed by the unfolding geography of uneven development (Smith, 1984), rather than in terms of binary oppositions of urban–rural, industrial–agrarian and so forth. The concept of uneven geographical development reframes these binaries in terms of dialectical relationships. By focusing the analysis of regional political ecologies on relations and processes, our research is better suited to address questions of ultimate causation. Impoverishment and wealth accumulation, environmental degradation and conservation, and urban development and rural crisis are linked processes, operating across scales ranging from the local to the global.

5
BIODIVERSITY CONSERVATION

In 1962, representatives from 63 different countries met in the cool summer days of the Pacific Northwest for the purpose of organizing 'the national park movement on a worldwide basis' (Adams, 1963: xxxii). At that meeting – the First World Conference on National Parks – the organizers laid out the conceptual foundation upon which twenty-first century biodiversity conservation is built. The most important of these ideas are that the establishment of national parks is the best and indeed only way to insure the survival of wild species and that parks 'should be looked upon as a *sanctum sanctorum*', where all settlement and natural resource exploitation is prohibited (Badshah and Bhadran, 1963: 30). In the face of concerns over extinction, conference goers likened national parks to 'nature islands' (Udall, 1963: 1) that could serve as protected refuges for wild species in a world dominated by human interests and activities. Participants at the meeting agreed that habitat modification was the primary reason for the extinction of species and that species loss was an international problem and therefore must be addressed through international cooperation and coordination. Four decades later, the conceptual foundations of nature protection remain intact though the nomenclature has changed, with 'biodiversity' replacing 'wild flora and fauna' and 'international' becoming 'global'.

The discursive construction of biodiversity as a discrete object of global concern can be traced to the 1980s and the more or less simultaneous maturation of the fields of genetic engineering and conservation biology. Technological and commercial advances in genetic engineering resulted in the commodification of genes as a resource, the raw material for a new industry as it were, subject to market forces. Conservation biology developed as an attempt to structure conservation practices on the scientific foundation of evolutionary biology, with its emphasis on the relationships among genetic variation, genetic exchange, species population sizes and species extinction rates (Frankel and Soulé, 1981; Soulé, 1986). Since the mid-1980s, when the term became the catchword for conservation planners, biodiversity has been discursively constructed in such a way to suggest a global perspective and 'top-down approaches in dealing with nature and natural resources' (Flitner, 1998: 6). This is clearly evident in the way that Third World protected areas have been planned and established through the interventions of First World scientists and managers.

Protected area planners have promoted the idea that parks will serve as the centrepiece of a global '*in situ*' genetic conservation scheme (McNeely and Miller, 1984). Participants at the 1992 United Nations Conference on Environment and Development (the Rio Summit) agreed that biodiversity loss was a 'global commons' problem that would need to be managed by global institutions operating under the directives of international conventions and treaties. The Convention on Biological Diversity (CBD), which resulted from the Rio Summit, now provides the framework and rationale for international efforts to stem biodiversity loss, focusing on *in situ* conservation in national parks and protected areas. Local commons of forest, pasture, and coastal waters are thus being reclassified as global commons to be managed for the protection and use of biodiversity for the 'global community'. Biodiversity has now become the main rationale for environmental interventions worldwide, with a corresponding fade in emphasis on other resources such as soil, water and energy.

Because national parks and equivalent reserves are viewed as the primary containers of the world's biodiversity, their currency has risen tremendously in the past few decades. Since the first World Parks conference 1962, there has been a nearly exponential rise in the number of officially designated national parks around the globe. The 1970s saw the greatest expansion of protected areas in history, with the number established between 1970 and 1990 exceeding the number created in all the decades previous (Harrison *et al.*, 1984; Wood, 2000). Most of the increase has occurred in tropical Third World countries, many of which are economically under-developed with populations that are predominantly rural and dependent on agriculture. There is an obvious geography to the distribution of biodiversity and the protected areas that enclose it, which links the global with the local. Tropical countries, particularly those that possess tropical rainforests, contain by far the largest share of the world's biodiversity. Global managers, technocrats and scientists covet the local commons where Third World pastoralists, swidden farmers, fishers and hunters have pursued their livelihoods for generations. The processes by which territory is designated as local or global commons and the symbolic and material struggles that result are the central concerns of the political ecology of biodiversity conservation.

This chapter explores the political ecology of biodiversity conservation through an examination of national parks and protected areas. As currently envisioned, biodiversity conservation is a territorially based strategy that is anchored in the proprietary claims of the state. It is widely acknowledged that for centuries, even millennia, non-state peoples have claimed, occupied or utilized virtually every part of the Earth with the exception of the most inhospitable environments. Beginning with the establishment of the world's first national park at Yellowstone in 1872, territorial forms of nature conservation have been deeply political because the state has claimed ownership over 'wilderness' areas that others considered to be their homeland (Dasmann, 1984). A political ecology analysis is a powerful way of examining both the ecological efficacy of this approach to biodiversity protection and of understanding the politics that produce and are produced by it. Parks and biodiversity conservation involve questions that are at the very core of political ecology. How is the relationship between society and nature defined and conceptualized, how is access to land and resources controlled, and how are environmental costs and benefits distributed?

The politics of global biodiversity conservation are driven by the interactions of three groups of actors: the state, international organizations and institutions, and civil society. The chapter thus begins by introducing the interests of each of these in relation to the history and practice of nature conservation. The focus then shifts to the mainstream or 'fortress' model (Neumann, 1997; Brockington, 2002; Adams, 2003a) of territorially based biodiversity conservation and explores how political ecology and related fields have critically evaluated the ideologies, assumptions and practices of its advocates. The following section examines some of the new biodiversity conservation models of 'nature–society hybrids' (Zimmerer, 2000: 356) that conservation planners have developed to address the political conflicts and ecologic limitations inherent in the fortress approach. A discussion of the conceptual and philosophical challenges surrounding biodiversity conservation that political ecologists are now exploring closes the chapter.

The role of the state

The state, specifically the modern nation–state as it developed from the eighteenth century onward, plays the central role in biodiversity conservation today. It is a role that is rooted in the history and very definition of the state as a form of spatial governance. Modern states claim sovereignty over the land and natural resources within their territorial boundaries and thus sole authority to regulate their use. States come into *being* by asserting control over mosaics of commons, dispossessing local, non-state entities of pre-existing claims and rights in the process (*The Ecologist*, 1993). States assert control through scientific and technical acts of surveying, inventorying, zoning and mapping the living resources of its territory, most relevantly forested lands (Vandergeest and Peluso, 1995; Bryant, 1997; Scott, 1998; Peluso and Vandergeest, 2001). These actions in effect enclose local commons and transfer ownership to the state, which then controls the allocation of benefits from the land and its biological resources.

The shift from local commons regimes to state property regimes can be recognized readily in the history of European colonization of tropical territories beginning in the second half of the nineteenth century. Peluso and Vandergeest (2001) capture the process perfectly in their notion of 'political forests' in their comparative historical study of state-led forestry in five regions of Southeast Asia. They found that in all the cases in their study, the governments declared that the state was sovereign owner of all land and resources and acted on this claim by demarcating state forests reserves. They label these reserves 'political forests', both to differentiate them from ecologically designated forests – since some state forest reserve lands were not forested and not all forested lands were included in reserves – and to highlight the political nature of their creation. Elsewhere, European colonial governments initiated parallel processes of state making. For example, in most of British colonial Africa, governments declared all uncultivated lands, forests and wildlife to be the property of the British Crown and secured this claim by creating various types of state reserves and enacting laws restricting access to wildlife and other living resources (Neumann, 1998). Today many of the game and forest reserves that colonial governments created are the national parks and protected areas of Third World tropical countries. Thus states now 'own' most of the key territory that is the locus of current global biodiversity conservation plans.

The process of state-making entailed the redefinition and reorganization of space within sovereign territorial boundaries. Censuses, surveys, resource inventories and maps are critical steps in making society and nature visible and governable. Forest and game reserves, resettlement schemes, villagization and similar designations reorder the landscape of the state in such a way as to promote legibility from 'above' (Scott, 1998; Neumann, 2001a). These spatial designations function to divide up and contain society and nature into discrete categories.

Present-day biodiversity conservation is founded on a historical process of state-making that spatially segregated society from nature, wilderness from civilization, conservation from development. State forest reserves, national parks and designated wilderness areas are the primary 'containers' of biodiversity in today's prevailing model of conservation. The ecological and political consequences of constructing a global biodiversity conservation strategy that accepts and builds upon this spatial categorization and simplification will be explored throughout this chapter.

International organizations and institutions

The crucial role of international organizations and institutions in conceptualizing, planning, funding and managing protected areas is one of the most distinctive features of biodiversity conservation in tropical Third World countries. International interest in Third World conservation and protected areas can be traced to the early years of the European colonial empire (Adams, 2001). Conservation advocates held a series of conferences in European capitals in the first decades of the twentieth century that were focused on the conservation of wildlife in the European colonies, initially in Africa and later in Asia. The individuals principally responsible for organizing the conferences were experienced African big game hunters, most of them privileged members of Europe's aristocracy. The most influential and effective of the international conservationists were British nationals organized through the London-based Society for the Protection of the Fauna of the Empire (SPFE), founded in 1903 and recognized as the world's first international wildlife conservation organization (Neumann, 1996). A conference they sponsored resulted in what came to be known as the 1933 London Convention, a critical document for the establishment of conservation standards and definitions in colonial Africa. Its most important features were the recommendations to outlaw most customary African hunting practices and create a system of national parks. The SPFE's focus on the establishment of conservation territories meant, 'national parks came to dominate state-run conservation almost everywhere in the former British colonial empire' (Adams, 2003a: 41). In neither the case of Africa nor Asia were indigenous residents of the colonies represented in the deliberations nor were they given any say in the formulation of conservation policies.

Following the formation of the United Nations and the rise of multilateralism in the aftermath of World War II, the number, types and agendas of international organizations and institutions interested in conservation multiplied. The first was the United Nations Educational, Scientific, and Cultural Organization (UNESCO) in 1946, which in turn helped found the IUCN in 1948, now known as the World Conservation Union. The membership of the IUCN is an eclectic mix of national governments, government agencies, private institutions and conservation NGOs. Two First World countries, the USA and the UK, account for over one-quarter of the total international NGO membership of the IUCN. Since 1959 when the United Nations delegated certain responsibilities to the organization – notably the listing and monitoring of a global network of national parks and protected areas – the IUCN has played a critical role in shaping the global geography of national parks and protected areas. Two of its actions have been critical both for implementing a global plan of biodiversity conservation and for understanding how local commons are claimed and discursively constructed as global commons by powerful international actors. First, it established the United Nations List of National Parks and Equivalent Reserves and created a protected area classification system to aid in coordinating a global system of conservation areas. Second, it established a system of biogeographic provinces that can be used to assess, map and plan protected area coverage worldwide. The system is based on Udvardy's (1975; 1984) scheme that scales the entire globe in terms of ecological zones, from the global scale of the biosphere, to biomes, to biogeographic provinces. The goal is representative coverage for all biogeographic provinces in each of eight 'realms' (primarily equivalent to continents).

The end of formal colonialism in the 1950s and 1960s heightened the importance of international organizations like the IUCN and UNESCO and deepened their influence on the conservation policies of Third World countries. The initial focus was on Africa where international conservationists grew anxious that the newly independent African leaders would abandon colonial conservation programmes altogether. The IUCN organized the 'African Special Project' in 1960, an effort to reach the new African leaders and generate public support for parks and wildlife conservation. A group of conservationists based in the USA, many of them wealthy big game hunters, started the African Wildlife Leadership Foundation in 1961 (now the AWF) to fund and train a cadre of African conservation bureaucrats and managers. Around the same time a group of largely British conservationists created WWF – or the World Wide Fund for Nature as it is now known – in an effort to attract donors through media blitzes and secret fundraising campaigns among the world's business and political elite (Bonner, 1993). WWF's fundraising efforts have been remarkably successful, if controversial (see Bonner, 1993; Ellis, 1994), and it is presently considered to be the world's best-funded international conservation organization. The majority of its projects involve protected areas in tropical Third World countries, a pattern that reflects and reinforces the top-down nature of global biodiversity conservation.

The number of international conservation organizations with projects in Third World countries has continued to grow since the 1960s. Along with UNESCO, whose Man and the Biosphere (MAB) programme is structured around a global network of biosphere reserves, there are a number of UN agencies with interests in biodiversity conservation and protected areas, including the Food and Agricultural Organization (FAO), and the UN Environmental Program (UNEP). There are also numerous First World-based non-governmental institutions and agencies, the most active and influential of which includes The Nature Conservancy (TNC), Conservation International (CI), the World Resources Institute (WRI), and the International Foundation for the Conservation of Wildlife (IFCW). The role of these organizations in the formulation of developing coun-tries' conservation policies and practices is fundamental. They typically work in cooperation with host government agencies and, increasingly, local organizations and communities, but their central role in conceptualizing, planning, organizing and funding conservation interventions cannot be over-stated. Among other activities, they have provided funds for protected area land acquisition, supplied arms and equipment for anti-poaching, designed and planned protected areas and offered a variety of technical and scientific training and advice. In addition to these groups, the World Bank in recent years has redefined its economic development role and cast itself as facilitator and financer of environmental interventions through the creation of its Global Environmental Facility (GEF). Political ecologists have ques-tioned the effectiveness of GEF policies, however, noting that they encourage the militarization of conservation and direct most funding towards supporting already existing protected areas, thus doing little to slow biodiversity loss in unprotected areas (Zerner, 1996; Bryant and Bailey, 1997).

Civil society

A focus on the politics of civil society has been a hallmark of political ecology (Peet and Watts, 1996a). Civil society here refers to the non-state organization of human action, specifically the practice of politics in the private sphere. Politics in the private sphere may manifest as social movements, which are often and increas-ingly represented by non-governmental organizations (NGOs), which in turn cooperate and compete for funds, influence and legitimacy. The most obviously important social movement with regard to biodiversity conservation is environ-mentalism, a movement generally traced to the First World countries of the

1960s. Other movements, however, have been important in the political ecology of biodiversity conservation, including the women's, civil rights, indigenous rights and human rights movements. In the realm of biodiversity conservation, the global environmental movement often intersects, overlaps or conflicts with local manifestations of these other movements.

Unlike traditional labour movements, the agendas of new social movements related to biodiversity conservation address qualitative questions about 'the right to sustenance and livelihood, the right to healthy and socially just forms of land use, and intergenerationally sustainable relations of production' (Goldman, 1998: 16). Globally, these social movements are fragmented and heterogeneous, and promote political agendas that are situational, contingent, and changeable. Classifying social movements and their NGO representatives is therefore difficult and prone to over-generalization. For example, Bryant and Bailey (1997) categorize Third World NGOs as focused on livelihood issues and First World NGOs on environmental concerns, a commonly accepted geographic differentiation that political ecologists working in the First World have challenged (Hollander, 1995; McCarthy, 2002).

To further complicate the analysis of civil society, the politics that often engulf biodiversity conservation do not necessarily constitute a 'movement' (Peet and Watts, 1996a). It is important, therefore, to keep in sight the 'micro-politics' within peasant communities (Moore, 1996: 126) and 'everyday forms of resistance' (Scott, 1985) that may shape the political ecology of conservation in specific locales (e.g., Bryant, 1997; Neumann, 1998). Theories of peasant economies are thus often critical when analysing the political ecology of conservation, particularly intra-household gender politics (e.g., Rocheleau, et al., 1996a; Schroeder, 1999).

In much of Third World political ecology, attention has been focused on various forms of peasant movements. Peasant communities often comprise the most active and vociferous opposition to ecologically destructive capitalist enterprises and state development initiatives because these threaten the foundation of their livelihoods. Thus such movements as Chipko in the Indian Himalayas and rubber tappers in the Brazilian Amazon appear to match environmental conservation with issues of social justice and livelihoods. Outsiders have attributed Chipko – the collective action of Himalayan forest village women of wrapping their arms around trees to prevent their harvest by commercial loggers – with a variety of meanings and goals. The movement was popularly understood in Western environmentalist circles as a grassroots conservation movement, demonstrating the possibilities for alliance of interests between First World environmentalists and Third World peasants. Scholars have framed it alternately as a women's movement, a critique of modernist development agendas, and a social justice movement (Guha, 1990; Shiva, 1989; Sinha et al., 1997). Rangan (1996) notes that the movement itself was complex and internally conflicted (and therefore difficult to categorize) but that at its heart was a concern with local control of access to forest resources. The other widely discussed movement, the Brazilian rubber tappers, gained much international attention in part because of its location in the Amazon rainforest, an iconic landscape in global biodiversity conservation. In this case, discussed later in this chapter, rubber tappers' interest in maintaining access to the resources of intact forests coincided with First World conservationists' interests in rainforest protection (Hecht and Cockburn, 1990).

Women were key actors in both the Chipko and rubber tappers movements, a common but often overlooked feature of social movements concerned with access and control to natural resources (Rocheleau et al., 1996a). Rocheleau et al. argue that prevailing gender relations, particularly in the areas of environmental science, property rights and political activity, shape many grassroots environmental movements worldwide (see Extract 12). They suggest a feminist political ecology perspective that views the motivations and goals of environmental social movements in different periods and places through the lens of gender, bridging the urban–rural and First World–Third World divides that often prevail in conceptualizations of nature–society relations. In sum, 'women's issues' and environmental conservation concerns often intersect in social movements in both First and Third World contexts.

extract 12

A feminist political ecology perspective

Gendered science can be viewed in terms of the definition of what is science and who does it, in terms of the different possibilities for defining the relation of people and 'nature,' and in terms of the apparently separate sciences and technologies of production and reproduction, public and private domains, and home, habitat, and workplace spaces ... In North America and Europe, feminist health movements and the 'housewives' environmentalist and anti-toxics movements have questioned the prevailing paradigm of professional science.

We recognize gendered environmental rights of control and access as well as responsibilities to procure and manage resources for the household and the community. These rights and responsibilities may apply to productive resources (land, water, trees, animals) or to the quality of the environment. In addition to the gender division of resources, there is a gender division of power to preserve, protect, change, construct, rehabilitate, and restore environments and to regulate the actions of others.

These grassroots organizations, with their significant involvement of women, are stressing the value of all human beings and their rights to satisfy basic human needs, including food security and health ... They emphasize ecological as well as economic concerns and the needs of future generations as well as those of diverse claimants on existing resources. There is a fundamentally humanitarian, egalitarian, pluralistic, and activist stance to many such organizations.
Source: Rocheleau et al. (1996: 7, 10, 18)

A final dimension of civil society that overlaps significantly with global biodiversity conservation and bridges First and Third World studies is indigenous peoples, specifically the indigenous rights movement. A pared-down definition of indigenous is 'native' or 'native origin', but in the postcolonial global order of nation–states, it has much greater cultural and political meaning. Paraphrasing the legal definition in the International Labor Organization's Indigenous and Tribal Peoples Convention 169, indigenous peoples are self-identified tribal peoples whose social, cultural and economic conditions distinguish them from the national society of their host state and who are regarded as descending from peoples present in the state territory at the time of conquest or colonization (ILO, 1989: Article 1.1). With respect to political ecology, the key concern is with indigenous peoples' historic claims to land and resource access (see Chapter 4). As Nietschmann has succinctly summarized, centuries of 'colonialism have stripped indigenous peoples of land, resources, and rights' and modern nation–states all over the world now lay claim to their territories (1985: 272). In recent decades, the United Nations has recognized and sought to address some of the injustices perpetrated against indigenous peoples during the colonial period and beyond, establishing the Working Group on Indigenous Populations in 1982. For their part, indigenous peoples have become increasingly organized (and successful) in their efforts to regain territorial autonomy and resource rights throughout the First and Third Worlds. They have, in short, become a recognizable social movement on a global scale, transforming 'formerly "domestic" disputes into international claims for recognition and rights' (Hodgson, 2002a: 1040).

Indigenous peoples' interest in controlling access to land and resources often appears to coincide with conservationists' agendas. In part, this reflects the reality that indigenous peoples often occupy the territories that Western scientists view as critical to global biodiversity conservation (an issue explored later in this chapter). For example, 85 per cent of the protected areas in Central America and 80 per cent in South America have resident indigenous populations (Alcorn, 1994). The relationship between indigenous land rights and biodiversity conservation is, however, not easily characterized. Rather, it is complex, fraught with contradictions and clouded by Western stereotypes that alternately romanticize and demonize indigenous cultures and their interactions with local ecologies (Colchester, 1994; Neumann, 1997; Hodgson, 2002a). What is clear, though, is that repressed and marginalized ethnic groups around the world are embracing the indigenous label as a means to defend and regain autonomous control of land and resources. Even in Sub-Saharan Africa, where the 'indigenous' label was only recently seen to be irrelevant, there is a growing movement among ethnic minorities to self-identify as indigenous (e.g., Watts, 2000b; Hodgson, 2002b; Sylvain, 2002).

As hinted at above, political ecologists consider questions of representation and discourse as key to understanding the relationship between indigenous land rights and biodiversity conservation. Within the discourse of biodiversity conservation one can identify a tendency to essentialize indigenous peoples as having a unique relationship to nature that qualifies them as stewards or guardians of the land (see Chapter 4). Marginalized ethnic groups have embraced this image of indigenous peoples as a way to reinforce and gain outside support for their proprietary claims on land and resources. These efforts to gain political agency have been labelled 'strategic essentialism' (Sylvain, 2002: 1081) or 'representational strategies' (Tsing, 1999: 160) in recognition of the way that indigenous peoples pick up on prevailing imageries and stereotypes and reflect them back to outside audiences. In this way, indigenous peoples' identity politics help position them as 'icons of resistance for environmentalists worldwide' (Brosius, 1997: 48; see also Chapter 4). While indigenous peoples may gain critical outside political support through such representational strategies, the internal conflicts, complexity, dynamism and heterogeneity of their society are often submerged. In the sections that follow, we will revisit some of these issues as indigenous peoples play key roles in both traditional models of fortress conservation and in the creation of new kinds of nature–society hybrids for biodiversity conservation.

Islands of nature?

The fortress model is based on the idea that biodiversity conservation can best be achieved by creating protected areas where ecosystems are allowed to function undisturbed by human activities. This is the 'nature island' concept that has dominated global protected area design and planning throughout the twentieth century and beyond. The implementation of this model in nearly all cases required the curtailment of local resource use and access and in many cases the eviction of entire communities. Political ecology studies have thus demonstrated that the establishment of protected areas often functions as a form of enclosure. Forests, bush and pastures that were held as communal property for community members to hunt, gather and graze have been enclosed and converted to state ownership for the conservation of wild flora and fauna and their touristic potential. Historically, this has been conducted with minimum involvement of the people most affected by enclosure. State agents have often resorted to force in order to curtail community access to the commons and to evacuate residents reluctant to relocate (e.g., Peluso, 1993; Hitchcock, 1995; Brockington, 2002). As a consequence, those communities located on the boundaries – more often than not having been displaced in the process of park establishment – are commonly antagonistic towards state-directed conservation policies. Political ecology is concerned with the issues of political conflict, social justice and ecological efficacy that surround state-directed biodiversity conservation.

A political ecology perspective stresses that the relative success of biodiversity protection strategies can only be fully explained through an analysis of the specific historical, cultural and political-economic contexts within which protected areas are embedded. Of particular interest in political ecology are the competing demands for material access to biodiversity (in all its forms) and the various symbolic meanings that the state, international conservationists and segments of civil society attach to parks and protected areas. In order to systematically survey some of this research, I have identified six areas of inquiry related to fortress-style biodiversity conservation. First, what has been the history of human use and occupation of protected areas and how has it influenced biodiversity? Second, how strong is the ecological evidence for prohibiting access and evicting resident communities? Third, what effect have protected areas had on the control of access to local commons and common property resources? Fourth, what is the relationship of mandatory evacuations of protected areas to state-directed schemes of segregations, resettlement and reservation? Fifth, how well does the fortress model of biodiversity conservation fit the reality of ecological change? Sixth, how do ideas of national parks and equivalent reserves relate to the social construction of collective identities? I will examine each of these questions in order in the following pages.

First, what has been the history of human use and occupation of protected areas and how has it influenced biodiversity? The human histories of national park landscapes have become increasingly contested and politicized. Advocates of fortress-style parks have tended to disregard or downplay historic human occupation and the role of human use and management on the ecology and landscape targeted for preservation (Hecht and Cockburn, 1990). Consequently, there is an explicit, almost ideological declaration that what is to be bounded and preserved is primaeval wilderness, and thus a product of nature and devoid of human agency. We see this pattern emerge with the world's first national park, Yellowstone, where early accounts by white explorers and naturalists denied any historic occupation by Native Americans (e.g., Chittenden, 1903), a position maintained decades later in official government histories of the park (Chase, 1987). Recent scholarship, however, details how various tribes had occupied, used and significantly shaped the ecology of the Yellowstone area (e.g., Spence, 1999). New environmental histories challenge the notion that other iconic North American landscapes, such as Glacier National Park were 'virgin wilderness', and instead emphasize a record of centuries of occupation by Native Americans (Warren, 1997: 134; Keller and Turek, 1997). These narratives suggest 'uninhabited wilderness had to be created before it could be preserved' (Spence, 1999: 4; see also Cronon, 1995). In Yosemite National Park, because authorities refused 'to recognize the importance of the Native Americans' use of fire in creating the open, park-like landscape scenery of Yosemite, the landscape became more and more overgrown … and the park became a fire hazard' (Olwig, 2002: 208). In none of these cases, it should be noted, have Native Americans abandoned their claims on lands and resources lost to the parks.

The debate over the presence and agency of human populations is also evident in other regions of the world. In East Africa, for instance, despite ample evidence of occupation and management by humans for centuries, areas targeted for protection are purported to be unspoiled wilderness that has retained its primaeval character (e.g., Turton, 1987; Neumann, 2001b). In the case of Omo National Park in Ethiopia (see Figure 5.1), for example, the main report advocating its establishment greatly under-estimated the existing population of Mursi agro-pastoralists and characterized it as 'Ethiopia's "most unspoiled" wilderness' (quoted in Turton, 1987: 179). Ecological research would reveal, however, that 'virtually every square inch of this country bears the imprint of human activity' (ibid.: 180). Indeed, eco-logical studies have determined that much of Africa's savanna grasslands, the pre-dominant ecological community of the most renowned wildlife parks in the region, are not wild landscapes, but rather have been shaped by centuries of pastoralists' herding and burning activities (Homewood and Rodgers, 1984; 1991; Moe et al., 1990). In West and Southern African landscapes as well, governments evacuated lands that had long been under the husbanding hand of herders and farmers in order to create national parks in the name of wilderness preservation (Ranger, 1999; Zuppan, 2000). In Nepal's Royal Bardia National Park a variety of ethnic groups historically relied on the park's land and resources, notably for cultivation of the *phantas* (open grasslands). Thus, the open grasslands, a significant habitat for some of the park's endangered species, 'are essentially abandoned agricultural landscapes' (Brown, 1998: 79).

Second, how strong is the ecological evidence for prohibiting access and evicting resident communities? This theme relates closely to the first. Recent studies have demonstrated that there is often a lack of empirical study and sound ecological jus-tification for government evictions of resident populations. In the case of Glacier National Park, for example, administrators complained that big game were 'being exterminated' by Blackfeet Indian hunters and argued for the expansion of the park into the Blackfeet reservation and the termination of hunting rights. The accusa-tions were proved groundless when, after opposing Native American hunting rights for years, park authorities were faced with exploding populations of elk and deer (Warren, 1997; Spence, 1999). In African studies there is increasing scrutiny of 'consensus views' and 'received wisdom' of environmental degradation narratives that have justified past evictions from protected areas (Beinart, 2000; Stott and Sullivan, 2000). In Matopos National Park in Zimbabwe, for example, government authorities claimed that residents were destroying the environment and pushed for their eviction. Ranger's study revealed that the government evicted residents 'despite the fact that successive investigations found that the Matopo Reserve was not, after all, in a state of [ecological] crisis' (1999: 80). In an investigation of one of the more recent mass evictions from a protected area, Mkomazi Game Reserve in Tanzania in 1988–89, researchers examined the empirical basis for eviction advocates' claims that the area was of exceptional ecological importance and was threatened by human use (Homewood and Brockington, 1999; Brockington and Homewood, 2001). They found a general lack of ecological data and an absence of studies on human–environment interactions that could substantiate the claims of environmentally destructive land use practices (see Extract 13).

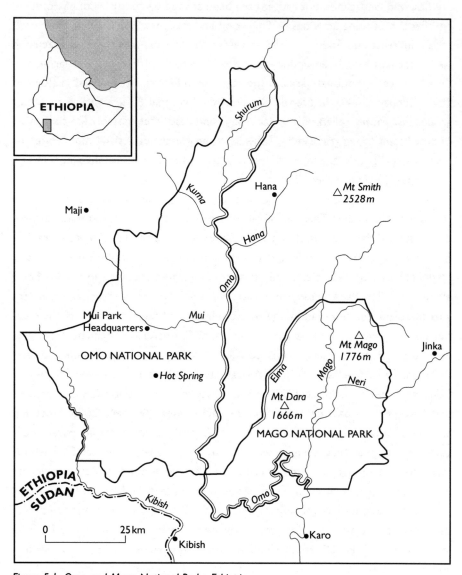

Figure 5.1 Omo and Mago National Parks, Ethiopia.

extract 13

Baselines for ecological change

Mkomazi [Game Reserve, Tanzania] manifests high levels of insect, bird and plant diversity that reflects its high habitat diversity, and its position on an eco-tone. It has been suggested that Mkomazi could be 'one of the richest savannas in Africa, and possibly the world' for birds, plants and insects. This is not sup-ported by the data ... More importantly, it is impossible to say that there has been any decline or improvement in these levels of biodiversity since eviction because there is no baseline against which to make comparisons ... The impli-cations are numerous. The high levels of diversity were monitored soon after the people were excluded. If people did reduce the biodiversity, then levels appear to have recovered sufficiently to be exciting to scientists within a relatively short time; the degradation people caused may have been short-lived. On the other hand, the current high levels may be but a remnant of much higher numbers of species that existed within the reserve before people lived there in large num-bers. It is also possible that some forms of human disturbance may foster biodi-versity, and human exclusion would be deleterious to that. However, current research simply does not allow us to offer an informed account of how human residence of Mkomazi may have affected its insect, bird and plant life.
Source: Brockington and Homewood (2001: 472)

Third, what effect have protected areas had on the control of access to local commons and common property resources? As noted previously, parks and pro-tected areas have functioned as a form of enclosure (see *The Ecologist*, 1993), often curtailing access to local commons and a variety of communal resources such as wildlife, pasture, water and fuelwood. Warren (1997) characterizes the historic change in human–environment relations in the American West as the (occasion-ally violent) transition from numerous local commons to a few centralized com-mons in the form of national parks and reserves. Similar historical shifts are observable elsewhere. In East Africa, for example, pastoralists have lost over 20,000 square kilometres of grazing commons to national parks and game reserves in Kenya and 3,234 square kilometres in Tanzania's Mkomazi Game Reserve alone (Igoe and Brockington, 1999). These conservation enclosures alter pastoralists' livelihood strategies in numerous ways, including greater reliance on subsistence agriculture, petty trade and ultimately migration to urban areas for low wage employment (e.g., Brockington, 2002). Conservation enclosures in Africa may function in political-economic terms in much the same way as the historic enclosures in Great Britain, helping to 'free' labour in countries where labour for capitalist enterprises historically has been in short supply (Neumann, 1998; 2001b).

The creation of parks and equivalent reserves has produced conflicts over access to a range of common property resources such as fuelwood, building materials, medicines and wild animals, as well as important cultural sites (see Figure 5.2). In Third World agrarian communities, access to these resources is key to maintaining and reproducing rural communities and households. Particularly contentious are restrictions on hunting and trapping. Access to wild meat protein is a critical element in many African agrarian economies across the continent, especially in times of dearth (for a review, see Neumann, 2002). Hunting on forest and bush commons, however, is usually the first activity to be outlawed upon the declaration of new conservation enclosures. In various regions around the world, wildlife immediately adjacent to protected areas are often considered 'park animals' or 'park property', which raises conflicts and debates over communal property rights in wildlife conservation (Naughton-Treves and Sanderson, 1995). At Glacier National Park, for example, 'the National Park Service and the Blackfeet contested communal ownership of the animals regardless of their location' for most of the twentieth century (Warren, 1997: 126).

Fourth, what is the relationship of mandatory evacuations of protected areas to state-directed segregations, resettlement and reservation schemes? Governments have often combined conservation enclosures with other state policies of social control and segregation including various state schemes of relocation, 'native' reservation and settlement concentration. Historians recently have linked the establishment of US national parks to the concept of 'manifest destiny' and the dispossession and near genocide of hundreds of thousands of Native American peoples (Spence, 1999; Burnham, 2000; Germic, 2001). Through a careful study of the 'crown jewels' of the national park system, Yosemite, Yellowstone and Glacier, Spence (1999) details how the removal of resident Native Americans from parks and the establishment of a system of Indian reservations were complementary policies in the post-bellum West. Similar policies can be observed elsewhere. In contemporary Malaysia, the establishment of national parks is linked to the government's efforts to assert political and economic control over far-flung rural populations through resettlement schemes (Colchester, 1993). In colonial Central African Republic, French administrators employed the technique of *regroupment* in

Figure 5.2 An elder from a Meru community displaced from Arusha National Park, Tanzania, stands at a ceremonial site, now 'off limits' inside the park.

an effort to corral Africans into 'civilized' settlements in strict distinction from 'wild' forest areas and thereby reorder the landscape. More recently, the post-colonial state, in cooperation with WWF, implemented similar settlement policies as part of their programme to manage the Dzanga-Sangha National Park (Giles-Vernick, 2002). In South Africa, the evacuation of part of Kruger National Park was associated with the racial segregation policies of the former Apartheid regime (Carruthers, 1994). In a 1998 programme that tragically echoes the colonial reset-tlement schemes for 'Bushmen' in Namibia (Gordon, 1992), the Botswana government began a three-year campaign to forcibly remove nearly 3,000 resident Basarwa San from the Central Kalahari Game Reserve and relocate them in reset-tlement villages to facilitate their assimilation as Botswana citizens (Survival International, 2001). In general, governments in Africa have viewed the establish-ment of protected areas and the concentration of settlement as complementary policies to centralize political and economic control of its citizenry (e.g., Neumann, 2001b).

Fifth, how well does the fortress model of biodiversity conservation fit the reality of ecological change? As detailed previously, political ecologists have demonstrated that conservationists' over-riding preoccupation with protecting 'virgin wilderness' has meant that the histories of human use and occupation are forgotten and ignored. The eviction of populations resident for centuries, however, often sets in motion unanticipated ecological change in landscapes presumed to be products of nature. In East Africa, for example, where pastoralist land use practices have helped to create habitat conditions favourable for wildlife populations, their exclusion could actually be detrimental to biodiversity (see Little, 1996). Since the eviction of Native American populations from Yosemite and Yellowstone, these parks have experienced significant, complex and undesirable changes in vegetation and wildlife populations (Chase, 1987; Spence, 1999; Warren, 1997). Often park managers must implement practices such as controlled burning, wildlife culling and brush clearance in an attempt to slow undesirable ecological change, in effect, mimicking the influence of evicted populations (Neumann, 1998; Spence, 1999).

Political ecologists have also argued that the fortress conservation model is based on the presumption of steady state or stable equilibrium ecology that is challenged by new ideas of non-equililbrium ecology (Zimmerer, 2000; Adams, 2003b). As Adams explains, attempts to bound and 'preserve' nature through management interventions to halt ecological change are ineffective where 'biodiversity depends directly upon natural patterns of disturbance' (2003b: 227). In environments characterized by sudden and extreme shifts in abiotic parameters, resident populations can be blamed for ecological change that may have more to do with abiotic sources of flux (Homewood and Brockington, 1999). Zimmerer argues that the fixed bounding and static scaling characteristic of fortress conservation are at odds with 'the rescaling of fluxes that is identified as a key feature of landscapes' (2000: 361).

Finally, how do ideas of national parks and equivalent reserves relate to the social construction of collective identities? The national park concept has played a particularly important role in the construction of national identities. Building the 'nation' side of the nation–state requires that the state elite create an idea of national culture, a sense of individual and collective identification with the territorial state, and a standard set of national characteristics. Beginning with the establishment of the world's first national parks in the western United States at Yosemite and Yellowstone, national parks have played a critical role in helping to define a national identity rooted in the landscapes of nature (Runte, 1979; Olwig, 2002). The enclosure of Yosemite as a state park (1864) and Yellowstone as a national park (1872) occurred at a critical historical juncture in the evolution of the USA as a nation–state. The territorial unity of the country had been threatened by a civil war over the secession of the southern states and new waves of impoverished immigrants from the non-Anglo-Saxon regions of Europe were filling the eastern cities. The invention of national parks helped answer the questions, what was 'America' and who was 'American' (Runte, 1979; Cronon, 1995; Olwig, 2002)?

The geographer Kenneth Olwig explained how the establishment of the world's first national parks at Yellowstone and Yosemite linked ideas of landscape, nature and national identity in a way that has been emulated in nearly every country of the globe:

> A consequence of the burgeoning American interest in landscape scenery was that when explorers discovered vast areas in the west that resembled grand landscape parks, these areas became symbols of American national identity. Their enclosure as the world's first natural parks set a pattern that has since become paradigmatic for the national parks of the world.
>
> (2002: 182)

We can clearly recognize circumstances in colonial and post-colonial tropical countries that parallel that of the United States. Indeed, Adams suggests that many of today's Third World national parks 'exist because they served a political purpose' during the colonial era (2003a: 41). National parks were particularly important, for example, to the formation of national identity grounded in nature and natural landscapes in the European settler colonies of Africa. For instance, Kruger, established in 1926 as the continent's second national park, played an important role in the formation of a collective (white) national identity in the early years of the South African Republic (Carruthers, 1989; 1995). In Zimbabwe (formerly Southern Rhodesia), the location of Cecil Rhodes' grave in Matopos National Park helped mark the rugged landscape as a symbol of (white) nationhood and 'the ceremonial heart of the Rhodesian nation' (Ranger, 1999: 158). During Zimbabwe's civil war for majority rule in the 1970s, the meaning of the Matopos landscape was contested and it came to symbolize both white nationhood and the black nationalism of the resistance movement.

Political ecologists have also investigated the ways in which protected area policies and practices intersect with social constructions of class, ethnicity, and race. As noted above, the global conservation movement originated with a group of wealthy and politically powerful European and American hunter–naturalists. An important aspect of their class identity was their romantic treatment of wild nature and sporting approach to hunting, which differentiated them from the 'lower' classes (Neumann, 1996; 1998). Early ideas regarding US national parks were meant to appeal to bourgeoisie identity, suggesting that only the cultivated classes could fully appreciate the wild grandeur of nature (Germic, 2001). In colonial Africa, class superiority was transformed into racial and cultural superiority. Many of the parks and reserves in Africa, for example, allowed certain peoples – hunter–gatherers and nomadic pastoralists, primarily – to remain in residence as long as they maintained their 'primitive' lifestyles, as defined by racist colonial social categories. In the case of Tanzania's Serengeti National Park, colonial park authorities stipulated what resident Maasai pastoralists could and could not do based on a European stereotype of static Maasai culture (Neumann, 1995).

Peluso and Vandergeest (2001) found in their study of Southeast Asia that state policies for protected forests helped to construct ethnic and racial identities. They explain that

[the] ways colonial governments resolved the question of native or 'minority' rights to land and forest resources contributed to the creation of racialized colonial categories for people (as 'natives,' 'Foreign Orientals,' 'primitives,' or 'minorities') and frequently territorialized these identities as well as patterns of resource access.

(2001: 800)

In a similar, contemporary example from the Central African Republic, WWF officials in the Dzanga-Sangha Special Reserve determined – with little historical or ethnographic understanding – which ethnic groups were 'migrant' and which were 'indigenous', characterizing the former as destroyers and the latter as stewards of the forest (Giles-Vernick, 2002).

The above political ecology studies may appear overly critical of the global biodiversity conservation movement and unsympathetic to the severe political and ecological threats facing protected areas around the world. None of the authors, I think it is safe to say, would consider themselves 'anti-conservation', however. Some in fact have made clear that their critiques originate from a position of sympathy and support for the general goals of the conservation movement (e.g., Cronon, 1995; Adams and Mulligan, 2003). The primary concern with the fortress approach is that it is deeply flawed for both ecological and political reasons. In ecological terms, global biodiversity losses have accelerated during the same period in which the number of parks and equivalent reserves has increased exponentially.

The global conservation community now acknowledges that 'activities centered on a protected area and sustainable-use approach failed to conserve biodiversity in a meaningful and long-term way' (Wood, 2000: 8). In political terms, the obsession with the wilderness ideal has meant that communities are displaced and local commons are enclosed on principle. In the absence of reliable data on human activities and ecological change, the standard procedure has been to evict first and ask questions later, if ever. The political ramifications of 'coercing conservation' (Peluso, 1993) bode ill both for the long-term security of parks or for social justice (Zerner, 1996; Neumann, 2004). For these reasons, scientists and managers have proposed new approaches to biodiversity conservation. We turn to an analysis of some of these new approaches in the next section.

Nature–society hybrids

In response to the political challenges of the ongoing conflicts with rural and indigenous peoples around the world and to the ecological limitations of the fortress model, protected area planners and scientists have devised a variety of 'nature–society hybrids' (Zimmerer, 2000: 356). Nature–society hybrids are new conservation territories that, in contrast to fortress conservation, integrate human habitation and resource use with biodiversity conservation goals. Nature–society hybrids go by a number of generic labels including buffer zones, indigenous reserves, integrated conservation and development (ICD) and community-based natural resources management (CBNRM). Three ideas predominate across the globe in shaping these projects (Neumann, 1997; Hulme and Murphree, 2001). First, that conservation should directly involve communities in management and benefit sharing rather than being strictly state-driven. Second, that the object of conservation (i.e., biodiversity) can be sustainably managed and exploited to serve both conservation and development goals. Third, that markets and restructured property rights are crucial for shaping incentives for conservation. That is, if people receive direct material benefit from biodiversity, they will be motivated to conserve it. A critical characteristic that nature–society hybrids share with fortress models is that they are geographically bounded and fixed in space through a process of scaling, the principal scale being the 'zone' or 'community' (Zimmerer, 2000). These ideas have been institutionalized around the globe in such state-sanctioned programmes as Joint Forest Management (JFM) in India, extractive reserves in Brazil, and the Communal Areas Management Programme for Indigenous Resources (CAMPFIRE) in Zimbabwe and globally in such multilateral efforts as UNESCO's Man and the Biosphere Programme (MAB).

We will examine some of these from a political ecology perspective in the following pages.

Extractive reserves

The Brazilian government officially defines extractive reserves as 'forest areas inhabited by extractive populations granted long-term usufruct rights to forest resources which they collectively manage' (Schwartzman, 1989: 151). Thus extractive reserves in essence are state-owned land with access and use rights legislatively allocated to local groups or communities, specifically to resident populations of rubber tappers. The basic appeal in terms of forest conservation is that traditional resident populations extract renewable commercial forest products (rubber and Brazil nuts) in an ecologically sustainable manner that leaves the forest intact (Browder, 1992). The extractive reserves in Brazilian Amazonia exist due to an organized social movement that invented them as a strategy to deal with immediate pressing social problems (Schwartzman, 1992). The movement began among rubber tappers in the state of Acre in the mid-1970s. It was the manifestation of organized resistance to growing deforestation and the concentration of land holdings through violence and corrupt land acquisition practices (Hecht and Cockburn, 1990). As Fearnside (1989) stresses, the fact that the extractive reserve idea emerged from a grassroots movement makes it nearly unique among Amazon development projects. The first extractive reserve was established in 1987 and by the early 1990s, seven and a half million acres of extractive reserves had been created in the Brazilian Amazon.

Following the implementation of extractive reserves in Amazonia in the late 1980s, there have been a number of efforts to analyse the socio-economic and conservation implications of this tenure arrangement. Some have argued that the usefulness of extractive reserves for socio-economic improvement and forest conservation was limited because the vast majority of rubber tappers are financially indebted to land-owners and patrons, remain among the poorest of the Amazon's non-indigenous rural population, and are residentially unstable (Browder, 1992; Lescure et al., 1994). Others have noted that extractive economies are notoriously volatile, and therefore reserves cannot guarantee that residents will not destroy the forest to meet short-term needs (Anderson, 1992). Despite these misgivings, one study found that a much larger percentage of the forest (90 per cent) remains intact through extraction than is the case through logging (50 per cent) or ranching (50 per cent), the other predominant land uses in the region (Nepstad et al., 1992). Despite socio-economic limitations, there is evidence that the granting of secure usufruct rights to extractive reserves can transform exploitative social relations towards greater equity and social justice (Schwartzman, 1992).

Joint forest management

The South Asian counterpart of extractive reserves is known as Joint Forest Management (JFM), which the Indian government initiated to promote the participation of communities surrounding state-owned forests beginning in the 1970s after decades of deforestation, biodiversity loss and social conflict. One of the most successful efforts at participatory protected area management has been that of West Bengal, India (Malhotra, 1993; Malhotra et al., 1993; Ghatak, 1995). In 1953, the state enclosed most of the natural sal forests (Ghatak, 1995). Forest communities resisted their loss of access and confrontations and violence became endemic in forest reserves. By the 1960s, the degradation of these forests and the growing conflicts between forest-dependent communities and the forest staff had led to the search for an alternative management strategy.

Similar to the case of Brazilian extractive reserves, political ecologists emphasize that the emergence of JFM 'is grounded historically in tribal and peasant resistance movements' (Poffenberger, 1998: 368), in particular, the Nexalite Movement of 1967–70 that demanded land reform and forest access for the rural poor of West Bengal. Following a Forest Department conference in 1972, participants urged the government to set up local forest protection committees (Malhotra, 1993). As Rangan and Lane (2001) note, however, it was the progressive land reform policies of the Left-Front government that came to power in West Bengal in the 1970s that provided the critical context for JFM. The Left-Front government designed JFM to specifically address questions of equitable resource access for the rural poor, particularly the adivasis, or indigenous peoples, of the region. JFM, in sum, is based on the premise that 'both de facto uses and de jure rights [of local communities] to the forests need to be recognized and incorporated' into the management of state-owned forests (ibid.: 157).

Political ecology studies of JFM have indicated that it has been largely successful, both in improving conditions for biodiversity conservation and in reducing social conflict with surrounding communities. Most studies attribute particular importance to the social and political context of JFM, stressing how a progressive, leftist state government provided the political environment to implement new institutions for community-oriented forest management in the 1980s (Poffenberger, 1998; Rangan and Lane, 2001). The relative success of JFM should be understood

as one aspect of a larger political process that has promoted democratic participation at all levels of society and in all aspects of governance. Linking social justice
and political participation to forest management appears to have had positive outcomes for biodiversity. Studies have found that the implementation of JFM has
coincided with increases in the level of biodiversity, rates of natural regeneration
and the proportion of forest cover in the region (Malhotra, 1993; Poffenberger,
1998) (see Figure 5.3).

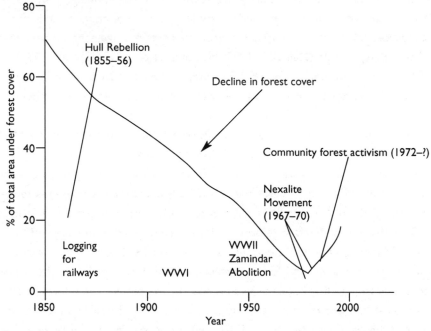

Figure 5.3 Changes in forest cover and community activism in Southwest Bengal, India.

At the same time, these studies show that interests may be fragmented within
local communities and intra-village conflicts can arise along gender, class and ethnic lines. Some of the communities involved are strongly patriarchal, for example.
Though JFM projects targeted women for involvement, the programmes have as
yet failed to truly integrate women's participation, partly because of the strength
of existing gender roles and gendered power relations within the communities
(Ghatak, 1995). In addition, Jewitt and Kumar (2000) observed that forest restrictions in JFM projects often increase women's labour burdens, an impact that is
rarely addressed in programme plans (see also discussion of Schroeder's (1999)
study in Chapter 4). They suggest that, in general, JFM only superficially addresses
gender–environment issues.

Community-based wildlife management

In Africa, one of the most widely discussed and debated of the new nature–society hybrids is Zimbabwe's CAMPFIRE. The origins of CAMPFIRE can be traced to Zimbabwe's 1975 Parks and Wildlife Act, which devolved the ownership of revenues from wildlife to the private landholders on whose land the wildlife occurs. At that time the country was still known as Southern Rhodesia and was ruled by a minority white settler class that was fighting a civil war with black anti-colonial forces. Beyond achieving majority rule for the country, the central issue in the black liberation struggle was the distribution of land, which had been structured unequally along racial lines during the colonial period. White settlers took the most productive agricultural lands, which individuals held under private title, and relegated the displaced black population to 'native reserves' in ecologically marginal areas where people held rights to land under communal tenure (Ranger, 1993). Following the 1980 Lancaster House agreement that brought Zimbabwe majority rule, the native reserves became 'communal areas' whose lands and resources are vested in the state under the 1982 Communal Lands Act. Significant redistribution of land to correct the racial inequities has yet to be realized. The 1982 amendment to the Parks and Wildlife Act extended the policy of devolution originally targeted for white landowners to rural district councils (RDC) which regulate land and resource use in the communal areas (Murombedzi, 2003; Murphree, 2004). In rough outline, then, this is the context for the postcolonial politics of land and resource control and for CAMPFIRE specifically.

CAMPFIRE became operational in 1988 when two districts were granted the right to collect revenues generated through commercial safari hunting of communal area wildlife. By 1995, a total of 25 districts had joined the programme, revenues were rising, and bilateral donor agencies such as USAID had begun to funnel funds into the programme (Jones and Murphree, 2001). The conceptual key to the programme was the devolution of property rights to wildlife revenues from the state level to the level of the RDC. In essence, the state granted the RDCs limited authority over a communally managed common pool resource. Funds generated from hunting and safari went directly to the RDCs, which were required to distribute at least 50 per cent to the wards where the revenue was produced and were allowed to retain the rest as a form of tax and to cover its costs for wildlife management. CAMPFIRE thus provided an economic incentive for wards to manage their lands for wildlife habitat and wildlife production. From the state's and the RDC's perspective, it was a lucrative tax programme that provided direct revenue, while simultaneously reducing expenditures on social welfare infrastructure when wards began to use CAMPFIRE money for local rural health clinics and the like.

While the programme has expanded geographically, success in terms of revenue generation and devolution of control has been uneven among and within the districts involved, while the overall contribution of CAMPFIRE to biodiversity conservation is unknown, but certainly limited. In a sharp but cogent critique of CAMPFIRE, Murombedzi (2003) proposes, first, that the programme has had the effect of strengthening the state's control over the countryside. The state retains control over communal lands, gains a means to intervene in the control of a profitable resource, and strengthens local state institutions. Second, Murombedzi points out that the programme tends to reinforce and strengthen the racial and class inequalities produced by colonialism over issues of resource access and control. The scheme does not question the existing colonial pattern of land distribution along race and class lines and the big money (profits from the safari hunting and tourism industries) is captured by a small, mostly white entrepreneurial class. CAMPFIRE has in essence made a formerly off-limits common pool resource (of the black communal lands) available to the (mostly white) private sector safari companies. Third, rather than promoting significant accumulation among individuals, the programme has the effect of blocking accumulation by individuals in participating wards. This is because the amount of revenue per individual household is too small to spark accumulation and because wildlife revenues serve mostly to subsidize local governments.

Indigenous reserves

One final, generic example of nature–society hybrids is the 'indigenous reserve' or 'indigenous protected area' (IPA). Not to be confused with Indian reservations in North America or native reserves of the European colonial empire, IPAs are based on the idea that the goals of biodiversity conservation and cultural survival can be mutually reinforcing. The evidence for this idea is substantially geographical. Lands with the highest biodiversity and most complete forest cover often overlap with territories claimed and inhabited by indigenous peoples who have managed and conserved the local ecology for generations (Nietschmann, 1992; Alcorn, 1994; Langton, 2003). Therefore, it is reasoned, one way to assure that biodiversity is maintained is to legally recognize the territorial claims of indigenous peoples within a circumscribed zone and to allow existing local land uses and management practices to continue, perhaps in consultation with outside scientists and conservationists.

Conservationists and indigenous rights advocates widely cite the case of the San Blas Kuna protected area on Panama's Caribbean coast as an example of a successful indigenous protected area, yet the specific local context within which it was established is not typical in the postcolonial world order. The San Blas Kuna had successfully resisted displacement and assimilation by the Panamanian state for decades and in 1945 the government officially recognized Kuna jurisdiction over their territory (*comarca*) (Nietschmann, 1985). They have enjoyed autonomy over their land and resources since that time. The idea to establish an IPA arose in the 1980s when Kuna leaders grew concerned that their forests might be cut down and overrun by non-indigenous squatters. Their response was to enlist the help of WWF and USAID in establishing an indigenous protected area on their lands as a way to demarcate and secure their territorial claims against outsiders. Though this has been relatively successful as an indigenous conservation and development project, the fact that the Kuna already had autonomous control over their territory and have unusually strong and active political structures means that this is not a readily transferable model (Davis and Wali, 1994).

In Australia, two initiatives have strengthened Aboriginal land claims and increased the involvement of indigenous peoples in conservation. First, the government in 1985 officially recognized Aboriginal ownership of four national parks that had been under state ownership and control. Political ecologists note, however, that a major stipulation of the agreement required that the Aboriginal owners lease back the land to the state to be managed as typical fortress-style parks (Colchester, 1994). Second, the government created the Indigenous Protected Area Programme, which was based on the voluntary inclusion of Aboriginal-owned lands in Australia's conservation estate. These areas are then managed through 'stewardship agreements' whereby the Aboriginal owners commit to manage the lands as protected areas for cultural and natural features and to support biodiversity conservation (Figgis, 2003: 208). By 2001, the programme included 13 designated areas, most of which were heavily dependent on continued funding and support from the state and private conservation community.

While indigenous peoples around the world have achieved significant advances towards regaining lost resources and rights, political ecologists and others have noted that their progress has been limited in the new models for biodiversity conservation. In the majority of cases, the state retains ownership and indigenous residents therefore do not possess secure permanent rights to their lands and natural resources (Davis and Wali, 1994). In such circumstances, indigenous peoples are commonly granted minimal say in protected area design or management decisions. In the rare case where land ownership is transferred to indigenous peoples, such as Australia, the state retains control over management decisions through lease agreements. Some have argued that the involvement of Aboriginals in the management of their reacquired territory is limited, and merely lends a flavour of cultural authenticity to the national parks for tourists' consumption (Colchester, 1994). Others have argued that indigenous peoples have a great burden of responsibilitmy to live up to the ideal of the 'noble savage' living in harmony with nature's rhythms. If they fail to demonstrate sufficient environmental sensitivity, as determined by a non-local authority, displacement looms. The state, in concert with outside conservationists, by and large retains the power to evict indigenous peoples whose land-use practices are deemed 'unsustainable' or incompatible with conservation goals (Stearman, 1994; Neumann, 1997).

Rethinking community-based conservation initiatives

The rise of interest in nature–society hybrids in conservation policy circles was evident by the time of the third World Parks conference in 1982. One of the steering committee members for that conference wrote that it was time for conservation planning to 'go beyond national parks to contribute to modern social, ecological and economic demands' (McNeely, 1984: 4). It appears, however, that the typical CBNRM project of today has not moved global biodiversity conservation very far beyond the fortress park model. Some of the most politically contentious and ecologically questionable characteristics of fortress conservation re-emerge in many of these nature–society hybrids. Some add new layers of bureaucratic control between residents and livelihood resources, more often than not the project design is predetermined for 'participating' communities, and most involve zoning and bounding that can result in contentious forced evictions (Colchester, 1994; Derman and Ferguson, 1995; Hitchcock, 1995; Neumann, 1996; Hill, 1996; Zimmerer, 2000). In a word, much of the community conservation planning functions as another form of enclosure.

What seems missing in conservation planners' conceptualization of nature–society hybrids is the recognition that the most socially and ecologically effective of the new experiments originate from the livelihood and justice struggles of displaced and impoverished rural groups. Global conservation planners widely view the cases cited previously as examples of new models of biodiversity conservation to be emulated in other geographic settings, yet each has its own unique political-economic and historical context. In the case of JFM, the support of a progressive state government focused on redressing historic inequities was key, in Brazilian extractive reserves, a vital social movement resisting the concentration of land ownership provided the initiative, and in the Kuna reserve, the indigenous residents made their land-use decisions under pre-existing conditions of autonomy and security of tenure. In the most thorough political ecology analysis of the transferability of the Brazilian model of extractive reserves, Peluso (1992a) argues that the political context and tenure arrangements in East Kalimantan's tropical forests provide a poor fit for the Brazilian model. To highlight just one important difference, independent unions, the organizing foundation of Brazilian extractive reserves, were banned in Indonesia. Although in several of these cases outsiders – particularly large international conservation organizations and bi-lateral aid agencies – provided technical support and funding, the projects did not originate with outsiders but were in fact grounded in local social movements. This is a key point in assessing the political and ecological consequences of the current growth in nature–society hybrids. In sum, the motivations, designs and effectiveness of these widely touted models are contingent and situational and therefore not easily transferable to other locations through the actions of states and global conservation organizations.

Despite the limited transferability of these would-be models, political ecologists do not dismiss the potential of nature–society hybrids to both raise the level of social justice and promote biodiversity conservation in specific locales. According to Zimmerer, the realization of this potential requires conservation planners to rethink, if not abandon, the ecological model of 'a balance or equilibrium-tending stability of nature' and the tendency towards rigid, fixed spatial boundaries that function as enclosures (2000: 357). His suggestion is to incorporate both the environmental politics of progressive social movements and the theoretical advances of non-equililbrium ecological science into new kinds of conservation planning. He calls for a perspective that is characterized by flux and fluidity. This would take the form of conservation boundaries that are flexible, multi-scalar and overlapping so as to accommodate the spatial and temporal heterogeneity of ecological processes as well as the extra-local geography of social and political movements (see Extract 14). This is no small order and would require something of a conceptual leap or even paradigm shift for conservation planners. To begin, it would require that the process of locating new conservation projects would start with identifying the environmental politics and development aspirations of social movements rather than merely identifying the geographic distribution of targeted species and habitats.

extract 14

Nature–society hybrids

Perspectives on cross-over hybrids and nonequilibrium landscapes can support a scope for conservation analysis that extends beyond the proclivity toward parks and other protected areas, and toward the fuller understanding of utilized or 'second nature'. For the field of geography, the importance of this conservation analysis may help renew interest in selective integrations or synthesis of human and physical geographies. Fullness is crucial to the framing of the millennial conservation boom offered by this essay. Fullness refers to an awareness of nature–society hybrids that characterizes the conservation boom and that is crucial to its geographical production. Fullness plays a sort of checking function on whether the policies and practices of conservation are amply informed by the close knit analysis of the many cross-overs of nature–society hybrids. This checking function cautions against the narrow type of conservation analysis that pries apart environmental and social attributes or that only rejoins them in block-like fashion (as in countless multidisciplinary technical reports). Central themes of conservation, such as territory, scale, boundaries, and environmental linkages, suggest that a fullness of multiple nature–society cross-overs is common. Similarly, the signs of fullness are demonstrated by the consideration of these conservation themes through the evolving ideas of nonequilibrium ecological science.

The fullness of conservation, particularly the emphasis on flux (rather than fixity) and crossing-over (rather than cordoning off), can contribute toward an enlarged and enhanced engagement with the politics of the environment. I would hope that, in the future, purely scientific or simply preset prerogatives will be thought of as unhelpful in guiding resource management, nature, protection, and environmental restoration.

Source: Zimmerer (2000: 364)

Living in a 'world of wounds'?

Political ecology studies suggest four conceptual or philosophical challenges for global biodiversity conservation. First, the 'nature islands' metaphor continues to haunt the design of both traditional-style protected areas and the new nature–society hybrids. The fact that the metaphor has a tenacious hold on conservation thought is not surprising for it reflects the Cartesian distinction of 'humans' and 'nature' as discrete, observable objects that is deeply embedded in the Western philosophy of science. In this worldview, nature can be cordoned off and contained. The primary effect is the spatial segregation of nature from human society that reflects and reinforces the modernist understanding of nature as 'non-present otherness' (Pred, 1998: 162). The island metaphor also reflects an adherence to equilibrium models in biological ecology, as in the case of MacArthur and Wilson's (1967) theory of island biogeography (discussed in Chapter 2). Numerous conservation biologists in the 1970s and 1980s attempted to derive the most effective protected area design strategy to assure species survival using island biogeography theory (e.g., Diamond, 1975; Abele and Connor, 1976; Miller, 1978; Simberloff and Gotelli, 1984).

Although the debate over the use of island biogeography theory in reserve design has gone out of fashion, ideas of equilibrium and 'balance of nature' have been key in the design and planning of biodiversity conservation (Adams, 2003b). If, as non-equililbrium ecology indicates, the geographical expression of biodiversity is the result of complex non-linear change occurring at different rates at multiple temporal and spatial scales, then the island in long-term stable equilibrium is precisely the wrong metaphor to guide biodiversity conservation. Zimmerer (1999; 2000) has suggested an alternative metaphor, 'overlapping patchworks', which reflects both a more dialectical understanding of human–environment relations and an engagement with non-equililbrium ecology. In this metaphor, biodiversity conservation would be driven by an emphasis on the flux, flexibility, heterogeneity and interactivity of nature–society relations.

Second, the discursive construction of biodiversity as a 'global' commons reflects and reinforces unequal North–South power relations and privileges the knowledge, authority and worldviews of First World environmental NGOs and scientists. This is particularly evident in the international agreements that control the realm of biodiversity prospecting (Flitner, 1998). The major international NGOs and multilateral institutions conceive and set conservation agendas long before they are introduced as projects at the national and local levels. These agendas reflect the interests and concerns of First World organizations and are highly selective in locating and prioritizing 'environmental problems' in the Third World (Bryant and Bailey, 1997; Stott and Sullivan, 2000; Adams, 2001). As Guyer and Richards (1996) noted, the vast bulk of knowledge of biodiversity in Africa comes from an expatriate perspective. Conservation programmes originating from First World organizations and institutions can at times, therefore, undermine local communities' cultural values, political interests and livelihoods (Neumann, 1998).

Issues of social and economic justice in North–South environmental relations have of late become more acute with the rise of 'environmental security' thinking in international affairs (Peluso and Watts, 2001a). A prevalent theme – embraced within some biodiversity conservation circles – is an emphasis on the militarization of environmental concerns accompanied by increased possibilities for authoritarian controls. Local communities tend to get caught in the crossfire in the 'war for biodiversity' (Neumann, 2004). Adams reminds us that although the First World conservationist's view does not necessarily have to work against the interests of the poorer and less powerful, it is 'simply that it often has done so, and sometimes still does' (Adams, 2001: 277).

Third, as currently conceptualized, most of the new community-oriented schemes do not adequately address the issues of land rights and resource access that have been the fundamental source of conflict between biodiversity conservation and local communities. Most projects are chiefly designed to redistribute benefits from conservation to local entities, more often than not through some form of market incentive. The conservation planners' assumption that this approach will lead to greater economic and social justice is hardly supported by the historical record of natural resource commodification (Hvalkof, 2000; Zerner, 2000). Schroeder argues that the conceptualization of buffer zones, extractive reserves and the like suffers from a weak theory of justice. He suggests that conservation must move 'beyond distributive justice' and address compensation for the forfeitures of rights, loss of land, intellectual property rights and provision of labour services (Schroeder, 2000: 52–3). Another way to think about reconceptualizing CBNRM projects is to recognize the difference between reformist and radical approaches. Reformist programmes and policies attempt to redistribute benefits from traditional state-directed conservation more directly to geographically proximate groups. This is the common distributive justice approach that Schroeder critiqued. Radical policies would actually reassign ownership of the national and global commons either jointly with the state or in total to the communities from which they were originally taken. The cases cited above in which park lands were transferred back to Aboriginals in Australia is one very rare example of a radical approach to justice. Radical and rare though the transfer of ownership and control may be, it is in the end at the core of the demands from local communities and indigenous peoples with which conservation planners must come to terms.

The fourth and final challenge for biodiversity conservation is to recognize the social and cultural origins of wilderness and understand the limitations of equating 'nature' with a wilderness empty of human history and imprint. Several of the studies cited above emphasized that wilderness was created through evacuations of human populations before it was protected in parks and reserves. Cronon observed that problems arise from the 'specific habits of thinking that flow from this complex cultural construction called wilderness' (1995: 81). The central habit of thought that he critiqued is the idea that a human presence in the landscape represents the denigration or fall of nature. This habit is inherent in conservation biology and is closely linked with neo-Malthusian ideas of human–environment relations (Guyer and Richards, 1996). Aldo Leopold, one of the major philosophical influences on the North American conservation movement suggested that, 'One of the penalties of an ecological education is that one lives in a world of wounds' (Aldo Leopold, quoted in Frankel and Soulé, 1981: 97). In other words, an ecological education predisposes one to see the degradation of nature everywhere, save for preserved wilderness. As Cronon pointed out, rather than being a universal truth, this way of thinking has very specific geographic, cultural and class origins. Where some see degraded nature, others may see a temporary stage in a dynamic nature–society dialectic.

The problems that the wilderness ideal raises for conceptualizing biodiversity conservation can be illustrated by referring to two empirical studies. Peluso and Vandergeest (2001) observed that what Western foresters and explorers took to be natural forests in Southeast Asia were actually the products of human activities of collection, production, protection and cultivation. The forests of the region, which are the fallow stage of the swidden agricultural cycle, can be viewed as a beginning or ending stage:

> If we see [the cycle] as starting with a forest cut, the forest itself gets naturalized. If we see it as the last in a series of stages starting from planting crops, the forest is a product of the process of fallowing after planting.
>
> (ibid.: 767)

The second example comes from Fairhead and Leach's (1996) study of the forest–savanna transition zone in West Africa (discussed in Chapter 3). In this case foresters and scientists have long viewed the islands of forest surrounded by savanna as isolated remnants of a once extensive primaeval forest that was rapidly disappearing as a result of human encroachment. Fairhead and Leach present convincing evidence that the opposite is true, that the forest islands are not natural remnants but the products of human occupation and land use. Forest islands grow, shrink, appear and disappear in the dynamic unfolding of a regional nature–society dialectic, resulting in an overall increase in the proportion of forest cover in the study area. The predisposition of scientists and officials from outside the region to see human settlement as destructive of nature led them to 'misread' the landscape as a degraded primaeval forest, rather than as the human-enhanced ecological mosaic that it is.

Three main lessons can be distilled. First, a focus on pristine nature may inhibit scientists and policy-makers from defining biodiversity and nature–society relations in alternative ways that allow for a more positive role for human populations (Cronon, 1995). Rare species may in fact be dependent on human derived habitats and biodiversity levels for certain taxa may be enhanced by the landscape patchworks and ecotones produced by human use (e.g., Kandeh and Richards, 1996). Second, that biodiversity cannot be conceptualized as something unconnected to human history (Zerner, 1996). The biodiversity that conservation biologists identify and covet in specific locations might very likely be the product of generations of local management and use. Evictions can thus be counter-productive, not only politically and socially, but also ecologically in efforts to keep the biodiversity of bounded conservation territories intact and 'pristine'. In the final analysis, most of the world's biodiversity occurs outside of state-designated protected areas (Nietschmann, 1992; Western, 1994). This fact alone should suggest to us that new models, theories and concepts are demanded. Third, the geography of protected areas reflects not only, or even primarily in many cases, their inherent biodiversity value. Rather, their geography is an expression of a complex set of power relations, operating across time and at scales ranging from the global to the very local. Understanding the social and ecological effects of their creation requires attention to the legacies of European colonialism, the role of institutions of global governance, the environmental politics of local social movements, and discourses of cultural and nature – in short, political-ecological analysis.

FUTURE DIRECTIONS

Predicting the future is a dangerous yet appealing exercise. Dangerous because one can so easily get things wrong and look terribly foolish, yet appealing for the opportunity to play the role of prophet with little fear that anyone will take the time to check up on you later. Thinking about the future directions of political ecology is partly an effort in surveying recent literature and searching for emerging new trends in research. But another, more difficult part, is thinking about what is not being addressed in research and about what sort of ecological, political, economic and cultural changes are underway in the world at large that may alter the direction of the field. Perhaps a productive way to start this exercise is to look for inspirational help from professionals whose stock in trade is predicting the future – science fiction writers. Margaret Atwood's (2003) recent foray into the science fiction genre, *Oryx and Crake*, because it deals explicitly with the future of nature–society relations, is a provocative example. It is a dystopian, but by no means unimaginable, vision. To loosely quote the author's wry description at a public reading in Coral Gables, Florida, it is a rollicking, joke-filled adventure story about the end of the human race.

In Atwood's future, there is a new disequilibrium ecology, where human-induced global warming and new human-engineered 'bioforms' constitute a second nature that is distinctly inhospitable to humans. Feral 'pigoons', genetically engineered as human organ donors and inadvertently programmed with new human-like cleverness, plot against their creators, perhaps driven by the very human need to avenge injustices. Accidentally mutated or purposefully engineered viruses and bacteria produce horrid deaths. Biotechnology firms constitute not only the predominant industry, but also the central institutions governing social relations. Scientific knowledge has been thoroughly privatized. In the place of local police is a global private security firm hired to combat bioterrorism and patent theft and defend the sealed compounds of the multinational corporations and their employees. New forms of socially produced environmental risk and scarcity are kept outside the enclave walls. These developments spawn a shadowy and loosely networked resistance movement that turns the science and technology of genetic engineering against the socio-economic system that created it. She imagines that:

> A new form of the common mouse addicted to the insulation on electric wiring had overrun Cleveland ... coffee bean crops were menaced by a new bean weevil found to be resistant to all known pesticides ... A microbe that ate the tar in asphalt had turned several interstate highways to sand.

> (Atwood, 2003: 216)

In short, she imagines a futuristic Luddite movement bent not on returning society to a romanticized rural past, but on hastening the apocalypse.

At the end of the day what Atwood has done, far more imaginatively than I ever could, was to assess current trends in privatization, socio-economic inequality, corporate influence on public life, climate change and biotechnology and project them into some unspecified future time. As she explained at her reading, she did not invent any bioform that either did not already exist, or could not exist, given today's technology. Her novel suggests some of the emerging concerns of political ecology, including new questions about genetically engineered ecologies, the political and ecological implications of increasing privatization of scientific knowledge, the ethical implications of bioengineering, environmental security, and forms of political resistance and social movements. Some of these will be addressed as we explore six themes in the future directions of political ecology: urban, landscape and meaning, environmental security and violence, ethics, identity and environment, and biotechnology and biodiversity. This list is not exhaustive nor is it meant to challenge or duplicate other efforts that suggest political ecology's future (e.g., Peet and Watts, 1996b; Zimmerer and Bassett, 2003c). It is hoped that it will provoke discussion and perhaps provide inspiration for new studies in political ecology.

Urban

Research in rural settings, particularly among agrarian or herding societies in the Third World, was a defining feature of early political ecology. Research in urban settings was initially rare, although there is nothing conceptually or theoretically inherent in political ecology that predetermines a rural focus. In fact, political ecology's 'chain of explanation' approach, its dialectical treatment of nature–society relations and its attention to theorizing the linkages among local social and environmental change and larger scale political-economic processes are highly conducive to urban research. The predilections and concerns of most early political ecologists, however, dictated that the linkages would be traced outward from rural, Third World locales and not from urban, First World locales. Even now, the vast majority of political ecology studies in Africa are rural, despite the continent's rapid urbanization (Freidberg, 2001). Predilections and concerns have been shifting in recent years and a strong urban political ecology focus has developed as a result (e.g., Pelling, 1999; Swyngedouw, 1999; Freidberg, 2001; Heynen, 2003; Robbins and Sharp, 2003; Swyngedouw and Heynen, 2003). With the rapid urbanization of large regions of the Third World and the accelerating expansion of global trade that is intensifying and multiplying the linkages between far-flung places around the world, urban political ecology is certain to form a major branch of the field. As Harvey maintains, 'the integration of the urbanization question into the environmental-ecological question is a *sine qua non* for the twenty-first century' (1996: 429).

One of the key inspirations for the new urban political ecology has been Marxist urban theory, notably Smith's (1984) elaboration on the concepts of uneven development and second nature (Pelling, 1999; Swyngedouw, 1999). Urban environments are the products of the intermingling of social and ecological forces, resulting in a hybrid form requiring vast inputs of capital and labour, yet still linked to and dependent upon biophysical processes. Urban environments – and the 'socioecological processes' (Swyngedouw and Heynen, 2003: 899) that govern their conditions – represent perhaps the most recognizable manifestation of second nature. Exposures to environmental hazards and access to environmental amenities in urban settings are products of political, economic and ecological processes that produce a geographic pattern of uneven development and a corresponding social pattern of winners and losers. In a recent introductory essay to a special issue on urban political ecology in the journal, *Antipode*, Swyngedouw and Heynen explain this perspective:

> From these perspectives, there is no such thing as an unsustainable city in general. Rather there are a series of urban and environmental processes that negatively affect some social groups while benefiting others. A just urban environmental perspective, therefore, always needs to consider the question of who gains and who pays and to ask serious questions about the multiple power relations – and the

scaler geometry of these relations – through which deeply unjust socioenviron-
mental conditions are produced and maintained.

(2003: 901)

One can readily observe in their perspective that urban political ecology addresses
many of the same concerns and brings to bear the same theoretical and methodological toolkits as 'classic' rural Third World political ecology studies (e.g., Watts,
1983a; Blaikie, 1985).

Indeed, recent studies in urban settings have demonstrated that the 'chain of
explanation' approach can serve just as well as a framework for unravelling the
ultimate causes of urban ecological problems as it has for explaining rural Third
World problems such as soil erosion and land degradation. Robbins and Sharp
(2003), for example, use a nested analysis to link urban ecological problems associated with pesticide use for lawn maintenance to the imperatives of the chemical
industry confronted by a contraction in the worldwide chemical trade. They argue
that:

> the propagation of the high-input lawnscape is structurally enforced by economic
> forces at many scales, with a synergy of production logics that facilitates the expan-
> sion of an expensive, high-maintenance, ecologically unstable environment. As such,
> the lawn is a political ecology not unlike that of other industrial agrarian systems,
> both in the challenges it faces and the opportunities it exploits.
>
> (Robbins and Sharp, 2003: 972)

As is common in many political ecology studies, they begin with the 'land manager'
– in this case the urban and suburban homeowner – and work outward to larger
and larger geographic scales and upward through non-place-based processes to
explain local land-use decisions. Thus, they show how urban household decisions
on land use are influenced by normative aesthetic considerations combined with
local zoning laws, which in turn are influenced by broader pressures on marketing
and production in the global chemical industry.

Since relatively little political ecology research has been conducted in urban settings, there is a wide range of questions to be explored in future research. These
studies will challenge the contradictory stance in ecological science that holds that
'everything in the world relates to everything else' while at the same time maintaining 'that the built environment and the urban structures that go with it are
somehow outside of both theoretical and practical consideration' (Harvey, 1996:

427). One of the key areas of investigation, then, will be exploring the socio-eco-logical interconnections that operate at multiple scales and that link cities to each other and to rural regions. Water, and the discursive, political and economic dimensions of its control, are already an important focus in urban political ecology and are likely increasingly to be so (e.g., Swyngedouw, 1999; Kaika, 2003). How does the production and functioning of socioecological processes reflect relations of power, what is the geographic distribution of amenities and risks that result, and who gains and loses? Research of this sort will bring political ecology in closer dialogue with studies of environmental justice and environmental racism (e.g., Pulido, 1996a; 2000). What sorts of social movements arise from this socio-environmental milieu and what understanding of urban political ecology do they bring to their mobilization efforts? What roles do cities play in the destruction and conservation of biodiversity and in processes of global environmental change? Investigations of the latter question will benefit from an engagement with new ideas of non-equilibrium ecology. There are many other areas of investigation to be considered, ensuring that political ecology will increasingly integrate urban research with its more traditional focus on the rural Third World.

Landscape and meaning

Landscape is a keyword in human geography. In the 1980s scholars – in a field that came to be known as the 'new cultural geography' – re-theorized landscape as constituted not merely by its physical qualities but also by its symbolic meanings (Jackson, 1989; Cosgrove and Daniels, 1988). Their interests lay with investigating landscape both as a material phenomenon and 'as a cultural image, a pictoral way of representing, structuring or symbolizing surroundings' (Daniels and Cosgrove, 1988: 1). The attention in political ecology to the importance of discourse, representation, and imagery in structuring knowledge of the world (Peet and Watts, 1996a; Blaikie, 1996) would appear to have much in common with the approach to landscape in the new cultural geography. Yet political ecology's engagement with the idea of landscape has most frequently focused on the interactions of social practices and the biophysical environment over time and in the context of political and economic forces operating at multiple scales. Where landscapes *are* evaluated in terms of how they are imagined, it has been for the purposes of demonstrating that the neatly bounded 'abstract categories' of natural and social landscapes do not comport with the actual hybridity of material outcomes (Robbins, 2001: 637). The analysis remains focused on the material expression of landscape and how it does or does not support discursive constructions. Even in political ecology studies that approach landscape by invoking the new cultural geography, the analysis remains focused on the use of 'scientific techniques and geomatics' to measure the material 'outcomes of the interplay of forces over time' (Batterbury, 2001: 438, 439).

The manner in which most political ecology studies consider 'landscape' – as fundamentally a scientistic investigation of social and natural processes interacting to produce a particular spatial form – glosses over or neglects a significant aspect of the concept: its symbolic meaning. Landscape in the sense it is treated in most political ecology studies is more properly captured by terms such as land-use type, agro-ecosystems or simply 'the environment'. Landscape, as conceived in cultural geography, 'does not lend itself easily to the strictures of the scientific method' (Cosgrove, 1998: 32). An investigation of landscape meaning, representation and metaphors requires a very different methodology, one that gives attention to the way that aesthetic considerations enter into the politics of land and resource ownership and use. In failing to engage fully with cultural geography's conceptualization of landscape, political ecology analysis risks missing a significant explanatory tool. Two examples of political ecology studies that have attempted to analyse the aesthetic and symbolic importance of landscape will illustrate this point.

Neumann (1998) explored the way in which the lands historically occupied by Meru farmers and livestock keepers in Tanzania were enclosed in a national park by wildlife conservationists who valued their ecological and aesthetic qualities. Building on Raymond Williams' (1973) ideas of landscapes of production and consumption, he sought to demonstrate that the political conflicts between local communities and the national park were simultaneously and inseparably struggles over material access to land and its symbolic meaning. A more recent political ecological study in the Sierra Nevada mountains in California argues that differing landscape aesthetics are integral to the social and political conflicts over land use there (Walker and Fortmann, 2003). The most vociferous (and potentially violent) aspects of the conflict involve not material resources, but aesthetic values. 'These are especially subject to dispute because "ownership" of landscape qualities is often undefined. Deeply political contests emerge over the question of who will "possess" or "control" the landscape' (ibid.: 471). Walker and Fortmann cogently demonstrate that subjective values and aesthetic judgments are key to understanding struggles to gain political control over the future course of land use and development in the region.

There is much to be gained in political ecology from a fuller engagement with the concept of landscape. With the increasing interest in urban and First World settings in political ecology, questions of aesthetics, values and norms will likely prove to have as much or more explanatory value than a singular focus on material access and control and the political-economic structures that regulate them. Furthermore, as second home ownership and enclave communities for affluent consumers are being produced on a global scale, land in the rural Third World will be increasingly coveted for its aesthetic rather than its productive value. There will also be synergies among political ecology studies concerned with the questions of ethics and identity that have been outlined in this chapter, such as the relationship 'between landscape and Romantic nationalism' (Cosgrove, 1998: xxi). There are in fact deep connections between the theoretical roots of political ecology and the new cultural geography, specifically a Marxian approach to the relations of ideology, consciousness, and material life, best captured by Raymond Williams' notion of 'cultural materialism' (Jackson, 1989: 33). Future efforts to incorporate landscape ideas will largely be a question of fulfilling the promise and potential of a dialogue between the new cultural geography and political ecology.

Environmental security and violence

If the global political economy at the end of the twentieth century was shaped by the 'privatization of everything' (Watts, 1994: 371), the beginning of the twenty-first century is being marked by the 'securitization of everything'; everything, that is, that can be placed under the category of 'the environment'. The proposition that the environment should be conceptualized as a national security issue has taken on increasing popularity in national policy circles and in institutions of global governance since the end of the Cold War. It gained considerable momentum with the publication of journalist Robert Kaplan's (1994) article 'The Coming Anarchy' and its subsequent elevation to must-cite status among policy wonks in US President Bill Clinton's administration (Dalby, 1996; Peluso and Watts, 2001a). According to Kaplan, 'surging populations, spreading disease, deforestation, and soil erosion ... will prompt mass migrations and in turn incite group conflicts' (1994: 58). In short, environmental degradation will result in war.

The source for the core of Kaplan's thinking on the relationship of violence and environmental collapse was the writing of political scientist, Thomas Homer-Dixon (1991). Kaplan borrowed from Homer-Dixon the idea that resource scarcity acted as a direct causal mechanism of armed conflict and war, and that resource scarcity in turn was driven primarily by population growth. Homer-Dixon and his colleagues in the 'environmental security school' recently have provided more nuanced and complex models (e.g., Homer-Dixon, 1994; 1999), but resource scarcity and over-population remain critical to their analysis of violence. Environmental security study centres now have been established across North America and Europe, from Toronto to Paris, while Homer-Dixon and like-minded thinkers have become respected policy advisors (Peluso and Watts, 2001a). The story related in this book's introduction of the US Department of Defense's report on the security threats from climate change is just one more sign that environmental security thinking has become firmly rooted in public policy and statecraft. Since 'the environment' is inclusive of climate, air and water quality, forest ecosystems, genetic diversity and all other aspects of the world around us, we are witnessing literally the securitization of everything.

Political ecology has developed one of the most potent critical assessments of environmental security thinking and a cogent argument for an alternative analysis of the relationship between environmental change and war and armed conflict (Warner, 2000; Fairhead, 2001; Hartmann, 2001; Le Billon, 2001; Peluso and Watts, 2001a; Dalby, 2002). The key criticisms of environmental security include, first, that it relies heavily on discredited Malthusian ideas of resource scarcity. Environmental security thinking is 'informed by a deep fear of the poor and their claims on resources' that is grounded in a neo-Malthusian framework of scarcity and conflict (Peluso and Watts, 2001a: 7–8). As was stressed throughout this book, political ecology has rejected neo-Malthusian models that posit a direct causal relationship between population and resource scarcity or degradation as empirically unsubstantiated, simplistic, oblivious of intervening variables, and lacking in explanatory and predictive power. A second criticism is that the key variable in Homer-Dixon's environmental conflict model, 'environmental scarcity', is conceptualized in such a way as to encompass very different social and environmental processes and conditions, including renewable resource scarcity, environmental degradation, population growth and the social distribution of resources. Each one of these components in turn represents the agglomeration of complex social and ecological processes into a single homogeneous object. The result is a 'methodological muddle' (Hartmann, 2001: 44) and the conceptualization of a causal variable that is 'tantamount to analytical obfuscation' (Fairhead, 2001: 217). The third area of criticism is that environmental security thinking treats conflict as a problem internal to 'groups' or 'societies' with little or no analysis of interactions with the international political economy. The role of multinational corporations in resource extraction, the strains of structural adjustment on Third World states and First World industrial demand for Third World resources, to mention a few key externally derived pressures on resources, are largely overlooked (Dalby,

1996; Fairhead, 2001; Hartmann, 2001; Richards, 2001; Watts, 2004). Fourth and finally, the environmental security literature over-stresses the role of poverty and scarcity in their analysis of conflict while all but ignoring the role of wealth accumulation and resource abundance (e.g., Fairhead, 2001; Richards, 2001; Watts, 2001b).

Given our current state of perpetual 'war on terrorism' and because Kaplan, Homer-Dixon and other environmental security school proponents have been so influential in national and international policy circles, an important future role for political ecology will be to provide an alternative analysis of the relationship between war, violence and the environment. Recent political ecology studies – including edited volumes (Zerner, 2000; Peluso and Watts, 2001b) and a special issue on 'resource wars' in *Geopolitics* (Le Billon, 2004) – have begun to explicitly explore the relationships between violence, justice and the environment. The studies in each of these collections, to varying degrees, are concerned with linking non-place-based political and economic conditions to specific social and geographic contexts – how the particular qualities of resources and environments and webs of social relations influence the expression of violence – and with the role of discursive constructions of nature and cultural identity in framing violence and justice. Extract 15 from Dalby's (2002) *Environmental Security*, articulates some of the insights that political ecology can bring to an analysis of the relationship of violent conflict and the environment.

extract 15

Violence, justice and the environment

Specifically the dangers of environmental determinism and neo-Malthusian assumptions about production limits in particular environments need to be countered by a more sophisticated political ecology that understands environmental change as a series of complex social processes in specific geographical contexts. In the process, simplistic assumptions about the efficacy of states, markets, civil society, or projects of ecological modernization to provide solutions to environmental difficulties are put in doubt.

If processes of resource capture are explained in their larger political economic context, within a discourse sensitive to changing resource ownership and control, then understandings of conflict, environmental change, and policy issues are likely to become much more insightful. But they do not fit easily into the frame-work of environmental degradation leading to conflict. The policy implications are also very different, not least because the modern assumption of scarcity as the general ontological condition of humanity is no longer the unquestioned premise for analysis. Scarcity, or notions of environmental stress, are now under-stood as in part political processes, and as such they are amenable to social change in more complex ways than those premised on conventional resource management assumptions.

All this is also coupled to the complex workings of the international financial sys-tem, the frequent encouragement of export agriculture as a development strat-egy, rural distress, elite manipulation of international aid, and structural adjustment fund conditionalities. In sum, this suggests a complex situation of rural dispossession and political violence. The Rwanda genocide of 1994 has complex roots, but understanding that these factors contributed to the violence is important if the simplistic portrayal of these events in Malthusian terms is to be avoided. The crucial point is that the specific factors in one state are related to the larger political economy within which food, land, and violence are enmeshed. To fully criticize the Malthusian assumption of scarcity requires understanding that the political ecology of poverty and violence is about more than an endogenous situation within the bounds of a single autonomous space, however important the specific actions of elites are in particular states.
Source: Dalby (2002: 80, 88–9, 89–90)

It bears emphasizing that one of the principal ways that a political ecology analysis differs from the environmental security school is in its attention to the biophysical qualities and geographical characteristics of specific natural resources and envi-ronments. Resources may be mobile or fixed, finite or renewable, diffuse or con-centrated, or near or distant from centres of power and these qualities influence the social relations of extraction and exploitation, the possibilities for violent con-flict for control, and a resource's 'lootability' by armed rebel forces (Fairhead, 2001; Watts, 2001b; Le Billon, 2004: 8). Take, for example, the case of forests, which represent a diffuse resource, often distant from centres of power, and therefore relatively difficult for states to control. Rebel forces commonly use forests as a refuge from government armies and exploit forest resources to fund their insurgencies. But the particular material qualities of the resource (i.e., large, cumbersome logs) require complex and expensive systems of transport, the cooperation of government authorities (e.g., forest managers), and access to markets. 'The lootability of timber thus often rests on a high degree of collusion between rebels, governments, and businesses' (Le Billon, 2004: 11). Le Billon (2001) has perhaps carried the investigation of geographical characteristics furthest by developing a typology that relates a resource's qualities (proximate or distant, point or diffuse) to types of conflicts (state control, rebellion, secession, and warlordism). Efforts to test the validity of this typology to explain or predict conflicts could provide the basis for many future investigations into the political ecology of 'resource wars'.

Efforts to securitize the environment show no signs of letting up and will most likely expand and intensify in the near term. It is important, given the analytical and explanatory limitations of environmental security thinking, for political ecologists to critique and question the ecological and political consequences of this trend. Political ecology can offer an alternative analysis from the environmental security school that may improve progress towards understanding and resolving violent conflicts that involve the environment or natural resources. It can also help in evaluating the consequences for environmental politics, especially in terms of the participation of civil society. What are the consequences, for example, of reducing the role of government bureaucracies, legislative bodies, and courts in environmental regulation and placing greater control under the purview of the military or government intelligence and security apparatuses? How will democratic governance be affected when land-use maps and environmental management plans are removed from easy public access for 'security reasons' (a process that is already underway on government websites in the US)? What are the effects of securitization of the environment on the politics of environmental social movements? Will states increasingly categorize environmental social movements as 'security threats' and, if so, what will be the effects on the frequency, forms and targets of environmental violence? How does ecological violence – that is the environmental degradation wrought by destructive extraction practices – relate to different forms of violence against people? These are just a sample of the difficult and weighty questions to be explored in the area of environmental security and violence, questions that political ecology is well suited to address.

Ethics

Towards the end of the 1990s, scholars were paying increasing attention to the development of a 'moral turn' in human geography and social sciences more generally (Smith, 1997). The concerns of 'moral geography' include exploring the connection between ethics and geographic distance, the ways in which places are morally coded, and the spatial particularity of the application of moral codes (ibid.: 2001). Within political ecology, interests in the moral economies of subaltern groups and the exploration of who gains and who loses in resource allocation have long been important normative concerns (e.g. Watts, 1983a; Blaikie, 1985). The 'chain of explanation' approach (Blaikie and Brookfield, 1987) that has been central to much political ecology writing carries an intimation of an ethical argument in the sense that it challenges the fixation on proximate causation as a blame-the-victim account of environmental degradation. However, these early explorations of moral economies and social justice were conducted largely through political-economic analysis – typically Marxist or neo-Marxist – rather than through a formal engagement with a philosophy of ethics.

Low and Gleason, in their 1998 book, *Justice, Society and Nature*, provided the first fully-fledged engagement with ethics within political ecology. Their main effort was directed towards theorizing the relationship between the distribution of environmental amenities and risks within human society and human society's interactions with the non-human world, with the practical goal of formulating a 'political ethic of justice' (ibid.: 21).

> The struggle for justice as it is shaped by the politics of the environment, then has two relational aspects: the justice of the distribution of environments among peoples, and the justice of the relationship between humans and the rest of the natural world. We term these aspects of justice: *environmental* justice and *ecological* justice. They are really two aspects of the same relationship.
>
> (ibid.: 2, emphasis in the original)

According to the authors, any attempt to address questions about environmental and ecological justice must necessarily make reference to ethical standards, a task that they painstakingly undertake over the course of the book. Their efforts result in a significant contribution to political ecology. Through their careful articulation of different philosophical positions, their attempts to develop ethical principles for environmental and ecological justice, and their treatment of justice as a dialectical process they have established a point of departure for further explorations within political ecology.

Indeed, recent developments within and outside of the academy suggest that an engagement with formal ethics will provide an important trajectory in the evolution of political ecology. For example, the rise of new social movements for environmental justice in the 1980s and 1990s pushed political ecology towards an exploration of 'the emancipatory potential of environmental ideas' (Peet and Watts, 1996a: 37) and thus closer to an explicit engagement with ethics. Environmental justice movements challenge the notion that 'disinterested, neutral observers are the best environmental experts' (Seager, 1996: 277) by asserting the legitimacy of moral and ethical concerns for determining the outcomes of environmental conflicts. As Low and Gleason (1998) argue, questions concerning the distribution of environmental 'goods' and 'bads' can only be addressed with reference to ethical standards.

Another key development has been the recent 'discovery' of global biodiversity, which has raised new questions about the expansion of our moral community (O'Neil, 1997). What is our moral duty with regard to biodiversity? Under what conditions and in what contexts is species extinction morally acceptable? What ethical standards guide the use of violence against people in efforts to protect biodiversity? The rise of the animal rights movement is another factor raising troubling issues regarding our moral relationships with the non-human world and influencing a deeper engagement with ethics in political ecology. Within the movement there is a new initiative to extend full moral standing to individual members of certain higher primate species. Organizations have taken the Anti-Slavery Society as their political model and seek to include chimpanzees, gorillas and orangutans with human beings in an expanded moral community where all members have equal rights to life and liberty (Neumann, 2004). This would fundamentally remake our moral relationship with non-human species, in essence, shifting the legal standing of individuals of some primate species from that of 'property' to that of 'person'. Finally, the increasing possibilities for mixing human and non-human genes in bio-engineered organisms raises fundamental concerns about the rights and moral standing of such hybrid creatures (Castree, 2003).

These sorts of ethical and moral issues are only just beginning to be explored in political ecology, but clearly are rooted in the field's tradition of a dialectical treatment of human–environment relations, particularly the relationship between marginalized environments and marginalized people. New studies in the field are now probing the ethics of human–environment relations from a variety of philosophical perspectives, exemplified by a recent special issue on ethics and political ecology in the journal *Political Geography* (Bryant and Jarosz, 2004). The topics that contributors to this issue explore include the possibilities for developing ethical relations in consumer behaviour, both with distant others and with distant environments. Another concern addressed is the moral and ethical dimensions of discourses and narratives of environmental degradation and conflict that sustain policies and programmes harmful to the least powerful community members. Finally, the issue raises questions about ethics in the practice of political ecology, both in terms of research strategies and classroom pedagogy. This special issue, though confronting but a fraction of the ethical and moral questions surrounding human–environment relations, signals the emergence of a compelling new branch of political ecology.

Identity and environment

Political ecology, we have observed, has long been concerned with questions of how social identities, particularly gender, race, ethnicity and nationalism, relate to ideas of nature, the perception and causes of environmental degradation, exposure to environmental hazards and risks, and rights claims to the control and ownership of land and resources. Particular strains of political ecology, exemplified by Moore's concern with micropolitics and the mobilization of local cultural idioms in contestations over land and resources (Moore, 1996; 2000), stress the interplay between global and national environmental discourses and local identity. As one manifestation of this interplay, politically and economically marginalized ethnic minorities are increasingly adopting the label of 'indigenous peoples' in defence of their land claims, in no small part because some aspects of environmentalist discourse have portrayed indigenous inhabitants as able land stewards and knowledgeable environmental managers (see Chapter 4). Debates over indigeneity, property rights and stewardship have sparked a range of fascinating new work in political ecology that is beginning to probe more deeply the relationship of identity and environment, raising new questions about the way we theorize culture and nature and about the politics of conservation and resource management.

Conservation scientists, environmental NGOs, academic researchers and state agencies have focused a great deal of attention on a social group's 'ecological legitimacy' (Pulido, 1996b: 37). Ecological legitimacy refers to whether or not a 'culture', indigenous peoples or ethnic group are considered able land stewards and resource managers and therefore are entitled to recognition of tenure and ownership rights (see also Neumann, 1997). Ecological legitimacy is based on the assumption that there is something inherent in a culture's or a group's identity that provides them with the knowledge, skills and values to manage their land sustainably. While such a designation is a form of essentialism, Pulido (1996b) has argued in her study of Hispano grazing in New Mexico that local marginalized groups can appropriate this identity as a form of resistance to threats from powerful outsiders. Sundberg's (2003) study of a similar process of a local group adopting a green identity in the Maya Biosphere Reserve in Guatemala presents a somewhat different analysis and conclusion. For Sundberg, it is not a question of resistance but of the way competing segments of a society position themselves to take advantage of shifting power relations to advance their interests. In this case, when the biosphere reserve was implemented, environmental NGOs became the new arbiters of proper land and resource use. Under the new power structure, certain long-term residents of the area 'seek to establish their legitimacy as caretakers of the Petén's forest through discourses of authenticity and locality that draw from and feed into North American idealizations of the *bon sauvage*' (Sundberg, 2003: 63). Furthermore, these discourses of authenticity are articulated most powerfully by educated men, two effects of which are the sharpening of internal divisions along class, gender and ethnic lines and the conversion of large swaths of forest into men's space.

A major danger for studies of identity in political ecology would be to conclude that claims of indigeneity and ecological legitimacy are the product of environmentalists' romantic fantasies and are 'just political' or merely 'invented' and therefore provide insufficient grounds for awarding control and management authority. Future political ecology studies will need to be aware of the instabilities and cultural constructedness of group self-identification while at the same time remaining sensitive to the validity of local historical narratives, practices, meanings and attachment to place. A riveting and cogent example of such an approach is Li's (2004) study of two rural locations in Indonesia's Central Sulawesi, both of which were inhabited by culturally similar people, but only one of which has persuasively articulated themselves as indigenous peoples. To explore these cases Li draws on two concepts – positioning and articulation – the former referring to the way local meanings and practices are employed in positing the group identity boundaries of inside and outside, while simultaneously assembling the elements of what lies inside. According to Li, 'Articulation is a key word of political ecology because it recognizes the structured character of distinct entities (means of production, social groups, ideologies) but highlights the contingency of the ways in which they are brought together – articulated – at particular conjectures' (ibid.: 339). Through a careful reading of news accounts and NGO documents, she demonstrates how, in the context of a proposed dam project, one community presented themselves as indigenous Lindu peoples by highlighting particular elements of their lives and history in a strategic alliance with environmental activists. The documents reveal:

how group boundaries were defined, and how elements from the local repertoire of cultural ideas and livelihood practices were selected and combined to character-ize the group. They reveal, that is, the 'cut' of positioning, its arbitrary closure at a highly politicized moment. They point to the uniqueness and contingency of articu-lation, and its necessary occlusion of the larger flows of meaning and power, the practices of everyday life and work, the differences according to gender or class position, and the structures of feeling which form the larger canvas within which positioning occurs.

(ibid.: 355)

The second community was just as 'indigenous', but did not take up the discourse of indigeneity in the absence of a similar constellation of events, actors and height-ened tensions brought on by a major state-sponsored project.

A final example of recent work on social identity in political ecology takes us back to New Mexico and the conflicts between Anglo and Chicano groups over environmental management and conservation. Kosek's (2004) approach, however, is quite different from that of Pulido's (1996b) discussed above. In a compelling presentation of the writings of key North American conservation thinkers – from Marsh to Leopold to Edward Abbey – Kosek demonstrates the role that ideas of whiteness and racial purity played in the formulation of the wilderness preserva-tion movement. In tracing these ideas Kosek travels a well-trodden path, but his study makes an important contribution to political ecology by revealing how racialized notions of nature–society relations fester barely below the surface in contemporary conflicts between Anglo and Chicano groups over forest manage-ment in the Western USA. 'At issue are historically sedimented fears and under-standing regarding nature, race, and class, and they are made manifest in material, often violent struggles over the forest' (Kosek, 2004: 154). A principal difficulty in resolving these struggles is the inability or unwillingness of environmental activists to recognize how their vision of the West's future is inseparable from their essen-tialist constructions of white and non-white racial identities.

The theoretical complexity and empirical and ethnographic detail of many of the studies constituting a new wave of attention to identity in political ecology have set a high standard and suggest a range of inquiries for future work. Since very often the tactical logic of claiming indigeneity is based on alliances with powerful environmental NGOs and activists, it might be instructive to ask what happens – ecologically, politically, discursively – when these alliances fails? What other sorts of alliances are available, including coalitions of indigenous peoples (Ecuador comes to mind) or with certain segments of the state bureaucracy (see Conklin, 2002)? What are the differing environmental-political-economic conditions under which a claim of indigeneity will weaken or strengthen land and resource rights? Of particular interest are questions regarding environmental interventions and their effects on local social relations, such as changes in gender and ethnic relations, and the structure of local human–environment interactions. For example, some of the studies on indigeneity suggest that women are left out of ideas of the indigenous land steward (e.g. Sundberg, 2003). To what degree are indigenous identities constructed as male or female and what does that imply for control over land and resources? What sorts of claims and rights are denied by privileging indigeneity over other types of group identities and who gains and who loses in the process? Finally, and related to the ethical questions in political ecology, what role do researchers play in weakening or reinforcing self-defined group identities and what are our ethical responsibilities in such situations?

Biotechnology and biodiversity

The last, but far from the least important, area of future exploration to consider is the political-ecological implications and effects of the unfolding biotechnological revolution. This subject returns us to Clarence Glacken's (1967) fundamental questions on the relationships between nature and culture that were used to begin this book's exploration of political ecology. Biotechnology, particularly genetic engineering and cloning, pushes us to reconsider what nature is and what our emotional and ethical relationship with it will be. As Watts and Peet suggest in the Preface to the second edition of *Liberation Ecologies*, Glacken's questions are still relevant today, albeit in a new and heightened manner:

> Of course the capacity to transform is now incomparably vast in relation to Glacken's account of the Hellenistic world or early modern Europe. Indeed the very idea of design has now scaled heights that even some of the early nineteenth-century scientific boosters like Saint Simon could not possibly have anticipated. But curiously this has made Glacken's reference to environmental influence more compelling.
>
> (2004: xviii)

More compelling, that is, because nature is far from subdued and controlled by human technology. The unforeseen and unintended environmental consequences of bio-industrial production, such as in the case of 'mad cow' disease, continue to challenge science's Promethean ambitions. One could add that advances in genetic engineering also open governments, corporations and civil society to new vulnerabilities and new and terrible forms of resistance. Atwood's Luddites have gone well beyond uprooting a few genetically engineered plants here and there, or just wrenching a few gears, as it were. They have, in effect, turned the machine loose on itself.

There is a great deal for political ecology to address and in this short space only a few broad areas of inquiry can be raised. One key area of investigation in political ecology centres on questions of property rights, including intellectual property rights. Political ecologists have theorized bioprospecting in the South as a process of enclosure through which the ownership and control of access to raw materials – biodiversity in all its manifestations – are removed from local or indigenous communities living and working at the source (Zerner, 1996; Flitner, 1998; Parry, 2000; Boal, 2001). In the predominant Northern narratives, biodiversity is portrayed as a common heritage of humankind, a gift from nature while '[l]ocal peoples' potential property rights to knowledge of the natural environment are not mentioned' (Zerner, 1996: 74). Who will collect, control and profit from that biodiversity, much of which is the product of generations of testing and selecting by indigenous farmers? The declaration of biodiversity as global heritage also presents a distinct challenge to national sovereignty over land and resources and exposes the unequal relations of power between the North and the South (Flitner, 1998). One question to address, then, is how the scaling of property rights – that is, as local, national or global – in biodiversity discourse influences who gains and who loses in bioprospecting. It is also important to ask what happens to the resource after it is extracted from its geographic point of origin and how its ultimate destination and use affect property rights. As Parry (2000) points out, it is not only the material qualities of biodiversity resources that are commodified, but also the information embodied within them. The information extracted can then be stored, recombined, transported electronically and used repeatedly in a bio-industrial production process that is 'extremely difficult to monitor or track' for the purposes of awarding royalties for intellectual property rights (ibid.: 392).

This reference to royalty payments raises another set of questions regarding ethics, equity and justice in bioprospecting/biotechnology. The ethical questions range from issues of the distribution of benefits within and between Northern and Southern territories to the moral standing of genetically engineered bioforms, some of which will likely contain human genetic material or information. One question relates to the ethics of using botanical collections, which were collected without the permission of local owners and for very different purposes (ibid.). Should scientific institutions be allowed to sell access to the biodiversity resources they control while the communities and nations of origin remain uncompensated? Another set of ethical questions derives from the potential to mix human and non-human genetic material for the purposes of genetically engineering new bioforms. This potential also reinvigorates poststructural debates about hybridity, the social construction of nature and the nature–society dialectic (see Chapter 3).

> Will cloned humans have the same political rights as 'natural' humans? If animals are granted a certain political status, how does one judge the propriety of sacrificing a baboon so that its heart can be transplanted into a child.
>
> (Castree 2003: 209)

Far from being settled, the questions of where or whether to draw a boundary between nature and culture, and the moral and ethical implications of the answers, are only intensifying.

There is no better illustration of the equity and justice questions raised by genetic engineering than the case of the so-called 'terminator gene'. The terminator gene was the term given to the Delta and Pine Land Company's method of producing sterile seeds in the second generation through the application of genetic encoding. It was in effect an act of 'designing scarcity' (Boal, 2001: 153) so that Third World farmers would be required to purchase seeds every year. The wide adoption of terminator genes would in effect abolish participating farmers' ability to save seed for the planting of the next crop, an art and science that has been at the core of agriculture since the Neolithic revolution. Third World reaction to the terminator gene raised questions about the morality of exposing the livelihoods and lives of poor farmers to the perennial demands of the global seed industry. A related issue of justice and equity derives from the geo-historical structure of seed production in the global agro-industrial complex, succinctly articulated by Flitner.

> Thousands of so-called land races or primitive varieties were brought from Southern fields to Northern genebanks without any compensation, whereas the final products of 'scientific breeding' returned to Southern markets as commodities that had to be paid for in hard currency.
>
> (1998: 152)

Political ecologists are critically evaluating the international agreements that purport to share the benefits of bioprospecting with Third World regions and their impoverished farmers. Some suggest that bioprospecting agreements reflect and perpetuate colonial relations between the North and South 'by relegating developing countries to the role of supplying raw materials' (Parry, 2000: 396) and treating local people as sources of 'cheap labour' rather than owner/partners (Flitner, 1998: 159).

Bioprospecting and biotechnology have generated their own particular environmental politics. The scale of politics ranges from debates on global agreements for the management, distribution and use of biodiversity resources to the emergence of new social movements in specific localities. New struggles over the uses and control over biotechnologies are emerging that echo early struggles over the enclosure of commons and the introduction of agrarian technologies in the nineteenth century (Boal, 2001). On the consumption end, public protests over genetically modified organisms reflect both the politicization of the production and presentation of scientific knowledge and ethical concerns over tampering with nature (Forsyth, 2003). The questions that future political ecology studies must address include the following: What are the possibilities for new political alliances across class, ethnic and national lines and across multiple geographical scales to slow or inhibit further enclosure and privatization of genetic materials? What new forms of resistance are emerging? How might the discourse of environmental security and concerns over bioterrorism affect the possibilities for popular political mobilizations to control biotechnology? How are these discourses related to material interests: of multinational corporations, states, environmental activists, small-scale agricultural producers and local communities? What new hybrid ecologies are resulting or could result from the introduction of genetically modified plant and animal life forms and how might local livelihoods be affected? These are just a few of the questions that likely will occupy political ecology for years to come.

REFERENCES

Abel, N. and Blaikie, P. (1990) Land degradation, stocking rates and conservation policies in the communal rangelands of Botswana and Zimbabwe. *Pastoral Network Paper* 29a. London: Overseas Development Institute.

Abele, L. and Connor, E. (1976) Application of island biogeography theory to refuge design: making the right decision for the wrong reasons, in **Linn, R. M.** (ed.), *Proceedings of the First Conference on Scientific Research in the National Parks.* Washington, DC: US Government Printing Office.

Adams, A. (1963) How it began, in **Adams, A.** (ed.), *First World Conference on National Parks.* Washington, DC: US Department of Interior, xxxi–iii.

Adams, W. (2001) *Green Development: Environment and Sustainability in the Third World.* 2nd edn. London: Routledge.

Adams, W. (2003a) Nature and the colonial mind, in **Adams, W. and Mulligan, M.** (eds), *Decolonizing Nature: Strategies for Conservation in a Post-colonial Era.* London: Earthscan, 16–50.

Adams, W. (2003b) When nature won't stay still: conservation, equilibrium and control, in **Adams, W. and Mulligan, M.** (eds), *Decolonizing Nature: Strategies for Conservation in a Post-colonial Era.* London: Earthscan, 220–46.

Adams, W. and Mulligan, M. (eds) (2003) *Decolonizing Nature: Strategies for Conservation in a Post-colonial Era.* London: Earthscan.

Agnew, J. (1987) *Place and Politics: The Geographical Mediation of State and Society.* Boston: Allen & Unwin.

Agrawal, A. (1995) Dismantling the divide between indigenous and scientific knowledge. *Development and Change*, **26**(3): 413–39.

Alcorn, J. (1994) Noble savage or noble state? Northern myths and southern realities in biodiversity conservation. *Ethnoecologica*, **2**(3): 7–19.

Anderson, A. (1992) Land-use strategies for successful extractive economies, in **Cousell, S. and Rice, T.** (eds), *The Rainforest Harvest: Sustainable Strategies for Saving the Tropical Forests?* London: Friends of the Earth, 213–22.

Anderson, L. E. (1994) *The Political Ecology of the Modern Peasant: Calculation and Community.* Baltimore, MD: Johns Hopkins University Press.

Atkinson, A. (1991) *Principles of Political Ecology.* London: Belhaven.

Atwood, M. (2003) *Oryx and Crake.* New York: Nan A. Talese/Doubleday.

Badshah, M. and Bhadran, C. (1963) National parks: their principles and purposes, in **Adams, A.** (ed.), *First World Conference on National Parks.* Washington, DC: US Department of Interior, 23–34.

Barnes, T. and Duncan, J. (eds) (1992) *Writing Worlds: Discourse, Text, and Metaphor in the Representation of Landscape.* London: Routledge.

Barrows, H. (1923) Geography as human ecology. *Annals of the Association of American Geographers,* **23**(1): 1–14.

Bartels, G., Norton, B. and Perrier, G. (1993) An examination of the carrying capacity concept, in **Behnke, R. H., Scoones, I. and Kerven, C.** (eds), *Range Ecology at Disequilibrium: New Models of Natural Variability and Pastoral Adaptation in African Savannas.* London: Overseas Development Institute, International Institute of Environment and Development, Commonwealth Secretariat, 89–103.

Bartram, R. and Shobrook, S. (2000) Endless/end-less natures: environmental futures at the Fin de Millennium. *Annals of the Association of American Geographers,* **90**(2): 370–380.

Bassett, T. (1988) The political ecology of peasant-herder conflicts in the northern Ivory Coast. *Annals of the Association of American Geographers,* **78**: 453–72.

Bassett, T. (1993) Introduction: the land question and agricultural transformation in sub-Saharan Africa, in **Bassett, T. and Crummey, D.** (eds), *Land in African Agrarian Systems.* Madison, WI: University of Wisconsin Press, 3–31.

Bassett, T. and Crummey, D. (eds) (1993) *Land in African Agrarian Systems.* Madison, WI: University of Wisconsin Press.

Bassett, T. and Koli Bi, Z. (2000) Environmental discourses and Ivorian savanna. *Annals of the Association of American Geographers,* **90**(1): 67–95.

Batterbury, S. (2001) Landscapes of diversity: a local political ecology of livelihood diversification in South-Western Niger. *Ecumene,* **8**(4): 437–64.

Bebbington, A. (1990) Farmer knowledge, institutional resources and sustainable agricultural strategies: a case study from the eastern slopes of the Peruvian Andes. *Bulletin of Latin American Research*, **9**: 203–28.

Bebbington, A. (1993) Modernization from below: an alternative indigenous development? *Economic Geography*, **69**(3): 274–92.

Bebbington, A. (1996) Movements, modernizations, and markets: indigenous organizations and agrarian strategies in Ecuador, in **Peet, R. and Watts, M.** (eds), *Liberation Ecologies: Environment, Development, Social Movements*. London: Routledge, 86–109.

Bebbington, A. (2000) Reencountering development: livelihood transitions and place transformations in the Andes. *Annals of the Association of American Geographers*, **90**(3): 495–520.

Behnke, R. and Scoones, I. (1993) Rethinking range ecology: implications for rangeland management in Africa, in **Behnke, R. H., Scoones, I. and Kerven, C.** (eds), *Range Ecology at Disequilibrium: New Models of Natural Variability and Pastoral Adaptation in African Savannas*. London: Overseas Development Institute, International Institute of Environment and Development, Commonwealth Secretariat, 1–30.

Behnke, R., Scoones, I. and Kerven, C. (eds) (1993) *Range Ecology at Disequilibrium: New Models of Natural Variability and Pastoral Adaptation in African Savannas*. London: Overseas Development Institute, International Institute of Environment and Development, Commonwealth Secretariat.

Beinart, W. (2000) African history and environmental history. *African Affairs*, **99**: 269–302.

Berman, M. (1982) *All that is Solid Melts into Air: The Experience of Modernity*. New York: Simon and Schuster.

Bernstein, H. (1978) Notes on capital and peasantry. *Review of African Political Economy*, **10**: 60–73.

Bernstein, H. (1979) African peasantries: a theoretical framework. *Journal of Peasant Studies*, **6**(4): 420–44.

Bhaskar, R. (1975) *A Realist Social Theory of Science*. Leeds: Leeds Books.

Bird, E. (1987) The social construction of nature: theoretical approaches to the history of environmental problems. *Environmental Review*, **11**(4): 255–64.

Black, R. (1990) 'Regional political ecology' in theory and practice: a case study from northern Portugal. *Transactions of the Institute of British Geographers*, 15(1): 35.

Blaikie, P. (1985) *The Political Economy of Soil Erosion in Developing Countries*. New York: Wiley.

Blaikie, P. (1989) Explanation and policy in land degradation and rehabilitation for developing countries. *Land Degradation and Rehabilitation*, 1: 23–37.

Blaikie, P. (1995) Changing environments or changing views? A political ecology for developing countries. *Geography: Journal of the Geographical Association*, 348(3): 203–14.

Blaikie, P. (1996) Post-modernism and global environmental change. *Global Environmental Change*, 6(2): 81–85.

Blaikie, P. and Brookfield, H. (1987) *Land Degradation and Society*. New York; London: Methuen.

Boal, I. (2001) Damaging crops: sabotage, social memory, and the new genetic enclosures, in **Peluso, N. and Watts, M.** (eds), *Violent Environments*. Ithaca: Cornell University Press, 146–54.

Bonner, R. (1993) *At the Hand of Man: Peril and Hope for Africa's Wildlife*. New York: Vintage.

Botkin, D. (1990) *Discordant Harmonies: A New Ecology for the Twenty-first Century*. Oxford: Oxford University Press.

Brockington, D. (2002) *Fortress Conservation: The Preservation of the Mkomazi Game Reserve Tanzania*. Oxford: James Currey.

Brockington, D. and Homewood, K. (2001) Degradation debates and data deficiencies: the Mkomazi Game Reserve, Tanzania. *Africa*, 71(3): 447–80.

Brokensha, D., Warren, D. and Warner, O. (eds) (1980) *Indigenous Systems of Knowledge and Development*. Washington, DC: University Press of America.

Brosius, P. (1997) Endangered forest, endangered people: environmentalist representations of indigenous knowledge. *Human Ecology*, 25(1): 47–68.

Brosius, P. (1999) Analyses and interventions: anthropological engagements with environmentalism. *Current Anthropology*, 40(3): 277–309.

Browder, J. (1992) The limits of extractivism: tropical forest strategies beyond extractive reserves. *BioScience*, **42**(3): 174–82.

Brown, J. and Lomolino, M. (2000) Concluding remarks: historical perspective and the future of island biogeography theory. *Global Ecology and Biogeography*, **9**(1): 87–92.

Brown, K. (1998) The political ecology of biodiversity, conservation and development in Nepal's Terai: confused meanings, means and ends. *Ecological Economics*, **24**: 73–87.

Bruce, J. and Fortmann, L. (1988) Why land tenure and tree tenure matter: some fuel for thought, in **Fortmann, L. and Bruce, J.** (eds), *Whose Trees? Proprietary Dimensions of Forestry*. Boulder, CO: Westview Press, 1–10.

Bruntland, H. (1987) *Our Common Future*. Oxford: Oxford University Press (for the World Commission on Environment and Development).

Bryant, R. (1991) Putting politics first: the political ecology of sustainable development. *Global Ecology and Biogeography Letters*, **1**(6): 164.

Bryant, R. (1992) Political ecology: an emerging research agenda in Third World studies. *Political Geography*, **11**(1): 12–36.

Bryant, R. (1997) *The Political Ecology of Forestry in Burma, 1824–1994*. Honolulu: University of Hawaii Press.

Bryant, R. and Bailey, S. (1997) *Third World Political Ecology*. London: Routledge.

Bryant, R. and Jarosz, L. (2004) Introduction: thinking about ethics in political ecology. *Political Geography* (in press).

Burnham, P. (2000) *Indian Country, God's Country: Native Americans and the National Parks*. Washington, DC: Island Press.

Burton, I., Kates, R. and White, G. (1978) *Environment as Hazard*. Oxford: Oxford University Press.

Burwell, T. (1995) Bootlegging on a desert mountain: the political ecology of Agave (*Agave* spp.): demographic change in the Sonora River Valley, Sonora, Mexico. *Human Ecology*, **23**(3): 407.

Butzer, K. (1989) Cultural ecology, in **Gaile, G. and Willmott, C.** (eds), *Geography in America*. Columbus, OH: Merrill Publishing Co., 192–208.

Carney, J. (1993) Converting the wetlands, engendering the environment: the intersection of gender with agrarian change in the Gambia. *Economic Geography*, **69**(4): 329–48.

Carney, J. and Watts, M. (1990) Manufacturing dissent: work, gender, and the politics of meaning in a peasant society. *Africa*, **60**(2): 207–41.

Carruthers, J. (1989) Creating a national park, 1910–1926. *Journal of Southern African Studies*, **15**(2): 188–216.

Carruthers, J. (1994) Dissecting the myth: Paul Kruger and the Kruger National Park. *Journal of Southern African Studies*, **20**(2): 263–83.

Carty, R. and Eagles, M. (1998) The political ecology of local party organization: the case of Canada. *Political Geography*, **17**(5): 589.

Castree, N. (2003) Environmental issues: relational ontologies and hybrid politics. *Progress in Human Geography*, **27**(2): 203–11.

Castree, N. and Braun, B. (1998) The construction of nature and the nature of construction, in **Braun, B. and Castree, N.** (eds), *Remaking Reality: Nature at the Millennium*. London: Routledge.

Chambers, R. (1983) *Rural Development: Putting the Last First*. Harlow: Longman.

Chase, A. (1987) *Playing God in Yellowstone: The Destruction of America's First Park*. New York: Harcourt, Brace, Jovanovich.

Chittenden, H. (1903) *The Yellowstone National Park*. 4th edn. Cincinnati, OH: The Robert Clark Company.

Churchill, W. ([1908] 1990) *My Africa Journey*. New York: W. W. Norton.

Clarke, W. (1977) The structure of permanence, in **Bayliss-Smith, T. and Feachem, R.** (eds), *Subsistence and Survival in the Pacific*. San Francisco: Academic Press, 363–84.

Clements, F. E. (1916) Plant succession, an analysis of the development of vegetation. *Carnegie Institution of Washington Publication*, **242**: 1–512.

Cockburn, A. and Ridgeway, J. (1979) *Political Ecology*. New York: Times Books.

Colchester, M. (1993) Pirates, squatters and poachers: the political ecology of dispossession of the native peoples of Sarawak. *Global Ecology and Biogeography Letters*, **3**(4/6): 158.

Colchester, M. (1994) *Salvaging Nature: Indigenous Peoples, Protected Areas and Biodiversity Conservation.* UNRISD Discussion Paper. Geneva: United Nations Research Institute for Social Development.

Collins, J. L. (1986) Smallholder settlement of tropical South America: the social causes of ecological destruction. *Human Organization,* **45**(1): 378–92.

Conklin, B. (2002) Shamans versus pirates in the Amazonian treasure chest. *American Anthropologist,* **104**(4): 1050–61.

Cosgrove, D. (1998) *Social Formation and Symbolic Landscape.* Madison, WI: University of Wisconsin Press.

Cosgrove, D. and Daniels, S. (eds) (1988) *The Iconography of Landscape.* Cambridge: Cambridge University Press.

Cronon, W. (1990) Modes of prophecy and production: placing nature in history. *Journal of American History,* **76**(4): 1122–31.

Cronon, W. (1992) A place for stories: nature, history, and narrative. *The Journal of American History,* **78**(4): 1347–76.

Cronon, W. (1995) The trouble with wilderness, or getting back to the wrong nature, in **Cronon, W.** (ed.), *Uncommon Ground: Toward Reinventing Nature.* New York: W.W. Norton & Co., 69–90.

Dalby, S. (1996) The environment as geopolitical threat. *Ecumene,* **3**(4): 472–96.

Dalby, S. (2002) *Environmental Security.* Minneapolis, MN: University of Minnesota Press.

Daniels, S. and Cosgrove, D. (1988) Introduction: iconography and landscape, in **Cosgrove, D. and Daniels, S.** (eds), *The Iconography of Landscape.* Cambridge: Cambridge University Press, 1–10.

Dasmann, R. (1984) The relationship between protected areas and indigenous peoples, in **McNeely, J. and Miller, K.** (eds), *National Parks, Conservation, and Development: The Role of Protected Areas in Sustaining Society.* Washington, DC: Smithsonian Institution Press, 667–71.

Davis, M. (2001) *Late Victorian Holocausts: El Niño, Famines and the Making of the Third World.* New York: Verso.

Davis, S. and Wali, A. (1994) Indigenous territories and tropical forest management in Latin America. *Indigenous Affairs,* **4** (Oct.–Dec.): 4–14.

Dedina, S. (1995) The political ecology of transboundary development: land use, flood control and politics in the Tijuana River Valley. *Journal of Borderlands Studies*, **10**(1): 89.

de Janvry, A. (1981) *The Agrarian Question and Reformism in Latin America.* Baltimore, MD: Johns Hopkins University Press.

Demeritt, D. (1998) Science, social constructivism and nature, in **Braun, B. and Castree, N.** (eds), *Remaking Reality: Nature at the Millennium.* London: Routledge, 173–93.

Derman, B. and Ferguson, A. (1995) Human rights, environment and development: the dispossession of fishing communities on Lake Malawi. *Human Ecology*, **23**(2): 125–41.

Diamond, J. (1975) The island dilemma: lessons of modern geographical studies for the design of nature preserves. *Biological Conservation*, **7**(2): 129–46.

Eagles, M. (1998) The political ecology of representation in English Canada: MPs and their constituencies. *The American Review of Canadian Studies*, **28**(1/2): 53.

Ehrlich, P. (1968) *The Population Bomb.* New York: Ballantine.

Ellis, J., Couhenour, M. and Swift, D. (1993) Climate variability, ecosystem sustainability, and the implications for range and livestock development, in **Behnke, R. H., Scoones, I. and Kerven, C.** (eds), *Range Ecology at Disequilibrium: New Models of Natural Variability and Pastoral Adaptation in African Savannas.* London: Overseas Development Institute, International Institute of Environment and Development, Commonwealth Secretariat, 31–41.

Ellis, J. and Swift, D. (1988) Stability of African pastoral ecosystems: alternative paradigms and implications for development. *Journal of Range Management*, **41**(6): 450–9.

Ellis, M. (1994) Of elephants and men: politics and nature conservation in South Africa. *Journal of Southern African Studies*, **20**: 53–69.

Enzensberger, H. (1974) A critique of political ecology. *New Left Review*, **8**: 3–32.

Escobar, A. (1995) *Encountering Development: The Making and the Unmaking of the Third World.* Princeton, NJ: Princeton University Press.

Escobar, A. (1996) Constructing nature: elements for a poststructural political ecology, in **Peet, R. and Watts, M.** (eds), *Liberation Ecologies: Environment, Development, Social Movements*. London: Routledge, 46–68.

Escobar, A. (1999) After nature: steps to an antiessentialist political ecology. *Current Anthropology*, **40**(1): 1–30.

Fairhead, J. (2001) International dimensions of conflict over natural and environmental resources, in **Peluso, N. and Watts, M.** (eds), *Violent Environments*. Ithaca, NY: Cornell University Press, 213–36.

Fairhead, J. and Leach, M. (1996) *Misreading the African Landscape: Society and Ecology in a Forest-Savanna Mosaic*. Cambridge: Cambridge University Press.

Fearnside, P. (1989) Extractive reserves in Brazilian Amazonia. *BioScience*, **39**(6): 387–93.

Ferguson, A. and Derman, B. (2000) Writing against hegemony: development encounters in Zimbabwe and Malawi, in **Peters, P. E.** (ed.) *Development Encounters: Sites of Participation and Knowledge*. Cambridge, MA: Harvard Institute for International Development.

Ferguson, J. (1990) *The Anti-Politics Machine: 'Development,' Depoliticization, and Bureaucratic Power in Lesotho*. Cambridge: Cambridge University Press.

Figgis, P. (2003) The changing face of nature conservation: reflections on the Australian experience, in **Adams, W. and Mulligan, M.** (eds), *Decolonizing Nature: Strategies for Conservation in a Post-colonial Era*. London: Earthscan, 197–219.

Fitzsimmons, M. (1989) The matter of nature. *Antipode*, **21**(2): 106–20.

Flitner, M. (1998) Biodiversity: of local commons and global commodities, in **Goldman, M.** (ed.), *Privatizing Nature: Political Struggles for the Global Commons*. New Brunswick, NJ: Rutgers University Press.

Forsyth, T. (2003) *Critical Political Ecology: The Politics of Environmental Science*. London: Routledge.

Fortmann, L. and Bruce, J. (1988) *Whose Trees? Proprietary Dimensions of Forestry*. Boulder, CO: Westview Press.

Foucault, M. (1979) *Discipline and Punish: The Birth of the Prison*. New York: Vintage Books.

Foucault, M. (1980) *Power/Knowledge: Selected Interviews and Other Writings, 1972–1977.* New York: Pantheon Books.

Frank, A. (1967) *Capitalism and Underdevelopment in Latin America: Historical Studies in Chile and Brazil.* New York: Monthly Review Press.

Franke, R. and Chasin, B. (1980) *Seeds of Famine: Ecological Destruction and the Development Dilemma in the West African Sahel.* Totowa, NJ: Allenheld and Osman.

Frankel, O. and Soulé, M. (1981) *Conservation and Evolution.* Cambridge: Cambridge University Press.

Freidberg, S. (2001) Gardening on the edge: the social conditions of sustainability on an African urban periphery. *Annals of the Association of American Geographers,* **91**(2): 349–69.

Germic, S. (2001) *American Green: Class, Crisis, and the Deployment of Nature in Central Park, Yosemite, and Yellowstone.* Lanham, MD: Lexington Books.

Ghatak, S. (1995) A recipe for success: women and non-timber forest products in Southwest Bengal, India, in **Fox, J., Donovan, D. and DeCoursey, M.** (eds), *Voices from the Field: Sixth Workshop on Community Management of Forest Lands.* Honolulu: East-West Center, 164–79.

Giddens, A. (1984) *The Constitution of Society: Outline of the Theory of Structuration.* Cambridge: Polity.

Giles-Vernick, T. (2002) *Cutting the Vines of the Past: Environmental Histories of the Central African Rain Forest.* Charlottesville, VA: University of Virginia Press.

Glacken, C. (1967) *Traces on the Rhodian Shore.* Berkeley, CA: University of California Press.

Glanz, J. (2004) At the center of the storm over Bush and science. *New York Times,* March 30: D1–4.

Goldman, M. (1998) The political resurgence of the commons, in **Goldman, M.** (ed.), *Privatizing Nature: Political Struggles for the Global Commons.* New Brunswick, NJ: Rutgers University Press, 1–19.

Goodman, D. and Redclift, M. (1991) *Refashioning Nature: Food, Ecology and Culture.* London: Routledge.

Gordon, R. (1992) *The Bushman Myth: The Making of a Namibian Underclass.* Boulder, CO: Westview Press.

Gramsci, A. (1971) *Selections from the Prison Notebooks.* New York: International Publishers.

Gregory, D. (1994) Social theory and human geography, in **Gregory, D., Martin, R. and Smith, G.** (eds), *Human Geography: Society, Space, and Social Science,* 78–109.

Grossman, L. (1984) *Peasants, Subsistence Ecology, and Development in the Highlands of Papua New Guinea.* Princeton, NJ: Princeton University Press.

Grossman, L. (1998) *The Political Ecology of Bananas: Contract Farming, Peasants, and Agrarian Change in the Eastern Caribbean.* Chapel Hill, NC: University of North Carolina Press.

Guha, R. (1990) *The Unquiet Woods: Ecological Change and Peasant Resistance in the Himalaya.* Berkeley CA: University of California Press.

Guyer, J. and Richards, P. (1996) The invention of biodiversity: social perspectives on the management of biological variety in Africa. *Africa,* **66**(1): 1–13.

Hansis, R. (1998) A political ecology of picking: non-timber forest products in the Pacific Northwest. *Human Ecology,* **26**(1): 67.

Hardin, G. (1968) The tragedy of the commons. *Science,* **163**(13): 1243–8.

Harding, S. (1996) Rethinking standpoint epistemology: What is 'strong objectivity'? in **Keller, E. and Longino, H.** (eds), *Feminism and Science.* Oxford: Oxford University Press, 235–48.

Haraway, D. (1988) Situated knowledges: the science question in feminism and the privilege of partial perspective. *Feminist Studies,* **14**(3): 581.

Haraway, D. (1996) Animal Sociology and a natural economy of the body politic, part II: The past is a contented zone, in **Keller, E. and Longino, H.** (eds), *Feminism and Science.* Oxford: Oxford University Press.

Harrison, J., Miller, K., and McNeely, J. (1984) The world coverage of protected areas: development goals and environmental needs, in **McNeely, J. and Miller, K.** (eds), *National Parks, Conservation, and Development: The Role of Protected Areas in Sustaining Society.* Washington, DC: Smithsonian Institution Press, 24–33.

Hartmann, B. (2001) Will the circle be unbroken? A critique of the project on environment, population, and security, in **Peluso, N. and Watts, M.** (eds), *Violent Environments*. Ithaca, NY: Cornell University Press, 39–64.

Harvey, D. (1973) *Social Justice and the City*. Baltimore, MD: Johns Hopkins University Press.

Harvey, D. (1993) The nature of environment: the dialectics of social and environmental change. *Socialist Register,* **29**: 1–51.

Harvey, D. (1996) *Justice, Nature and the Geography of Difference*. Oxford: Blackwell.

Hayles, N. (1995) Searching for common ground, in **Soulé, M. and Lease, G.** (eds), *Reinventing Nature? Responses to Postmodern Deconstruction*. Washington, DC: Island Press, 47–64.

Hayward, T. (1994) The meaning of political ecology. *Radical Philosophy,* **66**(2): 11–20.

Heaney, L. (2000) Dynamic disequilibrium: a long-term, large-scale perspective on the equilibrium model of island biogeography. *Global Ecology and Biogeography,* **9**: 59–74.

Hecht, S. (1985) Environment, development and politics: capital accumulation and the livestock sector in eastern Amazonia. *World Development,* **6**: 663–84.

Hecht, S. (1990) Indigenous soil management in the Latin American tropics: neglected knowledge of native peoples, in **Altieri, M. and Hecht, S.** (eds), *Agroecology and Small Farm Development*. Boca Raton, FL: CRC Press, 151–8.

Hecht, S. and Cockburn, A. (1990) *The Fate of the Forest: Developers, Destroyers and Defenders of the Amazon*. New York: Harper Perennial.

Heynen, N. (2003) The scaler production of injustice within the urban forest. *Antipode,* **35**(5): 980–98.

Hill, K. (1996) Zimbabwe's wildlife utilization programs: grassroots democracy or an extension of state power? *African Studies Review,* **39**(1): 103–22.

Hitchcock, R. (1995) Centralization, resource depletion, and coercive conservation among the Tyua of Northeastern Kalahari. *Human Ecology,* **23**(2): 169–98.

Hodgson, D. (2002a) Introduction: comparative perspectives on the indigenous rights movement in Africa and the Americas. *American Anthropologist*, **104**(4): 1037–49.

Hodgson, D. (2002b) Precarious alliances: the cultural politics and structural predicaments of the indigenous rights movement in Tanzania. *American Anthropologist* **104**(4): 1086–97

Hollander, G. (1995) Agroenvironmental conflict and world food system theory: sugarcane in the Everglades Agricultural Area. *Journal of Rural Studies*, **11**(3): 309–18.

Hollander, G. (2004) The material and symbolic role of the everglades in national politics. *Political Geography* (forthcoming).

Holling, C. (ed.) (1978) *Adaptive Environmental Assessment and Management*. New York: John Wiley and Sons.

Holling, C. (1986) The resilience of terrestrial ecosystems: local surprise or global change, in **Clarke, W. C. and Munn, R. G.** (eds), *Sustainable Development of the Biosphere*. Cambridge: Cambridge University Press, 292–317.

Holling, C. and Sanderson, S. (1996) Dynamics of (dis)harmony in ecological and social systems, in **Hanna, S., Folke, C. and Maler, K.** (eds), *Rights to Nature: Ecological, Economic, Cultural, and Political Principles of Institutions for the Environment*. Washington, DC and Covelo, CA: Island Press.

Homer-Dixon, T. (1991) On the threshold: environmental changes as causes of acute conflict. *International Security*, **16**(1): 76–116.

Homer-Dixon, T. (1994) Environmental scarcities and violent conflict: evidence from cases. *International Security*, **19**(1): 5–40.

Homer-Dixon, T. (1999) *Environment, Scarcity and Violence*. Princeton, NJ: Princeton University Press.

Homewood, K. and Brockington, D. (1999) Biodiversity, conservation, and development in Mkomazi Game Reserve, Tanzania. *Global Ecology and Biogeography*, **8**: 301–13.

Homewood, K. and Rodgers, W. (1984) Pastoralism and conservation. *Human Ecology*, **12**(4): 431–41.

Homewood, K. and Rodgers, W. (1991) *Maasailand Ecology: Pastoralist Development and Wildlife Conservation in Ngorongoro, Tanzania.* Cambridge: Cambridge University Press.

Hulme, D and Murphree, M. (2001) Community conservation in Africa: an introduction, in **Hulme, D and Murphree, M.** (eds), *African Wildlife and Livelihoods: The Promise and Performance of Community Conservation.* Oxford: James Currey, 1–8.

Huntington, E. (1915) *Civilization and Climate.* New Haven, CT: Yale University Press.

Hvalkof, S. (2000) Outrage in rubber and oil: extractivism, indigenous peoples, and justice in the upper Amazon, in **Zerner, C.** (ed.), *People, Plants and Justice: The Politics of Nature Conservation.* New York: Columbia University Press, 83–116.

Igoe, J. and Brockington, D. (1999) *Pastoral Land Tenure and Community Conservation: A Case Study from North-east Tanzania.* Pastoral Land Tenure Series No. 11. London: International Institute for Environment and Development.

Illius, A. and O'Connor, T. (1999) On the relevance of nonequilibrium concepts to arid and semi-arid grazing systems. *Ecological Applications,* **9**(3), 798–813.

ILO. (1989) *Convention (No. 169) concerning Indigenous and Tribal Peoples in Independent Countries.* Geneva: International Labor Organization, online: http://www.unhchr.ch/html/menu3/b/62.htm

Jackson, P. (1989) *Maps of Meaning: An Introduction to Cultural Geography.* London: Routledge.

Jackson, C. (1993) Women/nature or gender/history? A critique of ecofeminist 'development'. *Journal of Peasant Studies,* **20**(3): 389–419.

Jameson, F. (1998) *The Cultural Turn: Selected Writings on the Postmodern, 1983–1998.* London and New York: Verso.

Jarosz, L. (1999) A feminist political ecology perspective. *Gender, Place and Culture,* **6**(4): 390–3.

Jewitt, S. and Kumar, S. (2000) A political ecology of forest management: gender and silvicultural knowledge in the Jharkhand, India, in **Stott, P. and Sullivan, S.** (eds), *Political Ecology: Science, Myth and Power.* London: Arnold, 91–116.

Jones, B. and Murphree, M. (2001) The evolution of policy on community conservation in Namibia and Zimbabwe, in **Hulme, D. and Murphree, M.** (eds), *African Wildlife and Livelihoods: The Promise and Performance of Community Conservation.* Oxford: James Currey, 38–58.

Kaika, M. (2003) Constructing scarcity and sensationalising water politics: 170 days that shook Athens. *Antipode,* **35**(5): 919–54.

Kalipeni, E. and Feder, D. (1999) A political ecology perspective on environmental change in Malawi with the Blantyre Fuelwood Project Area as a case. *The Journal of Politics and the Life Sciences,* **18**(1): 37.

Kandeh, H. and Richards, P. (1996) Rural people as conservationists: querying neo-Malthusian assumptions about biodiversity in Sierra Leone. *Africa,* **66**(1): 90–103.

Kaplan, R. (1994) The coming anarchy: how scarcity, crime, overpopulation, and disease are rapidly destroying the social fabric of our planet. *Atlantic Monthly,* February: 44–76.

Keller, E. (1996) Feminism and science, in **Keller, E. and Longino, H.** (eds), *Feminism and Science.* Oxford: Oxford University Press, 1–16.

Keller, R. and Turek, M. (1997) *American Indians and National Parks.* Tucson, AZ: University of Arizona Press.

Kirkpatrick, J. (2000) The political ecology of biogeography. *Journal of Biogeography,* **27**(1): 45–8.

Kosek, J. (2004) Purity and pollution: racial degradation and environmental anxieties, in **Peet, R. and Watts, M.** (eds), *Liberation Ecologies: Environment, Development, Social Movements,* 2nd edn. London: Routledge, 125–65.

Kuhn, T. (1970) *The Structure of Scientific Revolutions.* 2nd edn. Chicago: The University of Chicago Press.

Kuletz, V. (2001) Invisible spaces, violent places: Cold War nuclear and militarized landscapes, in **Peluso, N. and Watts, M.** (eds), *Violent Environments.* Ithaca, NY: Cornell University Press, 237–60.

Langton, M. (2003) The 'wild', the market and the native: indigenous people face new forms of global colonization. In **Adams, W. and Mulligan, M.** (eds), *Decolonizing Nature: Strategies for Conservation in a Post-colonial Era.* London: Earthscan, 79–107.

Leach, M. and Mearns, R. (1996) *The Lie of the Land: Challenging Received Wisdom on the African Environment.* London, Oxford and Portsmouth: The International African Institute, James Currey and Heinemann.

Le Billon, P. (2001) The political ecology of war: natural resources and armed conflicts. *Political Geography,* **20**(5): 261–84.

Le Billon, P. (2004) The geopolitical economy of 'resource wars'. *Geopolitics,* **9**(1): 1–28.

Lee, E. (1993) The political ecology of coastal planning management in England and Wales: policy responses to the implications of sea-level rise. *The Geographical Journal,* **159**(2): 169.

Lescure, J., Emperaire, L., Pinton, F. and Renault-Lescure, O. (1994) Nontimber forest products and extractive activities in the Middle Rio Negro Region, Brazil, in **Plotkin, M. and Famolare, L.** (eds), *Sustainable Harvest and Marketing of Rain Forest Products.* Washington, DC: Island Press, 151–7.

Li, T. (1996) Images of community. *Development and Change,* **27**: 501–27.

Li, T. (2004) Environment, indigeneity and translation, in **Peet, R. and Watts, M.** (eds), *Liberation Ecologies: Environment, Development, Social Movements,* 2nd edn. London: Routledge, 339–70.

Little, P. (1996) Pastoralism, biodiversity, and the shaping of savanna landscapes in East Africa. *Africa,* **66**(1): 35–51.

Little, P. (2004) Rethinking interdisciplinary paradigms and the political ecology of pastoralism in East Africa, in **Bassett, T. and Crummey, D.** (eds), *African Savannas: New Perspectives on Environmental and Social Change.* Oxford: James Currey Publishers (forthcoming).

Little, P. and Horowitz, M. (eds) (1987) *Lands at Risk in the Third World: Local Level Perspectives.* Boulder, CO: Westview Press.

Little, P. and Painter, M. (1995) Discourse, politics, and the development process: reflections on Escobar's 'anthropology and the development encounter'. *American Ethnologist,* **22**(3): 602–16.

Lomolino, M. (2000) A call for a new paradigm of island biogeography. *Global Ecology and Biogeography,* **9**(1): 1–7.

Low, N. and Gleeson, B. (1998) *Justice, Society, and Nature: An Exploration of Political Ecology.* London: Routledge.

Lowenthal, D. (1965) Introduction, in **Marsh, G. P.**, *Man and Nature: Or, Physical Geography as Modified by Human Action.* Cambridge, MA: The Belknap Press of Harvard University Press, ix–xxix.

MacArthur, R. H. and Wilson, E. O. (1967) *The Theory of Island Biogeography.* Princeton, NJ: Princeton University Press.

Mackenzie, A. F. (1993) 'A piece of land never shrinks': reconceptualizing land tenure in a smallholding district, Kenya, in **Bassett, T. and Crummey, D.** (eds), *Land in African Agrarian Systems.* Madison, WI: University of Wisconsin Press, 94–121.

Mackenzie, A. F. (1998) *Land, Ecology and Resistance in Kenya, 1880–1952.* Portsmouth, NH: Heinemann.

Malanson, G., Butler, D. and Walsh, S. (1990) Chaos theory in physical geography. *Physical Geography,* 11(4): 293–304.

Malhotra, K. (1993) People, biodiversity and regenerating topical sal (Shorea robusta) forests in West Bengal, India, in **Hladik, C., Hladik, A., Linares, O., Pagezy, H., Semple, A. and Hadley, M.** (eds), *Tropical Forests, People and Food: Biocultural Interactions and Applications to Development. Man and the Biosphere 13.* Paris: UNESCO, 745–52.

Malhotra, K., Deb, D., Dutta, M., Vasulu, T., Yadav, G. and Adhikari, M. (1993) The role of non-timber forest products in village economies of southwest Bengal, in *From the Field.* Network Paper 15d (Summer). London: Rural Development Forestry Network, 1–8.

Marsh, G. P. ([1864] 1965) *Man and Nature: Or, Physical Geography as Modified by Human Action.* Cambridge, MA: The Belknap Press of Harvard University Press.

Marx, K. (1967) *Capital.* New York: International.

McCarthy, J. (2001) Environmental enclosures and the state of nature in the American West, in **Peluso, N. and Watts, M.** (eds), *Violent Environments.* Ithaca, NY: Cornell University Press, 117–45.

McCarthy, J. (2002) First World political ecology: lessons from the Wise Use Movement. *Environment and Planning A,* 34(7): 1281–302.

McCay, B. and Acheson, J. (1987) Human ecology of the commons, in **McCay, B. and Acheson, J.** (eds), *The Question of the Commons: The Culture and Ecology of Communal Resources.* Tucson, AZ: University of Arizona Press, 1–34.

McCusker, B. and Weiner, D. (2003) GIS representations of nature, political ecology, and the study of land use and land cover change in South Africa, in **Zimmerer, K. and Bassett, T.** (eds), *Political Ecology: An Integrative Approach to Geography and Environment-Development Studies.* New York: Guilford Press, 201–18.

McEvoy, A. (1988) Toward an interactive theory of nature and culture: ecology, production, and cognition in the California fishing industry, in **Worster, D.** (ed), *The Ends of the Earth: Perspectives on Modern Environmental History.* Cambridge: Cambridge University Press, 211–29.

McNeely, J. (1984) Introduction: protected areas are adapting to new realities, in **McNeely, J. and Miller, K.** (eds), *National Parks, Conservation, and Development: The Role of Protected Areas in Sustaining Society.* Washington, DC: Smithsonian Institution Press, 1–9.

McNeely, J. and Miller, K. (eds) (1984) *National Parks, Conservation, and Development: The Role of Protected Areas in Sustaining Society.* Washington, DC: Smithsonian Institution Press.

Merchant, C. (1992) *Radical Ecology: The Search for a Livable World.* New York: Routledge.

Miller, R. (1978) Applying island biogeographic theory to an East African reserve. *Environmental Conservation,* **5**(3): 191–5.

Moe, S., Wegge, P. and Kapela, E. (1990) The influence of man-made fires on large wild herbivores in Lake Burungi area in northern Tanzania. *The African Journal of Ecology,* **28**: 35–45.

Moore, D. (1993) Contesting terrain in Zimbabwe's eastern highlands: political ecology, ethnography, and peasant resource struggles. *Economic Geography,* **69**(4): 380–401.

Moore, D. (1996) Marxism, culture, and political ecology: environmental struggles in Zimbabwe's eastern highlands, in **Peet, R. and Watts, M.** (eds), *Liberation Ecologies: Environment, Development, Social Movements.* London: Routledge, 125–47.

Moore, D. (2000) The crucible of cultural politics: reworking 'development' in Zimbabwe's eastern highlands. *American Ethnologist*, **26**(3): 654–89.

Moore, P., Chaloner, W. and Stott, P. (1996) *Global Environmental Change.* Oxford: Blackwell Science.

Murombedzi, J. (2003) Devolving the expropriation of nature: the 'devolution' of wildlife management in southern Africa, in **Adams, W. and Mulligan, M.** (eds), *Decolonizing Nature: Strategies for Conservation in a Post-colonial Era.* London: Earthscan, 135–51.

Murphree, M. (2004) CAMPFIRE, in **Tsing, A., Brosius, P. and Zerner, C.** (eds). *Representing Communities: Histories and Politics of Community-Based Resource Management.* New York and London: Altamira Press.

Myers, N. (1979) *The Sinking Ark: A New Look at the Problem of Disappearing Species.* New York: Pergamon Press.

Naughton-Treves, L. and Sanderson, S. (1995) Property, politics, and wildlife conservation. *World Development*, **23**(8): 1265–75.

Nepstad, D. C., Foster Brown, I., Luz, L., Alechandre, A. and Viana, V. (1992) Biotic impoverishment of Amazonian forests by rubber tappers, loggers and cattle ranchers, in **Nepstad, D. C. and Schwartzman, S.** (eds), *Non-Timber Products from Tropical Forest: Evaluation of a Conservation and Development Strategy.* New York: The New York Botanical Garden, 1–14.

Neumann, R. (1992) The political ecology of wildlife conservation in the Mount Meru Area, Northeast Tanzania. *Land Degradation and Rehabilitation*, **3**(2): 85–98.

Neumann, R. (1995) Ways of seeing Africa: colonial recasting of African society and landscape in Serengeti National Park. *Ecumene*, **2**(2): 149–69.

Neumann, R. (1996) Dukes, earls and ersatz Edens: aristocratic nature preservationists in colonial Africa. *Society and Space*, **14**: 79–98.

Neumann, R. (1997) Primitive ideas: protected area buffer zones and the politics of land in Africa. *Development and Change*, **28**(3): 559–82.

Neumann, R. (1998) *Imposing Wilderness: Struggles over Livelihood and Nature Preservation in Africa.* Berkeley, CA: University of California Press.

Neumann, R. (2000) *Research in NTFP Commercialization: Review and Analysis.* Bogor, Indonesia: Center for International Forestry Research, and Rome: UN Food and Agricultural Organization.

Neumann, R. (2001a) Disciplining peasants in Tanzania: from state violence to self-surveillance in wildlife conservation, in **Peluso, N. and Watts, M.** (eds), *Violent Environments.* Ithaca, NY: Cornell University Press, 305–27.

Neumann, R. (2001b) Africa's 'last wilderness': reordering space for political and economic control in colonial Africa. *Africa,* **71**(4): 641–65.

Neumann, R. (2002) The postwar conservation boom in British colonial Africa. *Environmental History,* **7**(1): 22–47.

Neumann, R. (2004) Moral and discursive geographies in the war for biodiversity in Africa. *Political Geography* (in press).

Nietschmann, B. (1973) *Between Land and Water: The Subsistence Ecology of the Miskito Indians, Eastern Nicaragua.* New York: Seminar Press.

Nietschmann, B. (1979) Ecological change, inflation, and migration in the Far West Caribbean. *Geographical Review,* **69**: 1–24.

Nietschmann, B. (1985) Miskito and Kuna struggle for nation autonomy, in **Bodley, J.** (ed.), *Tribal Peoples and Development Issues: A Global Overview.* Mountain View, CA: Mayfield Publishing Co., 271–80.

Nietschmann, B. (1992) *The Interdependence of Biological and Cultural Diversity.* Center for World Indigenous Studies, Occasional Paper 21. Kenmore, WA: Center for World Indigenous Studies.

O'Connor, J. (1994) Is sustainable capitalism possible? in **O'Connor, M.** (ed.), *Is Capitalism Sustainable? Political Economy and the Politics of Ecology.* New York: Guilford Press, 152–75.

O'Connor, M. (ed.) (1994a) *Is Capitalism Sustainable? Political Economy and the Politics of Ecology.* New York: Guilford Press.

O'Connor, M. (1994b) Codependency and indeterminacy: a critique of the theory of production, in **O'Connor, M.** (ed.), *Is Capitalism Sustainable? Political Economy and the Politics of Ecology.* New York: Guilford Press, 53–75.

Olwig, K. (2002) *Landscape, Nature and the Body Politic: From Britain's Renaissance to America's New World.* Madison, WI: University of Wisconsin Press.

O'Keefe, P. and Wisner, B. (1975) African drought: the state of the game, in **Richards, P.** (ed.) *African Environment, Problems and Perspectives.* London: International African Institute, 31–9.

O'Neil, R. (1997) Intrinsic value, moral standing, and species. *Environmental Ethics,* 19(2): 45–52.

Onuf, N. (1989) *World of Our Making: Rules and Rule in Social Theory and International Relations.* Columbia, SC: University of South Carolina Press.

Parry, B. (2000) The fate of the collections: social justice in the annexation of plant genetic resources, in **Zerner, C.** (ed.), *People, Plants and Justice: The Politics of Nature Conservation.* New York: Columbia University Press, 374–402.

Paulson, S., Gezon, L. and Watts, M. (2003) Locating the political in political ecology: an introduction. *Human Organization,* 62(3): 205–20.

Peet, R. and Watts, M. (1993) Introduction: development theory and environment in an age of market triumphalism. *Economic Geography,* 68(3): 227–53.

Peet, R. and Watts, M. (1996a) Liberation ecology: development, sustainability, and environment in an age of market triumphalism, in **Peet, R. and Watts, M.** (eds), *Liberation Ecologies: Environment, Development, Social Movements.* London: Routledge, 1–45.

Peet, R. and Watts, M. (eds) (1996b) *Liberation Ecologies: Environment, Development, Social Movements.* London: Routledge.

Peet, R. and Watts, M. (eds) (2004) *Liberation Ecologies: Environment, Development, Social Movements.* 2nd edn. London: Routledge.

Pelling, M. (1999) The political ecology of flood hazard in urban Guyana. *Geoforum,* 30(3): 249–61.

Peluso, N. (1992a) The political ecology of extraction and extractive reserves in East Kalimantan, Indonesia. *Development and Change,* 23(4): 49–74.

Peluso, N. (1992b) *Rich Forests, Poor People: Resource Control and Resistance in Java.* Berkeley, CA: University of California Press.

Peluso, N. (1992c) The ironwood problem: (mis)management of an extractive rainforest product. *Conservation Biology,* 6(2): 210–29.

Peluso, N. (1993) Coercing conservation? The politics of state resource control. *Global Environmental Change,* 3(2): 199–217.

Peluso, N. (1996) Fruit trees and family trees in an anthropogenic forest. *Comparative Studies in Society and History*, **38**: 510–48.

Peluso, N. and Vandergeest, P. (2001) Genealogies of the political forest and customary rights in Indonesia, Malaysia, and Thailand. *The Journal of Asian Studies*, **60**(3): 761–812.

Peluso, N. and Watts, M. (2001a) Violent environments, in **Peluso, N. and Watts, M.** (eds), *Violent Environments*. Ithaca, NY: Cornell University Press, 3–38.

Peluso, N. and Watts, M. (eds). (2001b) *Violent Environments*. Ithaca, NY: Cornell University Press.

Peters, P. (ed.) (2000) *Development Encounters: Sites of Participation and Knowledge*. Cambridge, MA: Harvard Institute for International Development.

Peterson, G. (2000) Political ecology and ecological resilience: an integration of human and ecological dynamics. *Ecological Economics: The Journal of the Inter*, **35**(3): 323–36.

Poffenberger, M. (1998) The resurgence of community forest management in the Jungle Mahals of West Bengal, in **Arnold, D. and Guha, R.** (eds), *Nature, Culture, Imperialism: Essays on the Environmental History*. Delhi: Oxford University Press, 336–69.

Pred, A. (1998) The nature of denaturalized consumption and everyday life, in **Braun, B. and Castree, N.** (eds), *Remaking Reality: Nature at the Millennium*. London: Routledge, 150–68.

Proctor, J. (1998) The social construction of Nature: relativist accusations, pragmatist and critical realist responses. *Annals of the Association of American Geographers*, **88**(3): 352–76.

Pulido, L. (1996a) *Environmentalism and Economic Justice*. Tucson, AZ: University of Arizona Press.

Pulido, L. (1996b) Ecological legitimacy and cultural essentialism: Hispano grazing in the Southwest. *Capitalism-Nature-Socialism*, **7**(4): 37–58.

Pulido, L. (2000) Rethinking environmental racism: white privilege and urban development in southern California. *Annals of the Association of American Geographers*, **90**(1): 12–40.

Rangan, H. (1996) From Chipko to Uttaranchal: development, environment, and social protest in the Garhwal Himalayas, India, in **Peet, R. and Watts, M.** (eds), *Liberation Ecologies: Environment, Development, Social Movements.* London: Routledge, 205–26.

Rangan, H. and Lane, M. (2001) Indigenous peoples and forest management: comparative approaches in Australia and India. *Society and Natural Resources,* 14(2): 145–60.

Ranger, T. (1993) The communal areas of Zimbabwe, in **Bassett, T. and Crummey, D.** (eds), *Land in African Agrarian Systems.* Madison, WI: University of Wisconsin Press, 354–88.

Ranger, T. (1999) *Voices from the Rocks: Nature, Culture and History in the Matopos Hills of Zimbabwe.* Oxford: James Currey.

Rappaport, R. (1968) *Pigs for the Ancestors.* New Haven, CT: Yale University Press.

Redclift, M. (1984) *Development and Environmental Crisis: Red or Green Alternatives?* London: Methuen.

Reddy, S. (2002) Communal forests, political spaces: territorial competition between common property institutions and the state in Guatemala. *Space & Polity,* 6(3): 271–87.

Revkin, A. (2004a) Bush's science aide rejects claims of distorted facts. *New York Times,* April 3: A9.

Revkin, A. (2004b) NASA curbs comments on ice age disaster movie. *New York Times,* April 25: 14.

Revkin, A. and Seelye, K. (2003) Report by the E.P.A. leaves out data on climate change. *New York Times,* June 19: A1.

Richards, P. (ed.) (1975a) *African Environment: Problems and Perspectives.* London: International African Institute.

Richards, P. (1975b) 'Alternative' strategies for the African environment: 'folk ecology' as a basis for community oriented agricultural development, in **Richards, P.** (ed.), *African Environment: Problems and Perspectives.* London: International African Institute, 102–17.

Richards, P. (1985) *Indigenous Agricultural Revolution.* London: Hutchinson.

Richards, P. (1996) *Fighting for the Rainforest.* Portsmouth, NH: Heinemann.

Richards, P. (2001) Are 'forest' wars in Africa resource conflicts? The case of Sierra Leone, in **Peluso, N. and Watts, M.** (eds), *Violent Environments.* Ithaca, NY: Cornell University Press, 65–82.

Robbins, P. (1998) Authority and environment: institutional landscapes in Rajasthan, India. *Annals of the Association of American Geographers,* **88**(3): 410–35.

Robbins, P. (2001) Tracking invasive land covers in India, or why landscapes have never been modern. *Annals of the Association of American Geographers,* **91**(4): 637–59.

Robbins, P. (2002) Obstacles to a First World political ecology: looking near without looking up. *Environment and Planning A,* **34**(8): 1509–13.

Robbins, P. and Sharp, J. (2003) The lawn-chemical economy and its discontents. *Antipode,* **35**(5): 955–79.

Rocheleau, D. and Ross, L. (1995) Trees as tools, trees as text: struggles over resources in Zambrana-Chacuey, Dominican Republic. *Antipode,* **27**(4): 407–28.

Rocheleau, D., Thomas-Slayter, B. and Wangari, E. (1996a) Gender and environment: a feminist political ecology perspective, in **Rocheleau, D., Thomas-Slayter, B. and Wangari, E.** (eds), *Feminist Political Ecology: Global Issues and Local Experience.* London: Routledge, 3–23.

Rocheleau, D., Thomas-Slayter, B. and Wangari, E. (eds) (1996b) *Feminist Political Ecology: Global Issues and Local Experiences.* New York: Routledge.

Roth, M. (1993) Somalia land policies and tenure impacts, in **Bassett, T. and Crummey, D.** (eds), *Land in African Agrarian Systems.* Madison, WI: University of Wisconsin Press, 298–325.

Rothman, H. (2002) A decade in the saddle: confessions of a recalcitrant editor. *Environmental History,* **7**(1): 9–21.

Runte, A. (1979) *National Parks: The American Experience.* Lincoln, NE: University of Nebraska Press.

Sachs, W. (1992) Introduction, in **Sachs, W.** (ed.), *Development Dictionary: A Guide to Power as Knowledge.* London: Zed Books, 1–5.

Said, E. (1978) *Orientalism*. New York: Pantheon Books.

Sauer, C. (1924) The survey method in geography and its objectives. *Annals of the Association of American Geographers*, **14**: 17–33.

Sayer, A. (1980) *Epistemology and Regional Science*. Sussex: Sussex University School of Social Science.

Sayer, A. (2000) *Realism and Social Science*. London: Sage.

Sayre, N. (1999) The cattle boom in Southern Arizona: towards a critical political ecology. *Journal of the Southwest*, **41**(2): 239.

Schaffer, W. (1985) Order and chaos in ecological systems. *Ecology*, **66**(1): 93–106.

Schmidt, A. (1971) *The Concept of Nature in Marx*. London: New Left Books.

Schmink, M. and Wood, C. (1987) The 'political ecology' of Amazonia, in **Little, P. and Horowitz, M.** (eds), *Lands at Risk in the Third World: Local Level Perspectives*. Boulder, CO: Westview Press, 38–57.

Schroeder, R. (1993) Shady practices: gender and the political ecology of resource stabilization in Gambian gardens/orchards. *Economic Geography*, **69**(4): 349–65.

Schroeder, R. (1999) *Shady Practices: Agroforestry and Gender Politics in the Gambia*. Berkeley, CA: University of California Press.

Schroeder, R. (2000) Beyond distributive justice: resource extraction and environmental justice in the tropics, in **Zerner, C.** (ed.), *People, Plants and Justice: The Politics of Nature Conservation*. New York: Columbia University Press, 52–64.

Schroeder, R. and Suryanata, K. (1996) Gender and class power in agroforestry systems: case studies from Indonesia and West Africa, in **Peet, R. and Watts, M.** (eds), *Liberation Ecologies: Environment, Development, Social Movements*. London: Routledge, 188–204.

Schumacher, E. F. (1973) *Small is Beautiful: Economics as if People Mattered*. London: Blond and Briggs.

Schwartzman, S. (1989) Extractive reserves: the rubber tappers' strategy for sustainable use of the Amazon rainforest, in **Browder, J.** (ed.), *Fragile Lands of Latin America: Strategies for Sustainable Development*. Boulder, CO: Westview Press, 150–63.

Schwartzman, S. (1992) Social movements and natural resource conservation in the Brazilian Amazon, in **Cousell, S. and Rice, T.** (eds), *The Rainforest Harvest: Sustainable Strategies for Saving the Tropical Forests?* London: Friends of the Earth, 207–12.

Scoones, I. (1993) Why are there so many animals? Cattle population dynamics in the communal areas of Zimbabwe, in **Behnke, R. H., Scoones, I. and Kerven, C.** (eds), *Range Ecology at Disequilibrium: New Models of Natural Variability and Pastoral Adaptation in African Savannas.* London: Overseas Development Institute, International Institute of Environment and Development, Commonwealth Secretariat, 62–76.

Scoones, I. (1999) New ecology and the social sciences: what prospects for a fruitful engagement? *Annual Review of Anthropology,* **28**: 479–507.

Scott, J. (1976) *The Moral Economy of the Peasantry.* New Haven, CT: Yale University Press.

Scott, J. (1985) *Weapons of the Weak: Everyday Forms of Resistance.* New Haven, CT: Yale University Press.

Scott. J. (1998) *Seeing Like a State: How Certain Schemes to Improve the Human Condition Have Failed.* New Haven, CT: Yale University Press.

Seager, J. (1996) 'Hysterical housewives' and other mad women: grassroots environmental organizing in the United States, in **Rocheleau, D., Thomas-Slayter, B., and Wangari, E.** (eds), *Feminist Political Ecology: Global Issues and Local Experience.* London: Routledge, 271–83.

Semple, E. (1911) *Influences of Geographic Environment: On the Basis of Ratzel's System of Anthropo-geography.* New York: H. Holt & Co.

Shanin, T. (ed.) (1971) *Peasants and Peasant Societies.* London: Penguin.

Shiva, V. (1989) *Staying Alive.* London: Zed Press.

Simberloff, D. S. and Gotelli, N. (1984) Effects of insularization on plant species richness in prairie-forest ecotone. *Biological Conservation,* **29**(1): 27–46.

Smith, D. (1997) Geography and ethics: a moral turn? *Progress in Human Geography,* **21**(4): 583–90.

Smith, D. (2001) Geography and ethics: progress or more of the same? *Progress in Human Geography,* **25**(2): 261–8.

Smith, N. (1984) *Uneven Development: Nature, Capital, and the Production of Space.* New York: Basil Blackwell.

Smith, N. (1996) The production of nature, in **Robertson, G., Mash, M., Tickner, L., Bird, J., Curtis, B. and Putnam, T.** (eds), *Future Natural: Nature, Science, Culture.* London: Routledge, 35–54.

Smith, N. (1998) Nature at the millennium: production and re-enchantment, in **Braun, B. and Castree, N.** (eds). *Remaking Reality: Nature at the Millennium.* London: Routledge, 271–85.

Soulé, M. (ed.) (1986) *Conservation Biology: The Science of Scarcity and Diversity.* Sunderland, MA: Sinauer Associates, Inc.

Soulé, M. (1995) The social siege of nature, in **Soulé, M. and Lease, G.** (eds), *Reinventing Nature? Responses to Postmodern Deconstruction.* Washington, DC: Island Press, 137–70.

Soulé, M. and Lease, G. (1995) Preface, in **Soulé, M. and Lease, G.** (eds), *Reinventing Nature? Responses to Postmodern Deconstruction.* Washington, DC: Island Press, xv–xvii.

Spence, M. (1999) *Dispossessing the Wilderness: Indian Removal and the Making of the National Parks.* Oxford: Oxford University Press.

Sprugel, D. (1991) Disturbance, equilibrium, and environmental variability: what is 'natural' vegetation in a changing environment? *Biological Conservation,* **58**(1): 1–18.

Staniland, M. (1985) *What is Political Economy? A Study of Social Theory and Underdevelopment.* New Haven, CT: Yale University Press.

Stearman, A. (1994) Revisiting the myth of the ecologically noble savage in Amazonia: implications for indigenous land rights. *Bulletin of the Cultural and Agricultural Group,* **49**: 2–6.

Stephen, L. (1998) Between NAFTA and Zapata: responses to restructuring the commons in Chiapas and Oaxaca, Mexico, in **Goldman, M.** (ed.), *Privatizing Nature: Political Struggles for the Global Commons.* New Brunswick, NJ: Rutgers University Press, 76–101.

Steward, J. (1955) *Theory of Culture Change: The Methodology of Multilinear Evolution.* Urbana, IL: University of Illinois Press.

Stipp, D. (2004) The Pentagon's weather nightmare. *Fortune*, **149**(3): 100–7.

Stoddart, D. R. (1986) *On Geography: And its History*. Oxford: Basil Blackwell Ltd.

Stonich, S. (1989) The dynamics of social processes and environmental destruction: a Central American case study. *Population and Development Review*, **15**(2): 269–96.

Stonich, S. (1993) *I am Destroying the Land!: The Political Ecology of Poverty and Environmental Destruction in Honduras*. Boulder, CO: Westview Press.

Stonich, S. (1998) Political ecology of tourism. *Annals of Tourism Research*, **25**(1): 25.

Stonich, S. (1999) Comments [on Escobar, After nature]. *Current Anthropology*, **40**(1): 23–4.

Stonich, S. and Vandergeest, P. (2001) Violence, environment, and industrial shrimp farming, in **Peluso, N. and Watts, M.** (eds), *Violent Environments*. Ithaca, NY: Cornell University Press, 261–86.

Stott, P. (1997) Dynamic tropical forestry in an unstable world. *Commonwealth Forestry Review*, **76**(3), 207–9.

Stott, P. (1998) Biogeography and ecology in crisis: the urgent need for a new metalanguage. *Journal of Biogeography*, **25**, 1–2.

Stott, P. and Sullivan, S. (eds) (2000) *Political Ecology: Science, Myth and Power*. London: Arnold.

Sullivan, S. (1996) Towards a non-equilibrium ecology: perspectives from an arid land. *Journal of Biogeography*, **23**, 1–5.

Sullivan, S. (2000) Getting the science right, or introducing science in the first place? Local 'facts', global discourse: 'desertification' in north-west Namibia, in **Stott, P. and Sullivan, S.** (eds), *Political Ecology: Science, Myth and Power*. London: Arnold, 15–44.

Sundberg, J. (2003) Strategies for authenticity and space in the Maya Biosphere Reserve, Petén, Guatemala, in **Zimmerer, K. and Bassett, T.** (eds), *Political Ecology: An Integrative Approach to Geography and Environment-Development Studies*. New York: Guilford, 50–69.

Survival International (2001) Survival International website on www.survival-international.org.

Swyngedouw, E. (1999) Modernity and hybridity: nature, *regeneracionismo*, and the production of the Spanish waterscape, 1890–1930. *Annals of the Association of American Geographers*, **89**(3): 443–65.

Swyngedouw, E. and Heynen, N. (2003) Urban political ecology, justice and the politics of scale. *Antipode*, **35**(5): 898–918.

Sylvain, R. (2002) Land, water, and truth: San identity and global indigenism. *American Anthropologist*, **104**(4): 1074–85.

Tansley, A. (1946) *Introduction to Plant Ecology*. London: Allen & Unwin.

Taylor, P. (1997) 'Appearances notwithstanding, we are all doing something like political ecology'. *Social Epistemology*, **11**(1): 111–27.

The Ecologist (1993) *Whose Common Future?: Reclaiming the Commons.* Philadelphia, PA: New Society Publishers.

Thomas, W., Sauer, C., Bates, M. and Mumford, L. (1956) *Man's Role in Changing the Face of the Earth*. Chicago, IL: University of Chicago Press.

Thomas-Slayter, B. (1994) Structural change, power politics, and community organizations in Africa: Challenging patterns, puzzles, and paradoxes. *World Development*, **22**(10): 1479–90.

Thompson, E. P. (1971) The moral economy of the English crowd during the eighteenth century. *Past and Present*, **50**: 76–115.

Thrupp, L. (1990) Environmental initiatives in Costa Rica: a political ecology perspective. *Society and Natural Resources*, **3**: 243–56.

Torgovnick, M. (1990) *Gone Primitive: Savage Minds, Modern Lives*. Chicago, IL: University of Chicago Press.

Torry, W. (1979) Hazards, hazes and holes: a critique of the *Environment as Hazard* and general reflections on disaster research. *Canadian Geographer*, **23**: 368–83.

Tsing, A. (1999) Becoming a tribal elder and other green development fantasies, in **Li, T.** (ed.), *Transforming the Indonesian Uplands*. London: Harwood, 159–202.

Turner, J. (1995) A land fit for Tories to live in: the political ecology of the British Conservative Party 1944–1994. *Contemporary European History*, **4**(2): 189.

Turner, M. (1993) Overstocking the range: a critical analysis of the environmental science of Sahelian pastoralism. *Economic Geography*, **69**(4): 402–21.

Turner, M. (2003) Environmental science and social causation in the analysis of Sahelian pastoralism, in **Zimmerer, K. and Bassett, T.** (eds), *Political Ecology: An Integrative Approach to Geography and Environment-Development Studies*. New York: Guilford, 159–78.

Turshen, M. (1984) *The Political Ecology of Disease in Tanzania*. New Brunswick, NJ: Rutgers University Press.

Turton, D. (1987) The Mursi and national park development in the lower Omo Valley, in **Anderson, D. and Grove, R.** (eds), *Conservation in Africa: People, Policies and Practice*. Cambridge: Cambridge University Press, 169–86.

Udall, S. (1963) Nature islands for the world, in **Adams, A.** (ed.), *First World Conference on National Parks*. Washington, DC: US Department of Interior, 1–10.

Udvardy, M. (1975) *A Classification of the Biogeographical Provinces of the World*. IUCN Occasional Paper No. 18. Morges, Switzerland: IUCN.

Udvardy, M. (1984) A biogeographical classification system for terrestrial environments, in **McNeely, J. and Miller, K.** (eds), *National Parks, Conservation, and Development: The Role of Protected Areas in Sustaining Society*. Washington, DC: Smithsonian Institution Press, 34–8.

Vandergeest, P. and Peluso, N. L. (1995) Territorialization and state power in Thailand. *Theory and Society*, **24**(3): 385–426.

Vivian, J. (1994) NGOs and sustainable development in Zimbabwe: no magic bullets. *Development and Change*, **25**(1): 167–93.

Waddell, E. (1977) The hazards of scientism. *Human Ecology*, **5**: 69–76.

Walker, P. (2003) Reconsidering 'regional' political ecologies: toward a political ecology of the rural American West. *Progress in Human Geography*, **27**(1): 7–24.

Walker, P. and Fortmann, L. (2003) Whose landscape? A political ecology of the 'exurban' Sierra. *Cultural Geographies*, **10**: 469–91.

Wallerstein, I. (1974) The rise and future demise of the world capitalist system: concepts for comparative analysis. *Comparative Studies in History and Society*, **16**: 387–415.

Warner, J. (2000) Global environmental security: an emerging 'concept of control'? in **Stott, P. and Sullivan, S.** (eds), *Political Ecology: Science, Myth and Power.* London: Arnold, 247–66.

Warren, A., Batterbury, S. and Osbahr, H. (2001) Soil erosion in the West African Sahel: a review and an application of a 'local political ecology' approach in South West Niger. *Global Environmental Change – Human and Policy Dimensions,* 11(1): 79–95.

Warren, L. (1997) *The Hunter's Game: Poachers and Conservationists in Twentieth-Century America.* New Haven, CT: Yale University Press.

Watts, M. (1983a) *Silent Violence: Food, Famine and Peasantry in Northern Nigeria.* Berkeley, CA: University of California Press.

Watts, M. (1983b) On the poverty of theory: natural hazards in context, in **Hewitt, K.** (ed.), *Interpretations of Calamity from the Viewpoint of Human Ecology.* Boston, MA: Allen & Unwin, 231–62.

Watts, M. (1985) Social theory and environmental degradation: the case of Sudano-Sahelian West Africa, in **Gradus, Y.** (ed.), *Desert Development: Man and Technology in Sparselands.* Dordrecht: D. Reidel Publishers.

Watts, M. (1987) Drought, environment and food security: some reflections on peasants, pastoralists and commoditization in Dryland West Africa, in **Glantz, M. H.** (ed.), *Drought and Hunger in Africa: Denying Famine a Future.* Cambridge: Cambridge University Press, 171–211.

Watts, M. (1990) Review of land degradation and society, by Piers Blaikie and Harold Brookfield, 1987. *CNS,* 4 (June, 1990).

Watts, M. (1993) Idioms of land and labor: producing politics and rice in Senegambia, in **Bassett, T. and Crummey, D.** (eds), *Land in African Agrarian Systems.* Madison, WI: University of Wisconsin Press, 157–93.

Watts, M. (1994) Development II: the privatization of everything? *Progress in Human Geography,* 18(3): 371–84.

Watts, M. (1998) Nature as artifice and artifact, in **Braun, B. and Castree, N.** (eds), *Remaking Reality: Nature at the Millennium.* London: Routledge.

Watts, M. (2000a) Political ecology, in **Sheppard, E. and Barnes, T.** (eds), *A Companion to Economic Geography.* Oxford: Blackwell, 257–74.

Watts, M. (2000b) Contested communities, malignant markets, and gilded gover-
nance: justice resource extraction, and conservation in the tropics, in **Zerner,
C.** (ed.), *People, Plants, and Justice: The Politics of Nature Conservation.* New York:
Columbia University Press, 21–51.

Watts, M. (2001a) Author's response: lost in space. *Progress in Human Geography,*
25(4): 625–8.

Watts, M. (2001b) Petro-violence: community, extraction, and political ecology
of a mythic commodity, in **Peluso, N. and Watts, M.** (eds), *Violent
Environments.* Ithaca, NY: Cornell University Press, 189–212.

Watts, M. (2004) Resource curse? Governmentality, oil and power in the Niger
Delta, Nigeria. *Geopolitics,* **9**(1): 50–80.

Watts, M. and Peet, R. (2004) Preface to the second edition, in **Peet, R. and
Watts, M.** (eds), *Liberation Ecologies: Environment, Development, Social Movements.*
2nd edn. London: Routledge, xiii–xviii.

Western, D. (1994) Ecosystem conservation and rural development: the case of
Amboseli, in **Western, D., Wright, R. M. and Strum, S.** (eds), *Natural
Connections: Perspectives in Community-Based Conservation.* Washington, DC:
Island Press.

White, G. (1974) *Natural Hazards: Local, National, Global.* New York: Oxford
University Press.

White, R. (1990) Environmental history, ecology and meaning. *Journal of American
History,* **76**(4): 1111–16.

Whiteside, K. H. (1997) René Dumont and the fate of political ecology in
France. *Contemporary French Civilization,* **21**(1): 1–17.

Whittaker, R. H. (1975) *Communities and Ecosystems.* New York: Macmillan
Publishing Company.

Whittaker, R. J. (2000) Scale, succession, and complexity in island biogeography:
are we asking the right questions? *Global Ecology and Biogeography,* **9**(1): 75–85.

Wiens, J. (1984) On understanding a non-equilibrium world: myth and reality in
community patterns and processes, in **Strong, D., Simberloff, D., Abele, L.
and Thistle, A.** (eds), *Ecological Communities: Conceptual Issues and the Evidence.*
Princeton, NJ: Princeton University Press, 439–57.

Williams, R. (1973) *The Country and the City.* New York: Oxford University Press.

Williams, R. (1976) *Keywords: A Vocabulary of Culture and Society.* New York: Oxford University Press.

Willems-Braun, B. (1997) Buried epistemologies: the politics of nature in (post)colonial British Columbia. *Annals of the Association of American Geographers,* **87**(1): 3–32.

Wisner, B. (1976) *Man-made Famine in Eastern Kenya: The Interrelationship of Environment and Development.* Institute of Development Studies Discussion Paper No. 96. Sussex: IDS.

Wolf, E. (1972) Ownership and political ecology. *Anthropological Quarterly,* **45**(3): 201–5.

Wood, A. (2000) An emerging consensus on biodiversity loss, in **Wood, A., Stedman-Edwards, P. and Mang, J.** (eds), *The Root Causes of Biodiversity Loss.* London: Earthscan, 1–10.

Worster, D. (1990) Transformations of the earth: toward an agroecological perspective in history. *Journal of American History,* **76**(4): 1087–106.

Worster, D. (1995) Nature and the disorder of history, in **Soulé, M. and Lease, G.** (eds), *Reinventing Nature? Responses to Postmodern Deconstruction.* Washington, DC: Island Press, 65–86.

Zerner, C. (1996) Telling stories about biological diversity, in **Brush, S. and Stabinsky, D.** (eds), *Valuing Local Knowledge: Indigenous People and Intellectual Property Rights.* Washington DC: Island Press.

Zerner, C. (ed.) (2000) *People, Plants and Justice: The Politics of Nature Conservation.* New York: Columbia University Press.

Zimmerer, K. (1994) Human geography and the 'new ecology': the prospect and promise of integration. *Annals of the Association of American Geographers,* **84**(1): 108–25.

Zimmerer, K. (1999) Overlapping patchworks of mountain agriculture in Peru and Bolivia: toward a regional-global landscape model. *Human Ecology,* **27**(1): 135–65.

Zimmerer, K. (2000) The reworking of conservation geographies: nonequilibrium landscapes and nature-society hybrids. *Annals of the Association of American Geographers*, **90**(2): 356–69.

Zimmerer, K. and Bassett, T. (eds) (2003a) *Political Ecology: An Integrative Approach to Geography and Environment-Development Studies*. New York: Guilford Press.

Zimmerer, K. and Bassett, T. (2003b) Approaching political ecology: society, nature, and scale in human-environment studies, in **Zimmerer, K. and Bassett, T.** (eds), *Political Ecology: An Integrative Approach to Geography and Environment-Development Studies*. New York: Guilford Press, 1–25.

Zimmerer, K. and Bassett, T. (2003c) Future directions in political ecology: nature–society fusions and scales of interaction, in **Zimmerer, K. and Bassett, T.** (eds), *Political Ecology: An Integrative Approach to Geography and Environment-Development Studies*. New York: Guilford Press, 274–95.

Zuppan, M. (2000) Including herders in conservation management: reflections on both sides. *Development Anthropologist*, **18**(1–2): 3–17.

INDEX

9 780340 809396